Organization and Markings of United States Armored Units

1918-1941

Organization and Markings of United States Armored Units

1918-1941

Charles Lemons

Schiffer Military History
Atglen, PA

Photograph Credits

I would like to extend my thanks to the following people and organizations for their kind assistance in the creation of this book. Without their help and assistance it would have been nearly impossible to locate many of the photographs found in this volume. Their contributions are identified by the letter code shown to the right of their names.

Any photographs without a code or a code starting with **PM** were drawn from the Patton Museum photo collection.

Mr. Charles Oellig, Curator of the Pennsylvania National Guard Military Museum	**OC**
Mr. Z. Frank Hanner, Director of the National Infantry Museum at Fort Benning	NIM
CWO4 Clyde Newman, Director of the Colorado Military Heritage Museum	**CHM**
MAJ Mark Whitlock, Curator of the Illinois State Military Museum	**ISM**
LTC Emory Lehman, Director of the Washington NG State Historical Society Museum	**WNM**
Mr. Richard Hunnicutt, Author, California	**HC**
Mr. Doug Chilcote, Curator of the Patee House Museum in Missouri	**PH**
From the Private Collection of Mr. Mark Beveridge, Truman Library NARA	**MB**
The staff of the Tropical Lightning Museum at Fort Derussi, Honolulu, HI	**TLM**
The John Rowland Collection, 37th Infantry Division Historical Association	**JR**

Book design by Ian Robertson.

Library of Congress Catalog Number: 2004109418

Printed in China.
ISBN: 0-7643-2098-X

We are always looking for people to write books on new and related subjects. If you have an idea for a book, please contact us at the address below.

Published by Schiffer Publishing Ltd.
4880 Lower Valley Road
Atglen, PA 19310
Phone: (610) 593-1777
FAX: (610) 593-2002
E-mail: Info@schifferbooks.com.
Visit our web site at: www.schifferbooks.com
Please write for a free catalog.
This book may be purchased from the publisher.
Please include $3.95 postage.
Try your bookstore first.

In Europe, Schiffer books are distributed by:
Bushwood Books
6 Marksbury Ave.
Kew Gardens
Surrey TW9 4JF
England
Phone: 44 (0)20 8392-8585
FAX: 44 (0)20 8392-9876
E-mail: Info@bushwoodbooks.co.uk.
Free postage in the UK. Europe: air mail at cost.
Try your bookstore first.

Contents

	Introduction	6
Chapter 1	The Tank Corps 1917-1921	7
	Introduction to Chapters 2-4	*29*
Chapter 2	The Infantry (Tanks) Tank Battalions and Regiments 1921-1931	30
Chapter 3	The Infantry (Tanks) Light Tank Companies 1921-1935	43
Chapter 4	The Infantry (Tanks) National Guard Tank Companies 1921 -1935	56
Chapter 5	Infantry (Tanks) Tank Regiments and Battalions 1932-1935	64
Chapter 6	Mechanized Cavalry 1932-1935	74
	Introduction to Chapters 7-9	*81*
Chapter 7	Infantry (Tanks) Tank Regiments and Battalions 1936-1940	83
Chapter 8	Infantry (Tanks) Tank Companies 1936-1940	110
Chapter 9	Infantry (Tanks) National Guard Tank Companies 1936-1940	124
Chapter 10	Mechanized Cavalry 1936-1940	136
Chapter 11	The Armored Force - GHQ Tank Battalions 1940-1941	150
	Introduction to Chapters 12-15: The Armored Force	*167*
Chapter 12	1st Armored Division 1940-1941	173
Chapter 13	2nd Armored Division 1940-1941	185
Chapter 14	3rd Armored Division 1940-1941	201
Chapter 15	4th Armored Division 1940-1941	204
Chapter 16	U.S. Marine Corps Armor 1923-1940	207
	Appendices	
	Appendix A: Tables of Organization	214
	Appendix B: Organizations	216
	Appendix C: Federal Standard Color Equivalents	225
	Endnotes	226
	Bibliography	230

Introduction

The period between the two world wars has been a much-neglected period in the history of American armor. In this book I have attempted to shed light on the development of armored unit organization, as well as how these units painted and marked their vehicles in the years prior to World War II.

Army Regulations and the ever present need for security meant that, for the most part, unit tactical markings were not recorded. The markings recorded in this book are a result of extensive photographic research and, I believe, reflect the true colors and designs of American armor markings between the wars. It is not easy to find photographs of many of these units, especially those that existed in the first two decades of American armor. Units during that period tended to be small and, many times, they were stationed in out-of-the-way places. Even the large units were rarely photographed in the 1920s and early 1930s, and nearly all of the existing photographs are black and white.

The black and white film of the period did not always treat colors in the same manner, making color differentiation difficult. The changes in Army regulations were not always followed immediately and units sometimes exchanged vehicles with other units – further confusing identification.

I hope that this effort will be of use to both researchers and modelers in interpreting the look of American tank forces before World War II. I cannot absolutely guarantee that my choice of colors for the markings is correct – but I have worked hard to make it as accurate as possible.

1

The Tank Corps
1918-1921

Near the close of 1917, a tripartite agreement was made between American, French and British authorities in order to coordinate their tank programs, as well as cooperate in the production of the new weapon.[1] Following this agreement, the commander of the American Expeditionary Force (AEF), General Pershing established the AEF Tank Corps, with Colonel Samuel D. Rockenbach as its chief. At that point the organization consisted of exactly three officers, no enlisted personnel, and absolutely no tanks.[2]

Lacking any previous experience with tanks himself; Pershing made it the duty of his new Chief of the Tank Corps to, "...be responsible for all details concerning the instruction and training of tank units, and to supervise tank training centers (and)...the training of tank organizations until they join tactical units to which they may be attached."[3]

Meanwhile in the United States, and under that very same agreement, the U.S. Army established a Tank Branch under the Office of the Chief of Ordnance. The Tank Service was also authorized as part of the National Army, and placed under the control of the Chief of Engineers.[4] The 65th Engineers (Light and Heavy Tanks) was organized on February 18, 1918 at Camp Upton, New York. On March 5 the Tank Service was established as a new branch of the U. S. Army and, on March 22, it was renamed the Tank Corps. The original authorized strength for the corps was 925 officers and 13,911 enlisted personnel – enough to equip sixty light tank companies and fifteen heavy tank companies, as well as support, training, and carrier units.[5]

Training was of the utmost importance, and schools of instruction were quickly established both in the continental United States and in Europe. In Europe, the American Expeditionary Force (AEF) had made arrangements for the purchase of land near Bourg, France for the establishment of a light tank school. Crews for the proposed heavy tank battalions were sent to the well-established British Tank School at Wool, England.[6] In the United States, the Tank Corps Branch School was established on March 19, 1918 at Camp Colt, located near Gettysburg, Pennsylvania. By the end of the war, two additional training camps had been established, one at Camp Polk, Louisiana and another at Camp Tobyhanna, Pennsylvania.[7]

The first American heavy tank battalion: the 1st Separate Tank Battalion, Heavy Tank Service, 65th Engineers, was acti-

The American Tanker, American Expeditionary Force, 1918.

vated at Camp Upton, New York in February of 1918. It was quickly re-designated as the 1st Heavy Battalion; Tank Service in March of 1918 and just as quickly re-designated again as the 301st Tank Battalion, Tank Corps in April. It left the United States for the British Tank School at Wool, England in March of 1918.[8]

On March 10, 1918, the AEF Light Tank School at Bourg, France received its first light tanks, and driver training finally began. Its new commander, LTC George S. Patton Jr., was responsible, not only for the training, but also for the development of the syllabus and of combat tactics for the battalions. The last of its first ten tanks arrived at the school on 21 March 1918 and by June two light tank battalions had been organized and were in the process of training.

Across the ocean in America, driver training for the Tank Corps Branch School at Camp Colt was delayed until mid-June, as their FT17 light tanks did not begin to arrive until the 6th of June. The heavy tank training was also delayed until after the arrival of the first two heavy tanks (without armament) in mid-June.[9] Twenty-four light tank battalions and at least two heavy tank battalions had been organized in the United States by the end of the war. These delays in training were due to the fact that the American Tank Corps was completely dependent upon America's allies for equipment and initial training on both its light and the heavy tanks. In this matter the French turned out to be much more cooperative than did the British, selling the American army one hundred-fifty FT17 light tanks in March of 1918. The British supplied forty-five heavy tanks with the proviso that they be used only in the British sector of operations. The Army purchased an additional seventy-five FT17 tanks from the French in November of 1918 with twelve more second-hand heavy tanks being obtained from the British. These acquisitions comprised the total number of tanks used by the AEF Tank Corps in Europe.[10]

Although the U.S. Army had quickly established their own tank schools (at least for light tanks), the dependence on the French and British Armies for equipment continued until the end of the war. No domestically built tanks became available in the theater until after the signing of the armistice in November 1918.[11]

The AEF heavy tank battalions in Europe were trained entirely by the British Army, unlike the AEF light tank battalions for which the Americans organized their own training camps. As part of the agreement with the British for the tanks and the training, the only American heavy tank battalion to see combat was used only in the British sectors.

Of all the American tank battalions that were organized, only three actually saw combat in World War One. The 326th and 327th Light Tank Battalions saw their first combat action in the Meuse-Argonne Campaign in September of 1918. After rest and refitting, the units again saw combat in the St Mihiel Campaign in October of 1918. However, because of changes in unit designations in the United States, the two battalions were re-designated the 344th and 345th Tank Battalion respectfully in the period between their two combat engagements. Because of this change many people have assumed that four light tank battalions saw action in Europe rather than just the two. The only American heavy tank unit to see combat during the First World War was the 301st Heavy Tank Battalion. Equipped primarily with Mk V and Mk V* tanks, the unit went into action in support of British and American attacks during the last three months of the war.

Both the light and heavy tanks made use of tactical markings during their one-year of war, but at the signing of the Armistice, which ended the fighting on November 11, 1918, the use of such tactical markings on tanks was suspended by the U.S. Army. It was not taken up again for nearly ten years.

The Tank Corps began its peacetime decline with about 1000 light tanks and approximately 128 heavy tanks and in the months following the end of the Great War; it was reduced from its wartime high of 23,000 men to a mere 2,700 officers and men. In March of 1919, the overseas units began their return to the United States for demobilization or reassignment to Camp Meade, which had been chosen as the new home for the Tank Corps. These units brought back 218 FT17 Light Tanks and 29 British Mark V and Mark V* Heavy Tanks.[12] This, combined with the 942 M1917 Light Tanks built by the end of 1919 and the 100 Mk VIII Heavy Tanks, gave the Tank Corps a total of 1160 light tanks and 129 heavy tanks.

By mid 1919, the move of Tank Corps units back to the United States was complete. During 1919 and into the early 1920s, tanks were sent around the United States to boost recruiting for the Tank Corps. In April and May of 1919, several platoons of light tanks were shipped to Kansas City, Missouri where they participated in a parade and other events in the area. Stunts involving tanks, such as the FT17 that climbed Pike's Peak in Colorado, were all attempts to popularize the Tank Corps.

During 1919 to 1920, a number of camouflage paint schemes were used briefly, but their use was apparently was restricted to tanks of one, as yet unidentified unit at Camp Meade, MD. A particularly garish three-color paint scheme was developed by the U.S. Army near the end of World War I and was only used for a short time. In addition to the camouflage scheme, some tanks were painted with a company number on the upper front plate in twelve to fourteen-inch tall numerals.[13]

Under an act of Congress, passed on July 11, 1919 the Tank Corps, "...with their powers and duties as defined in orders and regulations in force and effect November 11, 1918, shall be continued to and until June 30, 1920." During this short grace period, the National Guard was authorized to organize four light tank battalions.[14] These battalions were to be organized along same lines as the regular army, but each of the companies in the battalions was to be divided among the several states. The proposed organization was laid out as follows:

1st Tank Battalion

Battalion Headquarters and Company A	New York
Company B	Pennsylvania
Company C	Massachusetts

2nd Tank Battalion

Battalion Headquarters and Company A	Texas
Company B	Tennessee
Company C	South Carolina

3rd Tank Battalion

Battalion Headquarters and Company A	Illinois
Company B	Ohio
Company C	Michigan

4th Tank Battalion

Battalion Headquarters and Company A	California
Company B	Washington
Company C	Minnesota

This organization ultimately failed to materialize because on June 2, 1920, the United States Congress stepped in and passed the National Defense Act of 1920. One portion of the act, Section 17, quietly dissolved the Tank Corps and relegated its men and equipment to the Infantry branch.[15] It would be twenty years before a separate Armor branch would, once again, be established.

Organization

When finally organized, the Tank Corps was part of the American National Army, as opposed to the Regular Army or National Guard. The numbering system used for Tank Corps battalions and other Tank Corps units was derived from War Department General Order Number 115, dated August 29, 1917: "The various organization of each class in the Regular Army, National Guard, and National Army will be numbered in separate series and the first number of each series will be as indicated in the following tables ...National Army ...301."[16] Thus, the first tank battalion organized was designated as the 301st Battalion (TC). Although some of the first organizations in AEF Tank Corps did not initially use this system of numbering,[17] by the end of 1918 all of the units had been brought into line.

The Light Tank Battalion

The tank battalion was the standard organization for American light tanks during the First World War. Each battalion was organized around a headquarters company and three light tank companies. Each of the tank companies consisted of a headquarters, with its nine replacement tanks and single signals tank, and three tank platoons of five tanks each. This organization was based on the French model with the exception of the signal tank, which substituted for one of the replacement tanks in the company headquarters. Throughout the war period and well into the 1930s, this organization remained the standard. It was not until the introduction of a more mechanically reliable tank that the light tank battalion and company were finally reorganized.

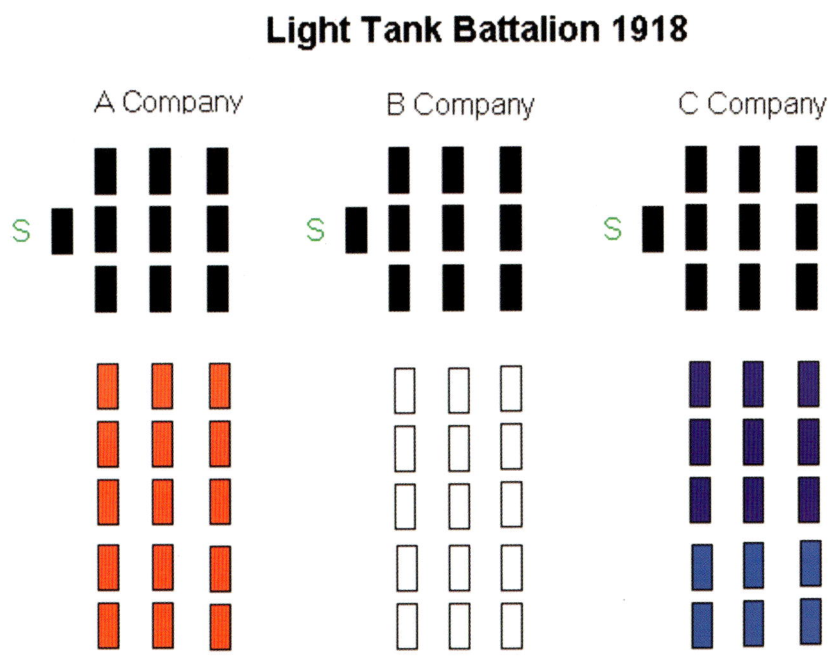

Table of Organization for the American Light Tank Battalion in 1918. The tank marked with an "S" is the signal tank assigned to the company headquarters.

Each battalion contained seventy-two French FT17 or FT18 light tanks, with an additional FT Signals tanks assigned to each company, making a total of seventy-five armored vehicles. As shown on the chart, each battalion contained three companies of twenty-five tanks each. The battalion headquarters itself contained no armored vehicles. Each of the companies was made up of three line platoons, each containing five tanks, and the headquarters section that held nine spare tanks and a single signal tank. The two light tank battalions that saw action in World War I were both assigned to the 1st (later 301st) Tank Brigade, commanded by Lieutenant Colonel George S. Patton Jr.

The Heavy Tank Battalion

Although the only American heavy tank battalion to see action in the First World War was organized along the British model, the proposed standard American heavy tank battalion was to be nearly twice as large. Rather than having three companies of sixteen heavy tanks, the proposed American battalion was supposed to consist of three line companies, each with a total of twenty-four tanks available to it. Each of the companies was to have three platoons of five tanks each, as well as a headquarters section with a signals tank and eight "spare" tanks.[18] Unlike the American light tank battalion, the battalion headquarters of the Heavy Tank Battalion was allotted a signal tank. This resulted in a battalion having a total of seventy-three heavy tanks, as opposed to the British battalion of forty-eight.

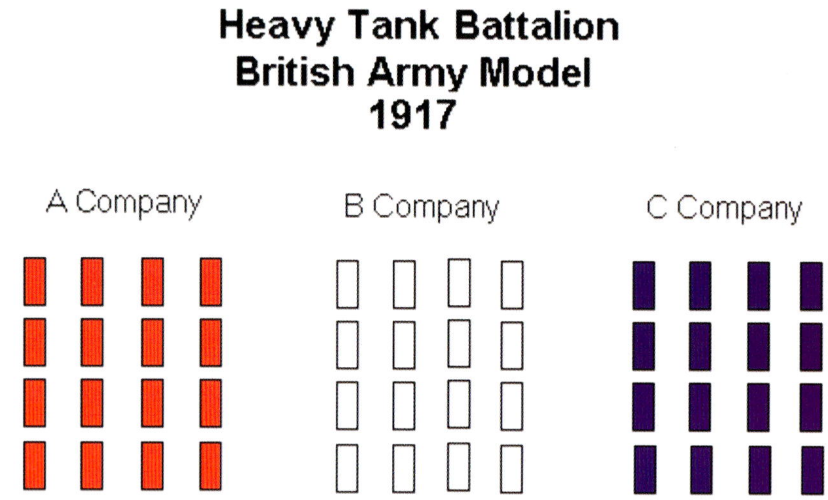

Table of Organization for the British Heavy Tank Battalion, 1917.

American mechanics service an FT17 at the AEF Tank School, circa August 1918. The vehicle is painted a solid olive-drab color with the serial number painted in white on each side. The vehicle's registration number (66316) is painted on the side of the suspension, as well as repeated on the very rear armor plate. This is a Renault built FT, as evidenced by the oval serial number plate bolted to the left suspension support. In the background is a second FT17 in a typical camouflage pattern.

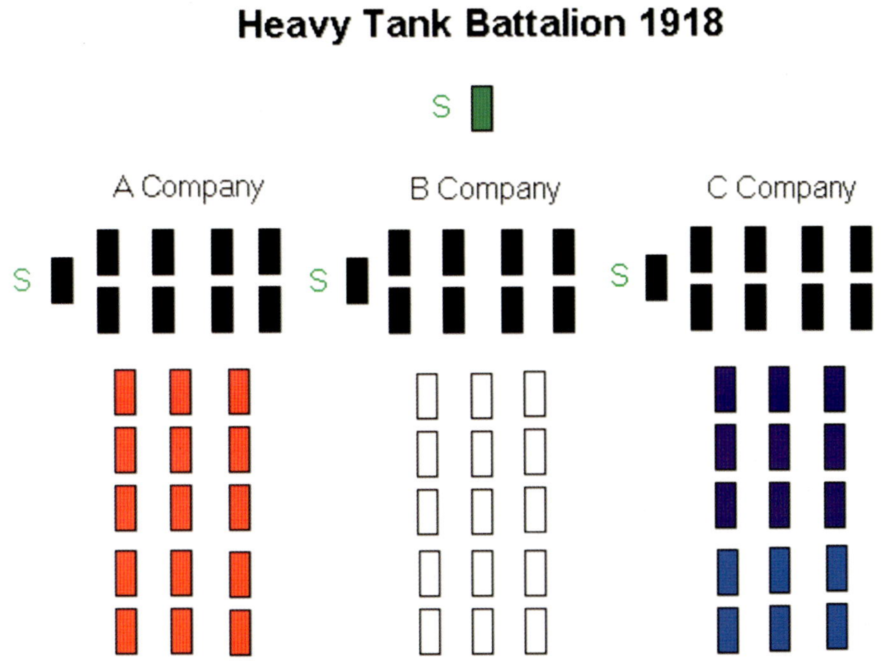

The proposed Table of Organization for an American Heavy Tank Battalion, 1918.

Colors and Markings

General

All of the tanks used by the AEF Tank Corps in Europe were delivered painted in the base color of the country that had supplied them. For the heavy tanks, this was a British Army dark earth color, with the serial number painted in white on both sides of the hull near the rear. For the light tanks, the French delivered these in a standard three or four-color camouflage. The serial number of each of the FT17 light tanks was usually painted in a six to eight-inch tall black outline on either side of the hull above the track. These numbers have also been known to appear as solid numbers and with some being applied in white paint.[19] American manned tanks often lacked this additional serial number stencil. In addition, the French also stenciled a white registration number, three to four-inches tall on the road wheel support bar on either side of the vehicle.

The AEF Tank Corps did paint the tank registration number in 1-inch block numbers on two locations on the FT17. The first location was on the plate forward of the driver – usually in white, the second location being across the rear of the hull. In both cases, the number was usually set to one side or the other, not centered, depending upon where the camouflage pattern would make it most visible.

An American manned FT17 in the three-color camouflage applied at the factory. The vehicle registration number (67006) is painted on the front slope of the vehicle in one-inch stencils.

Early pattern French Renault FT17 machinegun tank painted in French vert armeé (olive drab) at the Tank School, Camp Colt, PA, circa August 1918. This vehicle has the first pattern cast machinegun turret that was soon replaced by the riveted plate "omnibus" turret. Part of the vehicle registration number is visible in white on the track suspension bar.

FT17 and FT18 Light Tanks of the 301st Tank Center, AEF, being prepared for shipment back to the United States in early 1919. Each tank is stenciled on both sides of the engine compartment with the company letter and battalion number and with "US" below in white.

Tank park of returned FT17 and FT18 Light Tanks at Camp Meade, MD, in 1919. The various camouflage patterns are evident and, here and there, the tactical markings of combat units can been discerned.

Apparently, the light tanks that were shipped to the Tank School at Camp Colt were left in the French olive drab. The upper portion of the tank interiors, including the turret were painted in white to make the best use of what light there was available. However, the floor plates in the crew compartment, as well as the sidewalls, up to about 18-inches above the deck, was painted a light to medium gray color. The interior of the engine compartment was flat black. Much of the parts added to the vehicle during construction were installed in the red-lead primer and then painted after installation.

After the war, and in preparation for shipment to the United States, all of the tanks belonging to the U.S. Army were gathered together at a single location. The light tanks were marked on the either side of the engine compartment with "US" along with the battalion number and company letter.

Those tanks that returned from overseas in early 1919 were, for the most part, left in their original markings and camouflage. By 1920 the FT light tank was obsolete and many had their turrets removed, either as a form of demilitarization or for reuse. Their replacements, the new M1917 Six Ton Light Tanks, and the new Mark VIII Heavy Tanks were all issued in U.S. Army Quartermaster olive drab. The experimental Ford 3-ton Tanks, developed in 1918, were also issued to the units. Ford had hoped to construct 15,000 of these little tanks for the war, but ended up with only fifteen.

Group of FT series light tanks being stripped at Camp Meade, MD, in 1920. The markings applied overseas are still visible. The vehicle at center is marked for Company A, 345th Tank Battalion. The vehicles were being stripped for spare parts to keep a select number operational.

Ford Three-Ton Tank at Camp Meade, MD, in 1918. Painted Quartermaster olive drab, this is pilot vehicle number 7, as evidenced by the black stenciled marking on the rear of the engine compartment.

Light Tanks

The five colors used as camouflage by the French armored forces and, by extension, the American light tank battalions, consisted of a light to medium yellow, a medium olive-drab, black, red-brown, and a varying shade of blue-green. There were a large number of variations in the camouflage patterns applied to the French Renault FT17 and FT18, as much of the camouflage was hand applied by artists hired specifically for the job. Some tanks were painted in the field and these tend to appear to be less than artistic. In any case, they all show the sharp edges of brush painting. The camouflage patterns range from quite complicated and fanciful to a very simplistic rendering – depending on the skill (and the patience) of the artist. All of these camouflage colors were flat or lusterless oil based paints. The base coat for the French Renault light tanks was medium olive drab (also known as *vert armee*).

The use of tactical markings for light tanks was begun by the French Army, and the Americans quickly adopted a similar marking system. The tanks of the American 326th and 327th Tank Battalions could be easily identified by the location of their tactical markings. Light tanks assigned to the French Army were marked on either side of the engine compartment with a large geometric figure (Disk, Diamond, or Square) designating the company and a smaller "card" figure designating the section. The color of the card figure denoted the battalion to which the vehicle belonged. The Americans, using similar markings, placed the tactical markings on the rear turret door and on either side of the turret near the front.

The American Tank Corps hand painted their company designation markings without the use of a stencil for the most part, and these were applied in white paint in the three positions on the turret. The markings measured approximately 10"x10" with the card markings hand painted in the battalion color at the center.[20] In existing photographs, it can be discerned that the only difference between the markings of the two battalions is the color of the "card" figure. This was in line with the French practice. The tactical markings are poorly painted due mostly to the fact that the vehicles were delivered to the two battalions only days before their first combat.

An American crewman struggles to climb out of his ditched FT17 during training between battles in September of 1918. A typical four-color camouflage is very visible in the shot, as is the color and crudeness of the unit tactical marking on the turret. The vehicle serial number is painted in an outline stencil on the side of the hull. In this case, it would appear that the base color is the light dark yellow. This particular vehicle belonged to the American 326th Tank Battalion.

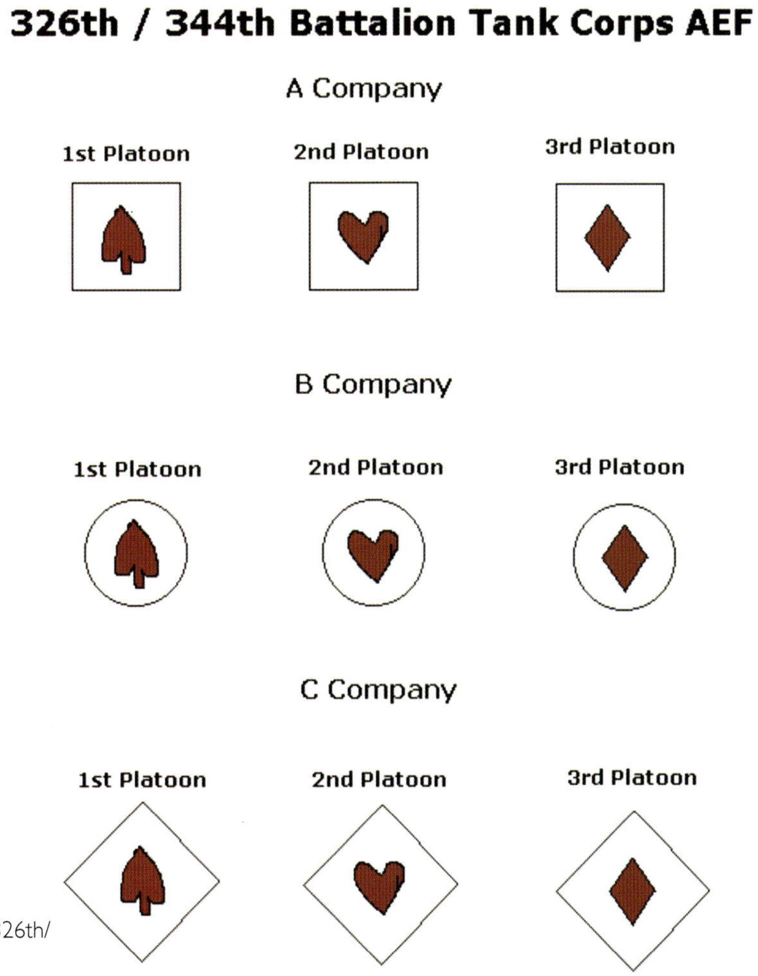

Colors and markings of the 326th/ 344th Tank Battalion.

Because no color pictures exist of the tanks as they were in World War I, it is difficult to differentiate between the two units. However, it would appear that, by comparing the shading values of the existing black and white photographs, the 326th Tank Battalion used the medium olive-drab color for their card markings – usually appearing as a dark shade in the black and white photos. The distinctive color used by the 327th is of a lighter value and would appear to be a shade of the bluish-green or of the red-brown camouflage color. Personally I believe that it is of the red-brown color. The Americans used only the spade, heart, and diamond in marking their vehicles within the combat platoons. However, the company commander was allowed the use of one of the tanks assigned to the headquarters – which was marked with the company background, then marked with the "club" symbol in the battalion color.

The famous "Five of Hearts" after its recovery from the battlefield in October 1918. This vehicle exhibits the French three-color camouflage, as well as the crudely painted unit tactical marking with the added white "5", typical of C Company, 327th Tank Battalion.

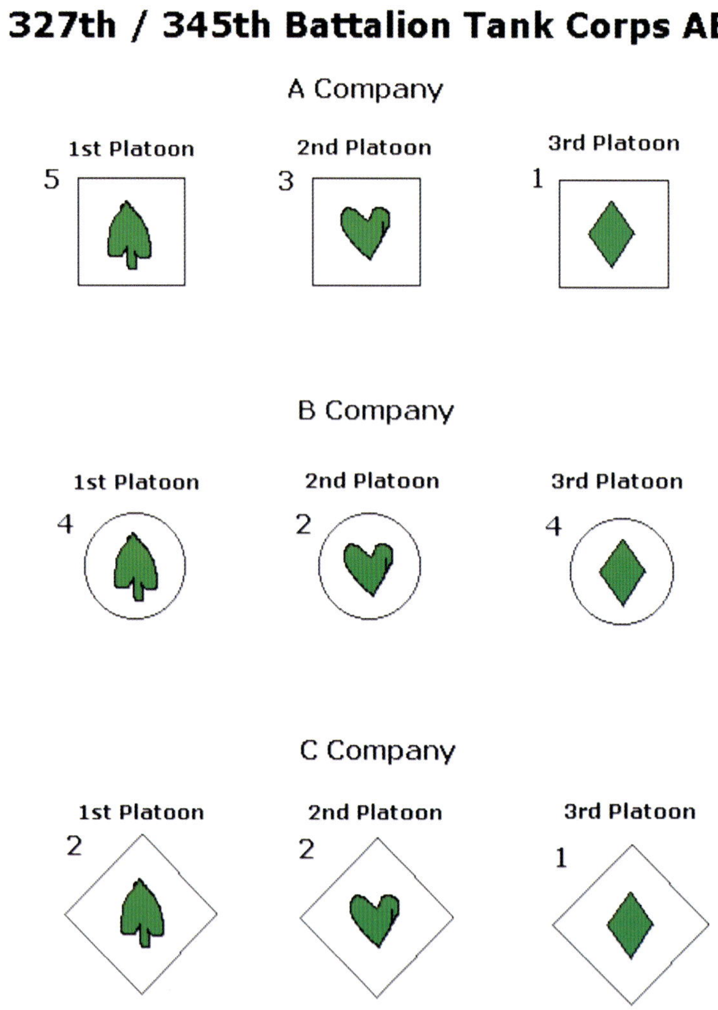

Colors and markings of the 327th/345th Tank Battalion.

Tanks of the 327th Tank Battalion parked at Verrennes after combat in the Meuse-Argonne, 26 September 1918. The tank in the foreground is marked with a white disk and a dark green or black club figure, with the numeral "2" in white off to the left side. This marks it as the B Company commander's tank.

While the color of the card marking identified the battalion, the shape of the white background figure identified the company within the battalion, with the card marking itself designating the platoon. Company A was given a white disk, Company B the white square, and Company C the diamond. The vehicles assigned to each company as "spare" vehicles received, for the most part, no tactical markings. The one exception was the tank set aside for use by the company commander, which was marked with the company background figure and the "club" card figure in the battalion color.

The only other marking that was used in conjunction with this system was a small white numeral painted above and to the left of the geometric company symbol. Based on the photographic evidence, the only unit that so marked its vehicles was the 327th Tank Battalion. These numbers, which ran from 1 through 5, designated the individual vehicles within each of the company's platoons.[21]

Only a single photograph of B Company, 327th Battalion has surfaced, but this may be due to the fact that the company took part in the Meuse-Argonne in an independent role, supporting the American 28th Division, while the rest of the battalion was assigned to support the 35th Division.[22]

Based on the known delivery dates for the tanks, and on existing photographic evidence, it would seem evident that these two tank battalions adopted their unit markings just prior to their first combat in late September of 1918.[23] It is interesting to note that the French and American light tank battalions were being organized at nearly the same time and that their final forms were almost identical.[24]

The American tank battalion consisted of three tank companies, totaling seventy-two light tanks and three signal tanks. Each of the line companies had three platoons of five tanks each, with the HQ section of the company retaining one signal tank and nine replacement tanks held in reserve.[25] The French light tank battalion differed only in the fact that they apparently did not use signal tanks, but instead rounded out their HQ section with ten rather than nine replacement tanks.[26] The Battalion Headquarters for both countries retained no tanks and consisted solely of support and administrative personnel and equipment.

The 326th and 327th Tank Battalions were the only American light tank battalions to see combat during the war, and they were also the only American light tank units to utilize tactical markings for identification. Some confusion has arisen as to the number of American tank battalions that took an active part in the First World War. Due to a problem with the numbering of several new battalions en-route from the United States, both the 326th and 327th were re-designated in October 1918. The

Rally area for the tanks of the American Expeditionary Force in late September 1918. The markings show that this is a mixture of FT17 and FT18 light tanks from both the 326th and 327th Tank Battalions. The different styles and patterns of camouflage—both three and four-color—are visible.

American officers standing next to a camouflaged FT17 at the American Expeditionary Force Tank School, Bourge, France, circa September 1918. This vehicle was base coated in the light dark yellow camouflage color, with the vehicle serial number painted in black or olive-drab on the side of the hull (98-) with the last digit obscured by camouflage paint. The registration number can be seen faintly painted on the track support bar. The camouflage pattern is of three colors, dark yellow, olive drab, and blue-green.

326th Battalion became the 344th, and the 327th became the 345th Tank Battalion. This re-designation, which took place between the two major campaigns of the Tank Corps, made it appear that four, rather than two, tank battalions had seen action. A number of other battalions were shipped overseas, but none arrived in time to participate in combat.

When these units returned to the United States, they brought all of their serviceable FT17 and FT18 Light Tanks with them. These were left in the original camouflage and markings. For the most part, by the end of 1919 all of the French tanks had been withdrawn from active service and had been replaced by the American M1917 Six-ton Light Tank.

The two combat veteran battalions, the 344th and 345th, remained on duty during this period and were stationed at Camp Meade, MD, equipped with the new M1917 Light Tank. The new tanks were delivered in the U.S. Army Quartermaster olive drab, a muddy looking light, grayish-green color.

One FT17 (left) and one FT18 (right) light tank at the AEF Tank School in the fall of 1918. The camouflage patterns are clearly visible. Both are painted in a three-color camouflage, which was hand applied by French artists at the factory. The tank jack can be clearly seen placed above the storage box on the FT17. Both appear to have the light dark yellow as a base coat. On each, the vehicle registration number is painted on the front slope in one-inch numbers. The differences, not only between the cast and plate turrets, but also the machinegun and 37mm gun mantlets, can clearly been seen.

FT18 of the American Expeditionary Force in France during late 1918. Note the storage box mounted on the side of the tank and the hard edge camouflage overall.

One of these two battalions was used to experiment with the particularly garish camouflage being developed by the U.S. Army. Shots of the tanks in parades in early and mid 1919 clearly show the camouflage pattern. In addition to the camouflage, the tanks are marked on the nose with a large vehicle lineal number. The battalion was issued, not only with the M1917 tanks but also with the Ford 3-ton Tank – which was also painted in this garish paint scheme.

These tanks were widely photographed due to their use in both parades and recruiting drives after the armistice in Europe. By the end of 1921, use of the pattern was abandoned.

An FT18 of Company A, 327th Tank Battalion in late September 1918. The unit tactical marking is clearly visible on the turret side. The camouflage is the atypical three-color pattern. The interior paint scheme can just been seen to the right of the driver—white uppermost, medium gray at the bottom.

An FT18 of the 345th Tank Battalion climbs out of a shell hole in October of 1918. The hand painted tactical marking for Company A is clear on the turret side and rear turret door.

Tank park of the 327th Tank Battalion after their first action in the Meuse-Argonne, late September 1918. Notice the mixture of FT17 and FT18 Light Tanks.

American M1917 Light Tank painted in the experimental camouflage pattern adopted in 1919. Photograph taken at Camp Meade, MD, circa 1920.

The other battalion continued to use a form of the World War I tactical markings, but I have not been able to establish which unit. As has always been the case for tactical markings, no record was kept of their meanings. However, the background markings – a white square or diamond have been identified and it can be assumed that the disk marking was also used – most probably designating the same companies. The square designated company A, the disk for Company B, and the diamond for Company C.

The available photographs have been too indistinct to allow positive identification of colored figures designating the platoons. Close inspection of the existing photographs under enhancement seem to indicate that the figures used to designate the platoons were also the diamond, square, and disk.

Just as the war was closing, a new tank was being tested for use by the United States Army. Ford had hoped to contract for 15,000 of these small machine-gun carriers, but in the end only 15 were built and accepted.

Two Ford 3-ton Light Tanks painted in an experimental camouflage pattern, setting on a rail car in 1919.

Dazzle camouflage pattern on an M1917 Light Tank being used to collect money for the Victory Loans of 1919. (MB)

M1917 Light Tank being used in a publicity stunt to sell Victory Bonds in 1919. The stunt involved driving the tank to the top of Pikes Peak in Colorado. Notice the camouflage pattern, as well as the white-circled "V" on the front armor.

A side shot of an M1917 Light Tank climbing Pikes Peak in 1919. The simple camouflage pattern is more clearly visible from this side angle. The tank's main armament has clearly been removed.

How embarrassing can it get? A camouflaged M1917 Light Tank awaiting equipment to right it after it fell over at the state capitol grounds in 1919 (state unknown).

Two tanks of Company A, 16th Light Tank Battalion at Fort Meade circa 1921. Both tanks are marked with a white square on side of the turret, probably both sides, with an indistinct dark figure at the center.

An unfortunately fuzzy photograph of two M1917 Light Tanks assigned to Company C, 16th Light Tank Battalion, circa 1921. Although the rear doors are open, a white diamond can be seen on the side of the turret of the right tank.

A collection of M1917 Light Tanks at Fort Meade, MD, in 1919. Most of the vehicles are painted a gloss olive drab, with a number painted in an American camouflage pattern. The tank at center has a stencil on the turret that begins "VETERAN TEAM" with the second line indistinct.

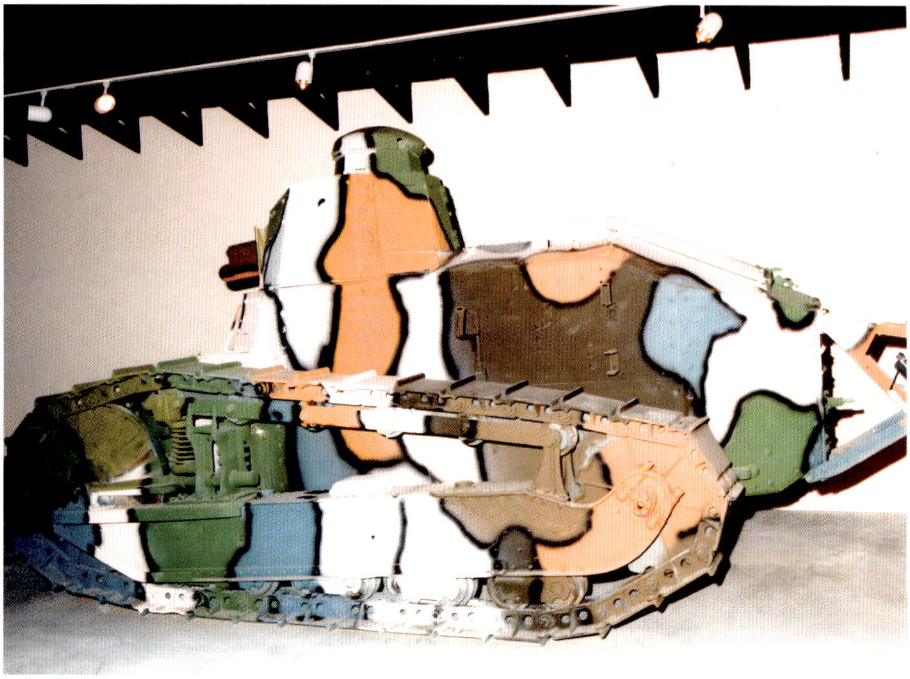

Recreation of the dazzle camouflage developed by the U.S. Army in 1919. (Courtesy of the Fort George G. Meade Museum, Maryland)

Heavy Tanks

The only American heavy tank battalion to see combat was the 301st Heavy Tank Battalion.[27] Trained and equipped by the British Army, the makeup of this particular unit followed the British system rather than the proposed American system. The battalion had three companies made up of four sections of four tanks each.[28] This resulted in companies containing sixteen tanks, for a battalion total of forty-eight heavy tanks. In practice, this was followed very closely, but the losses in combat and lack of replacements, soon reduced the battalion's strength to sixteen, and then twelve tanks. Near the end of its service, it was reduced to an ad hoc company.[29]

Because of the loss of so many heavy tanks to the Germans, the heavy tanks that made the final attacks in late 1918 were painted with bright recognition colors of red and white. This included the American heavy tanks. These markings consisted of a series of stripes in red and white on the front of the forward casemate and the back of the rear casemate, as well as on the front points of either side of the hull. Because of this, differentiation between the British Tank Corps vehicles, and those of the American 301st Tank Battalion is, at best, problematic. However, the Americans did not appear to have painted any company numbers or letters on their vehicles, and an incomplete list of vehicle numbers has survived which can positively identify most of the American tanks by company.[30]

The Americans were armed entirely with Mark V and Mark V* heavy tanks, in all the various combinations of armaments,

Close up view of a Mark V* Heavy Tank from the 301st Heavy Tank Battalion at Camp Meade, MD, in mid-1919, after their return from overseas. The stripes are red and white, marking the vehicle for company C.

Close up view of Mark IV and Mark V* Heavy Tanks of Company A, 301st Heavy Tank Battalion at Camp Meade in mid-1919, after their return from overseas. The striping—white red white—was applied in the United States.

A Mark V* Heavy Tank of the 301st Heavy Tank Battalion being driven through Camp Meade in 1919. The vehicle registration number (9602) is clearly visible in white on the side of the vehicle. The same number is repeated on the back of the vehicle, black on a white rectangle.

Mark V* Heavy Tank #9602 showing the unit markings on the front of the hull. Red and white stripes mark this vehicle as belonging to Company C, 301st Heavy Tank Battalion. These unit markings were used only in the United States for a short time.

including Male, Female, and composite vehicles.[31] Several photographs exist of tanks from the 301st, but the location and date at which they were taken is unknown. However, at least two photographs exist of the returned Mark V*s of the 301st, one from A company and one from B Company and both still painted in wartime colors.

The vehicle serial number was painted in 6-inch tall white numbers on both sides of the vehicle above the radiator vents. Additionally, on some vehicles, a white rectangle, approximately 6-inches tall and 24-inches wide, was painted centered on the back of the vehicle with the vehicle serial number painted on it in black, 4-inch tall numbers.

In the year following the war, American tanks continued to be marked with two or three vertical stripes, each approximately 12-inches wide, placed on the very front edge of each side. For a short time after the war in the United States, each company of the 301st Battalion utilized a different combination of stripes.[32]

When the battalion was sent back to the United States, it was posted to Camp Meade, MD. With little or no change in personnel and equipment, the vehicles remained in their wartime colors with perhaps one exception. Now back in the states, and in peacetime, each tank was combat locked with its own padlock. In order to keep track of which key fit which tank, the tanks were marked with a two-inch tall by twelve inch long rectangular white block upon which was stenciled the key number in black one-inch stencils. On tank #9602 it was "KEY SET 10". This was stenciled on the door that was locked – in the case of 9602, the right hand door.

By the middle of 1920, all of these tanks had been withdrawn from active service and replaced with the brand new Mark VIII "International" Heavy Tank, which were delivered in the U.S. Army Quartermaster olive-drab. The only markings that the Mark VIII received were its serial number, which was painted in white, six-inch tall numerals on either side of the hull near the rear.

Stripe markings for Company A, 301st Heavy Tank Battalion at Camp Meade in 1919-1920.

Stripe markings for Company B, 301st Heavy Tank Battalion at Camp Meade in 1919-1920.

Stripe markings for Company C, 301st Heavy Tank Battalion at Camp Meade in 1919-1920.

A popular vehicle to photograph—Mark V* #9602 of Company C, 301st Heavy Tank Battalion is demonstrated climbing out of a ditch at Camp Meade in 1919.

A veteran of the war. Mark V Composite #9136 of Company C, 301st Heavy Tank Battalion being worked on at Camp Meade in 1919. It remains marked for Company C, using only two stripes—one red, one white—painted on the forward part of the hull on each side.

301st Tank Battalion AEF
Heavy Tanks

A Company
9 Mk V* Male Tanks
2 Mk V* Female Tanks
4 Mk V* Composite Tanks

Vehicle#	Tank Commander	Type
9347	LT Colburn	Mk V
9524	LT Jones	Mk V*
9583	LT Frost	Mk V*
9586	LT Watts	Mk V*
9589	LT Taylor	Mk V*
9591	LT Hobbs	Mk V*
9593	LT Hart	Mk V*
9594	LT Goss	Mk V* Female
9603	LT Adams	Mk V*
9604	LT Webb	Mk V* Male
9606	LT Hillsey	Mk V*
9891	LT Moury	Mk V*
9892	LT Dean	Mk V*
9893	LT Mitchel	Mk V*
9893	LT Gutkowiski	Mk V*
9894	LT H. Taylor	Mk V*

B Company
7 Mk V* Male Tanks
2 Mk V* Female Tanks
3 Mk V Male Tanks
3 Mk V Female Tanks
3 Mk V Composite Tanks

Side#	Tank Commander	Type
9047	LT Haimbaugh	Mk V Male
9117	SGT Kittinger	Mk V
9352	LT McDonald	Mk V
9429	LT Jones	Mk V
9592	LT Ellingswood	Mk V*
9601	LT Kusener	Mk V*
	9602	Mk V* Male
9605	LT Forrel	Mk V*
9888	LT Kohr	Mk V*
9895	LT Lester	Mk V*

C Company
7 Mk V Male Tanks
9 Mk V Composite Tanks

Side#	Tank Commander	Type
9017	LT Brown	Mk V
9027	LT Holmes	Mk V
9043	LT Dinsmore	Mk V
9060	LT Parks	Mk V
9088	LT Logan	Mk V
9111	LT Budd	Mk V
9136	LT O'Kane	Mk V Composite
9191	LT Little	Mk V
9265	LT Dunning	Mk V Composite
9279	LT Williard	Mk V Male
9334	LT Potter	Mk V
9376	LT Vernon	Mk V
9390	LT Shonks	Mk V
9396	LT Latham	Mk V
9435	LT McKay	Mk V

Introduction
Chapters 2-4

With the demise of the Tank Corps in 1920, all responsibilities for tanks and tank training were transferred to the Infantry Branch, with the branch sub-designator of Infantry (Tanks).[1] In the draw down after the war, many of the existing light and heavy tank battalions had been simply decommissioned. Beginning early summer in 1921, the seven surviving tank battalions were reorganized, re-designated, and assigned to new home stations. In addition, thirteen National Guard tank companies were activated as support for the existing National Guard divisions.

As a result of this reorganization program, part of the veteran 345th Tank Battalion was re-designated as the Headquarters and Headquarters Company of the 16th Light Tank Battalion. At the same time, Company C of the 301st Tank Battalion was re-organized and re-designated as Companies A, B, and C, of the 16th Light Tank Battalion.

In the meantime, portions of the 344th Light Tank Battalion and Company A, 301st Heavy Tank Battalion was combined to form the 15th Composite Tank Battalion, as well as spinning off the 5th Tank Company. The 328th Light Tank Battalion and the remainder of the 345th Light Tank Battalion were broken up to form six additional divisional tank companies, which were then assigned to the regular Army divisions.[2]

Company A, 303rd Tank Battalion was re-designated as Company A, 17th Tank Battalion, and Companies B & C were re-designated as Company C, 17th Tank Battalion. Rounding out the battalion was Company B, 301st Tank Battalion, which was re-designated as Company B, 17th Tank Battalion.[3] The 329th Tank Battalion was re-designated, as a whole, as the 18th Tank Battalion.

In spite of the reorganization, the Tank School itself remained at Fort George G. Meade, MD, with the 16th Light Tank Battalion and 17th Heavy Tank Battalion assigned. The 15th Composite Tank Battalion was posted to the Infantry School at Fort Benning, GA.[4] The nine divisional tank companies that had been created during the reorganization,[5] as well as the newly formed National Guard tanks companies, were dispersed to their individual numbered divisions.[6]

During this early period tactical markings, per se, were not used to any great extent, and unit markings were still in the process of being standardized. In 1929 the Army consolidated the four surviving tank battalions into two tank regiments, one of light tanks and one of heavy tanks.[7] However, due to equipment and monetary constraints, these units rarely operated above a battalion level. In fact, the heavy tank regiment never exceeded company strength.

The Infantry (Tank) units of this inter-war period did little more than selectively recruit and train personnel. In 1931, the Tank School and part of its associated tank regiment, was formally transferred from Fort George G. Meade to the Infantry School at Fort Benning, GA. It would remain the home of armor until the advent of World War II.

2

The Infantry (Tanks) Tank Battalions & Regiments 1921-1931

Organization

The Light Tank Battalion and Company

The transfer of responsibility for tanks to the Infantry Branch did not initially affect the basic organization of tank units. The Light Tank Company in the period of 1919 to 1932 continued the wartime organization of twenty-five tanks divided between a Headquarters section and three line platoons. Each of the line platoons was made up of five M1917 Light Tanks, two armed with the 37mm gun and the remainder was armed with a .30 caliber machine-gun.[1] The Headquarters section contained the company's supply of nine reserve tanks (four armed with 37mm guns and five with light machine-guns).

The Light Tank Battalion was made up of three light tank companies, and a headquarters and headquarters company. The battalion Headquarters Company had only the single signals tank with no other armor attached. This gave the battalion a

The American Tanker, 16th Tank Battalion, 1922.

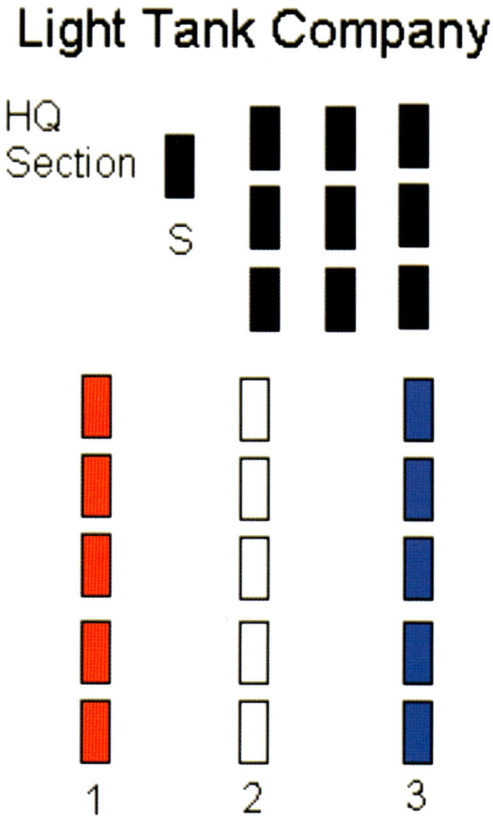

Light Tank Battalion 1927

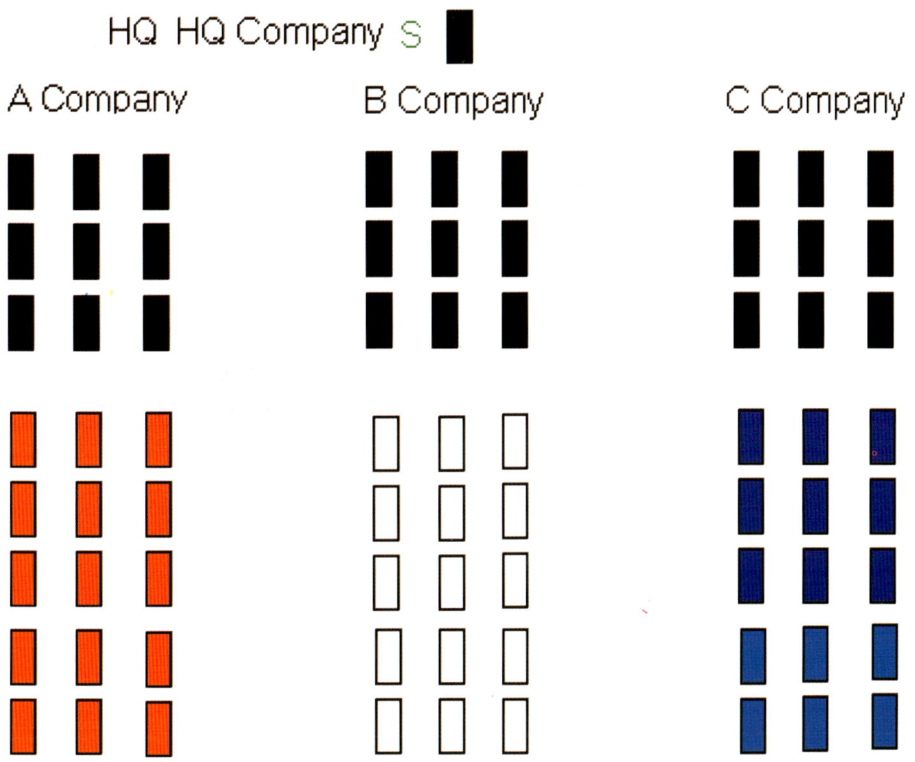

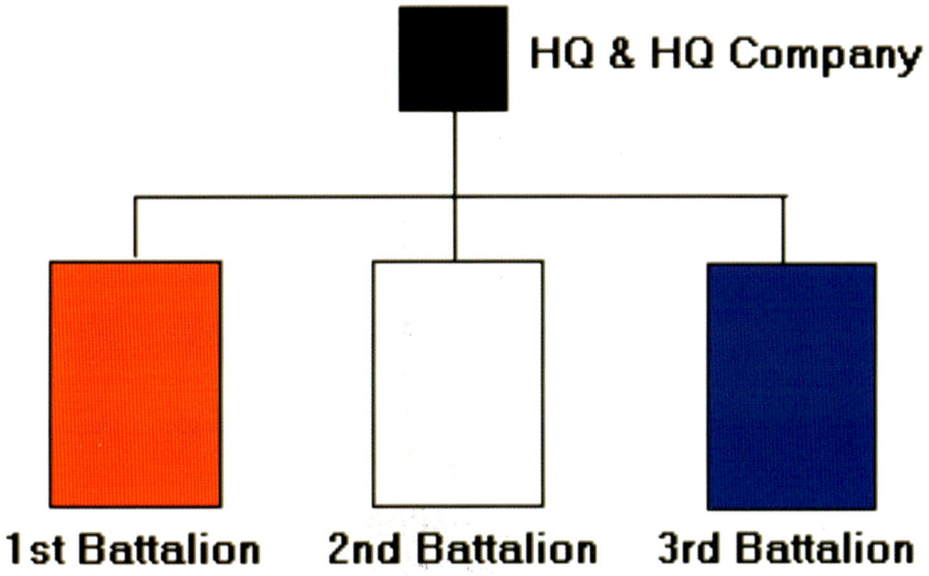

Light Tank Regiment 1927

Heavy Tank Company

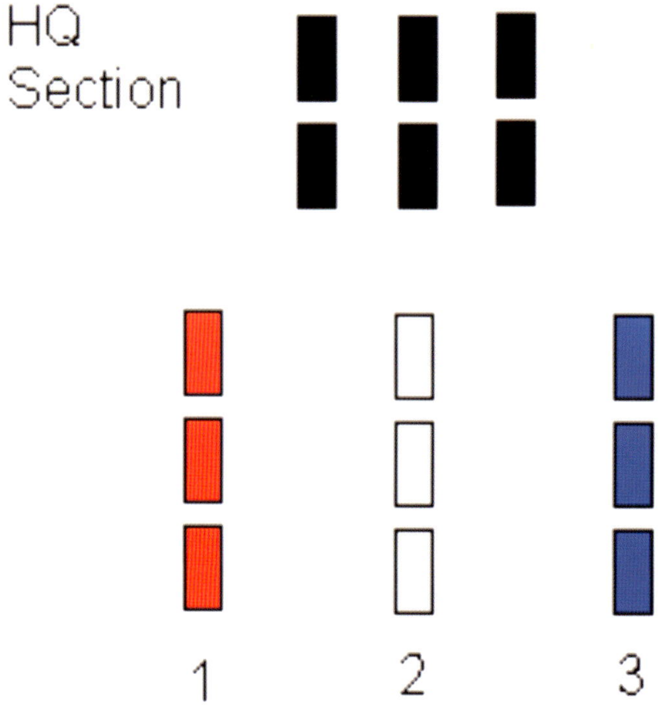

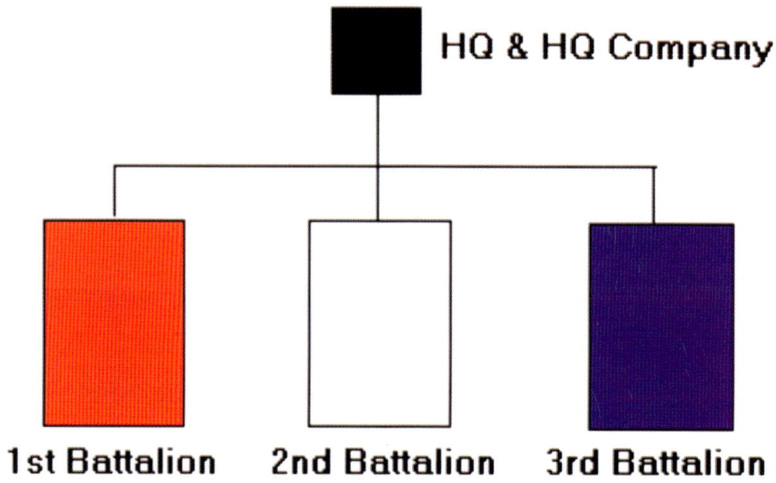

Heavy Tank Regiment
1927

total strength of seventy-five light tanks and signal tanks.[2] In 1927, the tank battalion was modified by the removal of the signal tanks from the individual companies and the assignment of a single signal tank in the battalion headquarters. The newly organized light tank regiment was supposed to contain three tank battalions, each having seventy-three tanks assigned, for a total of 249 tanks. In practice, only two of the battalions were activated – the first and second. The third battalion was not activated until 1931.

The Heavy Tank Battalion and Company

The Heavy Tank Company was modified from the original World War I model, which had three platoons of five tanks each and a HQ section with a signals tank and eight "spare" tanks. The old Mark V and Mark V* tanks were quickly replaced with the newer "International" Heavy Tank – the Mark VIII. By 1925 it consisted of a Headquarters section - with six reserve tanks, and three line platoons, each of which containing only three tanks rather than the original five. This gave the company a strength of fifteen Mk VIII heavy tanks, quite a drop from the twenty-four tanks originally authorized.

The Heavy Tank Battalion consisted of three of these tank companies, giving it a total combined strength of forty-five heavy tanks as opposed to the original proposed seventy-three heavy tanks.[3]

The heavy tank regiment was authorized in 1927 and, as with the light tank regiment, it was supposed to contain a total of nine tank companies, organized into three battalions. In practice, only one company was even activated in the regiment, F Company – part of the 2nd Battalion.

Colors and Markings

The color of American armor from 1919 and into the early 1920s continued to be Quartermaster Corps olive drab: basically a muddy, grayish-green color.[4] In 1920 the U.S. Army Quartermaster Corps issued Specification 3-1, which specified the twenty four standard colors to be used by the U.S. Army, one of these being olive-drab.[5] This new, lusterless color was a darker shade than the previous color of OD and would remain the standard color well through the Second World War. The interiors of the vehicles were normally painted white, with the doors being painted OD on both the inside and out, although during peacetime the doors were often left white.[6] This practice of painting tank interiors white continues to this very day.

The new lusterless olive drab, unfortunately, was easily scuffed and presented a rather rough appearance in service. Because of this the Ordnance Committee recommended in 1928 that spar varnish be added to, or applied over, the olive-drab paint used on Ordnance Corps vehicles to "give them an attractive appearance in time of peace." This treatment gave the paint a darker, glossy appearance as opposed to the lighter, flat finish that was normally applied during wartime.[7] Because of the use of linseed oil as base, the paints used prior to 1937 had a long drying time, tended to cover unevenly, and didn't blend well with previous coats.[8]

Tanks during the 1920s did not always receive unit markings, due to a proviso written into the army regulation governing the marking of property.[9] If the vehicles were marked, the markings were in white and were placed on the side plates of the turret (in the case of the light tanks) or on the sides of the sponsons (in the case of the heavy tanks).

Taking advantage of this proviso, most units never bothered to place unit markings on their tanks. Photographs of the Mk VIII Heavy tanks assigned to the 17th Heavy Tank Battalion reveal no markings other than the vehicle serial number.[10] The 16th Light Tank Battalion likewise did not mark their vehicles, except for a three-inch tall lineal number painted on the downward slope of the front hull armor plate.

If markings were used, there was a choice of two marking systems under AR 850-5 *Marking of Equipment, Vehicles, and Property*. The first system called for a straight line marking placed between two white horizontal lines. A full color rendition of the Division unit shoulder patch was painted to the left, with the sub-unit designation stenciled in white to the right. Numbers and capitals were three inches tall, while the small letters were one and one-half inches tall. These markings were applied on both sides of the tank turret. This system was designed primarily for use by units attached to an Army Division.

Under the second system, the marking for tanks consisted of the Infantry crossed rifles, approximately thirteen inches wide and nine inches tall, with the appropriate unit numbers and letters in three-inch stencils above or below the insignia. This system of markings was the most appropriate for the tank regiments and battalions, since these units existed independent of the Army Division. It was also a popular system, since it called for a simple stencil and only one color. In any case, the use of both of these marking systems continued until the eve of the Second World War.

In 1931, a change to AR 850-5 required that all U.S. Army vehicles be marked with unit markings. As part of the change, a special branch insignia was prescribed for the Infantry (Tanks): the emblem of crossed rifles with a Mark VIII Heavy Tank superimposed. For the M1917 Light Tank, the marking was stenciled in white on either side of the turret, just below the pistol port. On the Mk VIII Heavy Tanks, it was stenciled in white on each side of the main turret directly below the outlook turret. These markings apparently were supposed to supercede the previously prescribed markings, however some units persisted in using the older system of marking their tanks.

In addition to this branch marking, the company identification number was applied in three-inch tall numerals to the outside armor: centered on the nose of the M1917 Light Tank, and within the triangular splash angle at the front of the Mk VIII Heavy Tank.[11] In the 1st Tank Regiment, all of the light tanks were stenciled in accordance with regulations, with a white three inch tall "1" above the tank emblem and a white three inch tall company letter below.

15th Composite Tank Battalion

Composed, as it was, of two companies of light tanks and a single heavy tank company, the 15th Composite Tank Battalion apparently did not mark either its light tanks or heavy tanks with any recognizable unit markings until at least 1927. It can be assumed, however, that the light tanks were stenciled on the front slope with a company or platoon lineal number. By 1927, the unit had created and adopted a marking system that was soon adopted (with modifications) by the 16th Tank Battalion at Fort Meade, MD. Although no description of the markings have been discovered, it can probably be assumed that it involved the use of colored stripes around the turret cupola on the light tanks and on the driving cupola on the heavy tanks. Vehicle lineal numbers were probably applied in white. It is assumed that red, yellow, and blue – the colors of the Tank Corps – were probably utilized for the stripes.

16th Light Tank Battalion

The battalion was, for the most part, equipped with M1917 Light Tanks. Little is known of their marking scheme of the early 1920s. Because of their size of the unit, it may be assumed that they at least used vehicle lineal numbers – but no record of their marking scheme has yet surfaced for the period prior to 1927.

In 1927, the 16th Tank Battalion (Light) at Fort George G. Meade began using a new system of home grown tactical markings to identify its tanks.[12] Under this system, each tank within the battalion had a color stripe painted around the base of the tank tower[13] to designate the company to which it belonged; red for "A", yellow for "B", or blue for "C". In addition, each tank assigned to a combat platoon was equipped with two twelve inch diameter metal plates, painted in the platoon color; red for 1st platoon, yellow for 2nd platoon, or blue for 3rd platoon. These plates were marked with a black or white number (depending on the background color), from 1 through 5, to designate the vehicle's linear number within the platoon and were designed to bolt into the loopholes (pistol ports) at either side of the turret. Because they were removable, this allowed the vehicles to be transferred between the Reserve and Training section of the company headquarters, and the combat platoons within the company. The company tanks were also marked with a four-inch tall number (from 1 to 25) on the front and on both sides of the engine compartment.[14]

When the unit was re-designated as the 1st Battalion, 66th Infantry Regiment (Light Tanks) in 1932, the use of the stripes around the turret continued – but the markings on the engine compartment were increased in size from four inches to nearly

Mark VIII Heavy Tank of the 15th Composite Tank Battalion at Fort Benning, GA, circa 1920. The tank is painted in a flat Quartermaster olive drab with no visible markings except for the white registration number at either side of the hull.

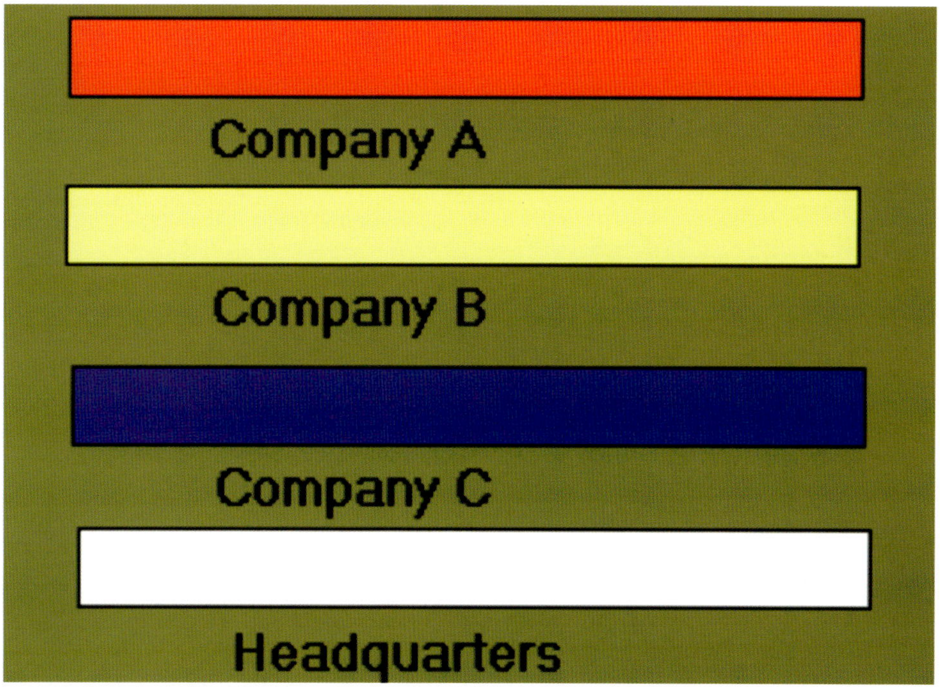

Striped markings used around the base of the cupola on 16th Tank Battalion tanks.

Example of vehicle lineal number for 16th Tank Battalion tanks. The blue color, counter shaded with white, indicates company C.

Examples of the painted steel plates inserted into the pistol port on the M1917 Light Tank turrets of the 16th Tank Battalion.

twenty-four inches. The numbers were applied in the company color with Companies A and C often being additionally painted with a white shadow, since the red and blue colors did not show up well against the olive-drab background. Photographs of the tanks assigned to that unit shows similar stripes being used on their M1917 Light Tanks.[15] Many tank units simply did not mark their vehicles with unit designations until the late 1920s.

1st Tank Regiment (Light Tanks)

Created by the amalgamation of the 15th Composite Tank Battalion and 16th and 17th Light Tank Battalions, the 1st Tank Regiment (and its subsequent re-designations) was the U.S. Army's only light tank regiment until the eve of World War II. Formed on 1 September 1929, it was equipped entirely with M1917 Light Tanks. Since Army Regulations initially did not mandate the marking of tanks, the unit's tanks were left unmarked except for the obligatory unit lineal number painted on the front of the light tanks. With the adoption of a new AR 850-5 in March of 1931, the entire unit was re-painted in a dark, gloss olive-drab paint with the Infantry (Tanks) insignia painted on either side of the turret in white paint. The regimental number was painted above the insignia, with the company letter painted below.

It is very probable that all three of the battalions adopted a form of the marking system used by the 16th Tank Battalion (which was based on a system developed by the 15th Composite Tank Battalion). This would involve marking the cupola of the light tank with a stripe to designate the company within the battalion: red for 1st company, yellow for 2nd company, and blue for 3rd company. This has not been confirmed, but photographic evidence seems to support this assumption.

Attack by M1917 Light Tanks of the 1st Battalion, 1st Tank Regiment and Company I of the regiment in mid-1931. Several of the lead vehicles exhibit the markings of Company I – the white stripe and white lineal numbers. Vehicles further in the background are evidently part of Company B, as the blue color of its stripe marking does not show up well against the gloss olive-drab finish coat. The lineal numbers for the vehicles are clearly visible on the front slope.

1st Battalion

When the 16th Tank Battalion was re-designated as the 1st Battalion, 1st Tank Regiment in 1929, it continued to use its previous marking system in a modified form. The use of the metal designator plates was dropped, but the use of the colored stripes continued.

What is interesting to note is that when the battalion was ordered to supply tanks for the experimental Mechanized Force at Fort Eustis, the tanks from Company A arrived there with absolutely no markings on them at all – not even the company lineal number. The adoption of the new regulation in March of 1931, however, resulted in the proper markings being applied.

In 1932 the entire regiment was re-designated to bring it into line with the rest of the Infantry Branch, and it was renamed the 66th Infantry Regiment (Light Tanks).

M1917 Light Tank of Company A, 1st Tank Regiment being transported while assigned to the Mechanized Force in early 1931. The stripe around the tower of the cupola is not visible at this angle, but should be red, designating Company A.

Offloading an M1917 Light Tank from its transporter for use by the Mechanized Force in early 1931. Assigned to Company A, 1st Tank Regiment, the vehicle lacks any markings at this point.

Light tank of Company A, 1st Tank Regiment operating with the Mechanized Force in early 1931. The vehicle lineal marking is clearly visible on the nose of the tank.

M1917 Light Tank of Company A, 66th Infantry Regiment (Light Tanks) being off-loaded from its transport truck at Fort Meade, MD, 1932. The red stripe around the turret, as well as the white counter-shaded red "5" are clearly visible in this photograph.

M1917 Light Tanks await loading onto the transport trucks at Fort Meade in 1932. The left tank is marked for Company I, while the right tank is marked for Company C of the 66th Infantry Regiment (Light Tanks). The blue color used for C Company tanks makes the lineal number "5", as well as the painted cupola and hatch of the signal tank barely visible. In contrast, the white cupola and hatch of the Company I signal tank are clearly visible, as is the vehicle lineal number.

M1917 Light Tank assigned to Company I, 3rd Battalion, 1st Tank Regiment. The vehicle lineal number is painted in white on the top of the engine compartment in back, with the Infantry – Tanks emblem on the turret. A broad white stripe is painted around the base of the cupola (tower). Circa 1930.

2nd Battalion

Formed from the 15th Composite Tank Battalion, it originally consisted of two companies of light tanks and one company of heavy tanks. This third company was re-equipped with light tanks when the battalion was re-designated as the 2nd battalion of the 1st Tank Regiment. It can be assumed that it continued to use, at least in part, the marking system the battalion had developed in 1929. It is believed that this included the use of the striped markings or either red, yellow, or blue, around the base of the light tank cupola, while white was used for the lineal markings on the hull.

3rd Battalion

The 3rd Battalion was activated in September of 1931 and was, for the most part, stationed at Fort Devens, MA. Few, if any photographs of the battalion have been found during this time period and its markings are presently unknown. However, Company I was stationed at Fort Meade, MD with the 1st Battalion.

Because of this fact, Company I was marked in a similar manner to those vehicles assigned to the 1st Battalion. Each of the tanks was marked on the sides of the turret with the tank and crossed rifles of the Infantry (Tanks) in white, with the regimental number above and the company letter below. In addition, the lineal number was painted on the front plate in four-inch numerals, as well as on top of the engine compartment at the very back of the hull. Because the three main colors of red, yellow, and blue had already been used by tanks of the 1st Battalion, tanks of Company I were painted with a wide white stripe around the cupola, and the lineal vehicle markings were also in white.

1st Tank Regiment
1 September 1929 to October 25 1932
1st Battalion: Formed from 16th Tank Battalion
2nd Battalion: Formed from 15th Tank Battalion
3rd Battalion: Formed from 17th Tank Battalion (inactive until 16 September 1931)
- Headquarters & Headquarters Company: Formed from HQ 17th Tank Battalion
  - G Company formed from A & C Companies 17th Tank
  - H Company formed from A & C Companies 17th Tank
  - I Company formed from A & C Companies 17th Tank

The entire unit was re-designated as the 66th Infantry Regiment (Light Tanks) October 25, 1932

2nd Tank Regiment (Heavy Tanks)

Created at the same time as the 1st Tank Regiment, this unit was created by re-designating three heavy tank battalions – only one of which that was in fact active. The 2nd Battalion, 2nd Tank Regiment consisted of a single heavy tank company – Company F. As far as can be told, the 2nd Tank Regiment never actually used the markings called for by AR 850-5. Their tanks began to be marked with the adopted unit crest of the

Mark VIII Heavy Tanks of the 2nd Tank Regiment in their storage barns at Fort Benning, circa 1930. Like most tanks of the period, no markings are visible from this distance. (NIM)

The variety of medium tanks assigned to the Company F, 2nd Tank Regiment in 1932. All are painted in a gloss olive drab with the vehicle designation painted on the front and sides of the hull.The unit designation and Infantry-tank insignia is painted on either side of the turret in white.

17th Tank Battalion, and this practice would continue until the unit was finally brought to full strength in 1940.

The unit was issued Mark VIII Heavy Tanks, but in 1932 a variety of tanks were tested with the unit. These received markings similar to those painted on the Mark VIII tanks.

Initially, the tanks were painted in the regulation flat olive drab with the unit lineal number painted in white, twelve-inch numerals on either side of the cupola and with the serial number painted in six-inch numerals on either side of the hull near the rear. Even with the adoption of the new AR 850-5 in March of 1931, the unit crest continued to be painted in full color on either side of the tank, centered on the sponson. The Infantry (Tanks) emblem was rarely applied to any of the tanks assigned to this unit.

2nd Tank Regiment
1 September 1929 - 31 September 1932
1st Battalion (Inactive): Formed from 19th Tank Battalion
2nd Battalion (Active): Formed from 17th Heavy Tank Battalion (active) 9-1-29
F Company formed from B Company 17th Tank Battalion
Re-designated F Company 67th Infantry Regiment (Medium Tanks) 1932
Inactivated 15 Sept 1931
3rd Battalion (Inactive): Newly constituted 9-1-29

All re-designated as 67th Infantry Regiment (Medium Tanks) October 25, 1932

Rear view of a T1 (Christie) Medium Tank assigned to Company F, 2nd Tank Regiment, 1932. The vehicle is painted in a flat olive-drab. Gloss shades of olive-drab always appear darker in black and white photography. (NIM)

Left rear quarter view of a T1 (Christie) Medium Tank assigned to Company F, 2nd Tank Regiment, 1932. Notice the regulation pattern white stencil on the side of the turret. (NIM)

3

The Infantry (Tanks) Light Tank Companies 1921-1935

The dissolution of Tank Corps in June of 1920 and the assignment of tanks as a component of the Infantry Branch eventually resulted in the formation of nine Regular Army divisional tank companies. Most of these companies were activated in January of 1921, and they were technically attached to the eight Regular Army divisions and one Cavalry Division, but in practice they normally belonged to the Corps Headquarters in the area where the division was stationed. Despite being of part of the Regular Army, only a small number of these companies were issued enough tanks to fill more than one platoon. This would normally consist of the five tanks assigned to a line platoon and three spare vehicles that would have been retained in the company headquarters, for a total of eight light tanks.

1st Tank Company - I Corps Area
(Miller Field, Staten Island, NY) 1st Division
2nd Tank Company - II Corps Area
(Fort Sam Houston, TX) 2nd Division
3rd Tank Company - III Corps Area
(Fort Lewis, WA) 3rd Division
4th Tank Company - IV Corps Area
(Fort McClellan, AL) 4th Division (1 platoon)
5th Tank Company - V Corps Area
(Fort Ben Harrison, IN) 5th Division (1st Platoon only)
6th Tank Company – VI Corps Area 6th Division
(Jefferson Barracks, MO) (1 platoon only)
7th Tank Company – VII Corps Area 7th Division
(Fort Snelling, MN) (1 platoon)
10th Tank Company – 1st Cavalry Division (Fort Bliss TX)[1]
11th Tank Company – Department of Hawaii
(Schofield Barracks, Hawaii) Hawaiian Division

The American Tanker, 5th Tank Company, 1935.

Organization

As was noted in the Light Tank Battalions and Companies section, the organization of the Tank Company remained nearly unchanged during this initial post-war period. The light Tank Company continued to consist of twenty-five tanks, divided between a Headquarters section and three line platoons. Each of the line platoons was made up of five M1917 Light Tanks, two armed with the 37mm gun and the remainder was armed with a .30 caliber machine-gun.[2] The Headquarters section contained one light signal tank (M1917) and also the company's supply of nine reserve tanks (four armed with 37mm guns and five with light machine-guns).

Colors and Markings

The regulation color for tanks of this time period was the U.S. Quartermaster olive drab, as made under QM Specification 3-1. It was applied, either in its original lusterless formulation or mixed with spar varnish to lend a glossy finish.[3] During the early years of this period, tanks had few, if any, markings. By 1926, Army Regulations noted that markings for the vehicles were optional. However, if markings were used there was a choice of two marking systems under AR 850-5 *Marking of Equipment, Vehicles, and Property*.

The first system called for a straight line marking placed between two white horizontal lines. A full color rendition of the Division unit shoulder patch was painted to the left, with the sub-unit designation stenciled in white to the right. Numbers and capitals and the unit patch were three inches tall, while the small letters were one and one-half inches tall. The second marking system called for painting the Infantry crossed rifles, approximately thirteen inches wide and nine inches tall, onto the vehicle. Above and/or below the insignia was painted the appropriate unit numbers and letters in white, three-inch stencils. These markings were applied to both sides of the tank turret.

From 1921 until the adoption of the new markings regulation in March of 1931, most of divisional tank companies did not mark their tanks with anything other than a white lineal number on the front-sloped hull armor of their M1917 Light Tanks. Since most of the companies consisted of only a single platoon, this presented little or no problem. Those Regular Army Tank Companies that possessed a full complement of vehicles generally adopted a variation of the first system, which involved painting the unit markings on the upper front nose plate of their light tanks.[4]

Photographs of several tank companies show the units using a variation of the first marking system, which was authorized by Army Regulations. Under this variation, the markings were usually painted on the front hull armor, and took the form of the divisional patch, in color, with unit designation below in white (*see* below).[5]

Although at first the army regulations had made the marking of tanks optional, this changed with the approval of the new AR 850-5 dated March 16, 1931. The new publication mandated that all tanks be marked, and authorized the newly designed Infantry (Tanks) emblem – crossed rifles with a Mk.VIII tank superimposed at the center.

For the M1917 Light Tank, the marking was stenciled in white on either side of the turret, just below the pistol port. In addition, the regulations called for a three-inch tall company identification number to be painted on the nose of the M1917 Light Tank.[6]

1st Tank Company

Located on Staten Island, New York, the 1st Tank Company, 1st Division, Regular Army, was one of two Regular Army tank companies that were issued a full complement (25) of M1917 Light Tanks. It used a variation of the authorized markings on their M1917 Light Tanks. This consisted of the unit insignia, a red "1" surrounded by a black outline in the shape of a shield, and surrounded by a white wreath, which was painted on either side of the turret beneath the pistol port. The unit linear number was then painted in white on the front hull armor and on either side of the engine compartment.[7]

Four M1917 Light Tanks assigned to the 1st Tank Company. The unit insignia is visible on only one of the four vehicles and is painted on the sides of the turret. The vehicle lineal number is painted in white on both the front of the vehicle and on either side of the engine compartment. (MB)

2nd Tank Company

Activated in late January 1921, the company was assigned to the 2nd Division out of Fort Sam Houston in Texas. Like most of the regular tank companies, the 2nd Tank Company was issued only a partial complement of eight M1917 light tanks when it was organized, but this was increased rather quickly to the full complement of twenty-five. The unit received its first tanks from Fort Meade, many of which apparently arrived in the experimental camouflage then in vogue. The only photographs that have surfaced of the company in this early time period were taken around 1921, showing the tanks painted in a three-color camouflage. The colors used were probably a dark yellow or tan, olive drab, and brown.

M1917 Light Tank of the 2nd Tank Company during a public demonstration and parade at Fort Brown Texas, circa 1922. The tank is in a three-color camouflage overall – probably olive drab, brown, and a dark yellow or tan. The five-pointed star is painted in white on both sides of the turret with the vehicle's lineal number (8) painted in black or olive-drab. The star is reminiscent of the shoulder patch of the 2nd Division.

Second photograph of the same vehicle in front of a Southern Pacific Railroad car at Fort Brown, Texas circa 1922. The camouflage pattern is much clearer in this particular shot.

Tank number 7 of the 2nd Tank Company during a public parade around 1922. The camouflage pattern is not clear in this photograph, but is present.

Another photograph of tank number 7, 2nd Tank Company, circa 1922. The camouflage pattern on the turret is clearly visible.

M1917 Light Tank of the 2nd Tank Company. The vehicle is painted flat olive drab with a very small white star, outlined in black, stenciled high on the side of the turret. Inside the star is a full color Indian-head looking forward. The photo was taken around 1923.

Members and tanks of the 2nd Tank Company in October 1931. The tanks are painted gloss olive drab with the white Infantry-Tanks emblem on both sides of the turret. The right tank shows the lineal number "15" painted in six-inch numerals on the nose of the hull.

Apparently the first markings for the unit were fairly crude, consisting of a large, five-pointed white star painted on either side of the turret. The idea for the star was drawn from the 2nd Division's unit patch, which uses a star as a background for the full color Indian-head motif. In the center of the star is a four to five inch tall vehicle lineal number, between one and eight, applied in either black or olive drab paint. No other markings were apparently used with this paint scheme.

When the vehicles were repainted in 1922-1923, they were painted in a flat olive drab paint and marked on the side of each turret with a small (approximately 4-inch diameter) white star outlined in black with a full color Indian head at the center. It is assumed that a vehicle lineal number was painted on the nose of the hull. In 1931, as a result of the revised AR 850-5, the entire company had the old markings painted out and the new required Infantry-tank emblem painted on either side of the turret with the company number below. The vehicle lineal number was painted on the nose of the vehicle in white.

In 1931 the company repainted and remarked their tanks in order to bring them into line with the new AR 850-5, the regulation that governs the marking of Army equipment. The vehicles were painted a gloss olive drab with the Infantry-tanks emblem painted in white on either side of the turret. The vehicle lineal number was painted on the nose of the hull. The highest number noted so far is "15."

Color example of markings for the 3rd Tank Company.

M1917 Light Tank of the 3rd Tank Company showing the markings on the front of the hull. The regulation markings are also just visible at the side of the turret.

3rd Tank Company

It is not known what markings were initially used by the 3rd Tank Company when it received eight M1917 Light Tanks in 1921. However, by 1932, the 3rd Tank Company was using a combination of both of the authorized marking systems, painting a large version of their unit patch on the front slope of the M1917 Light Tank, in full color, with the unit designation below in white. In addition, the Infantry (Tanks) insignia was painted on both sides of the turret, just below the pistol port, in white stencils, with "3" below it.

4th Tank Company

As with most of the Regular Army Tank Companies, the 4th Tank Company did not paint its tanks with identification markings prior to the adoption of the March 1931 version of AR 850-5. The unit did mark the vehicle's lineal number on the front slope in a four-inch white numeral.

The 4th Tank Company was issued, for a short time, a number of T4E1 Light Tanks for testing. No special markings, other than the unit lineal number on the front of the hull, were applied

M1917 Light Tank assigned to the 5th Tank Company on the firing line at Fort McClellan, AL, circa 1935. Due to the heavy dust and dirt covering the tanks, the only marking visible is the Infantry-Tank stencil on the sides of the turret. (PM - Scheller)

Three M1917 Light Tanks of the 5th Tank Company, Fort McClellan, circa 1935. On the side of the engine compartment is visible the vehicle's lineal number in white paint. (PM – Scheller)

When finally forced to mark their vehicles, the unit adopted the second marking system, painting the Infantry (Tanks) emblem in white on both sides of the turret on their M1917 Light Tanks with a four-inch tall "4" underneath. The company lineal number was painted on the front slope in four-inch white numerals.

5th Tank Company

From its inception in 1921, until it was forced to mark its vehicles in 1931, the 5th Tank Company simply painted a four-inch tall white company lineal number on the front and on either side of the engine compartment. In 1931, the unit finally painted the regulation Infantry (Tanks) emblem in white on both sides of the turret, as required by regulations – but did not include its company number.

6th Tank Company

Like the 5th Tank Company, the 6th Tank Company consisted of a single platoon (five tanks plus three spares for a total of eight) and did not place any unit markings on its vehicles except for the white company lineal number on the front of the tank. The unit went through several changes during its existence – being inactivated and re-activated at least twice.

M1917 Light Tank of the 6th Tank Company being used to familiarize Army Reservists at a National Guard Camp in Illinois, circa 1932. The vehicle lineal number is visible on side of the engine compartment. The tank commander's name is just visible stenciled on the left side of the turret in one-inch white letters. (PM - Smith)

Front of the same tank from the 6th Tank Company, showing the vehicle lineal number painted on the nose of the hull. (PM - Smith)

Five tanks of the 6th Tank Company during demonstrations for Army Reserve officers at a Camp in Illinois, circa 1932. (PM - Smith)

Newly issued M1917 Light Tanks of the 11th Tank Company at Fort Shafter in Hawaii. The tanks are painted in gloss olive drab and have yet to receive any stenciled markings. Photograph taken circa 1922. (TLM)

New M1917 Light Tank of the 11th Tank Company during an open house for the public, circa 1923. The tank has full equipment installed, with all of its doors open for easy inspection. No markings have been applied. (TLM)

7th Tank Company

With the adoption of the newest version of AR 850-5 in March of 1931, the 7th Tank Company began marking its tanks with the Infantry (Tanks) emblem on each side of the turret, but with a twist. Besides the "7" painted underneath the emblem, the unit also painted a three-inch diameter 7th Division patch just above it.

11th Tank Company

Constituted 16 November 1921 in the Regular Army as the 11th Tank Company, the unit was activated on 19 November 1921 at Camp George G. Meade, Maryland and assigned to the Hawaiian Division on 15 July 1922. It was relieved 1 October 1941 from assignment to the Hawaiian Division and finally disbanded on 23 April 1942 in Hawaii

The 11th Tank Company was the only other Tank Company (besides the 1st Tank Company) that received its full complement of tanks from the start. It was issued twenty-five M1917 Six-ton Tanks in 1921-1922, but it is not known whether the unit painted anything on their vehicles prior to 1931. Photographs of their first vehicles reveal no markings.

With the adoption of the new AR 850-5 in 1931, the 11th Tank Company began marking their tanks with a very elaborate white and black stencil of the Infantry (tanks) emblem. They continued to paint the company lineal number on the front slope of their vehicles. The vehicles themselves were painted in the regulation olive drab with a gloss finish.

M1917 Light Tanks of the 11th Tank Company, Hawaiian Division, circa 1932. In accordance with regulations, the Infantry-Tank emblem has been painted on either side of the turret. However, the stencil is extremely detailed, with the company number painted below. The stencil is outlined in black. Although not visible, the company letter is painted on the nose and on either side of the hull in white, four-inch numbers.

Closeup of the 11th Tank Company markings stenciled on the both sides of the turret. The black outlining is clearly visible. The vehicle is painted in a base coat of gloss olive drab. (TLM)

Hawaiian Division open house, circa 1935. This M1917 Light Tank has a new fresh paint job with fresh stenciling. The Infantry-Tank emblem is painted on either side of the turret in white and black. On the forward part of the turret is a full color divisional patch of green, black and red. On the side of the hull is painted a black "spade", evidently a platoon marking. Below this marking would be the lineal number of the vehicle – and these markings are duplicated on the nose of the hull. (TLM)

M1917 Light Tank of the 11th Tank Company being utilized as a monument vehicle at Fort Shafter, Hawaiian Territory, circa 1938. This tank is painted in the last scheme used for these light tanks. The tank has the Infantry-Tank emblem painted on either side of the turret, along with a full color rendition of the divisional shoulder patch. On the nose of the hull, and on either side of the engine compartment, is the platoon marking (a diamond) and the vehicle lineal number. These appear to be applied in black. TLM

4

National Guard Tank Companies 1921-1935

In addition to the formation of regular Army tank regiments and battalions, the establishment of the Infantry (Tanks) sub-branch in 1921 also resulted in the assignment of tanks to the individual Regular and National Guard Divisions throughout the United States. These companies were normally assigned to the division headquarters as Special Troops.

Several of these divisions (the 32nd, 33rd, and 37th) already had tank companies experimentally attached through the auspices of the Tank Corps. When the Tank Corps was dissolved in 1921, these existing companies were re-designated and permanently assigned.

Unit Designation and Assigned Headquarters of National Guard Tank Companies
(in order of date of organization)

32nd Tank Company (Janesville, WI) Company I Tank Corps 31 March 1920, 30 November 1921
33rd Tank Company (Maywood, IL) Company G Tank Corps 17 Nov 1920, 13 December 1921
37th Tank Company (Port Clinton, OH) Company H Tank Corps 21 June 1920, 1 July 1921
38th Tank Company (Harrodsburg, KY) 29 March 1921
39th Tank Company (Alabama NG) 11 May 1921 re-designated 31st Tank Co. 1 July 1923
27th Tank Company (New York, NY) 1 September 1921
29th Tank Company (Danville, VA) 17 October 1921
45th Tank Company (Denver, CO) Tank Co. Corps Troops 24 March 1921, 1 November 1921
28th Tank Company (Norristown, PA) 25 November 1921
35th Tank Company (St. Joseph, MO) 5 March 1923
31st Tank Company (Ozark, AL) 1 July 1923
26th Tank Company (Boston, MA) 11 March 1924
40th Tank Company (Salinas, CA) 18 June 1924
30th Tank Company (Forsyth, GA) 15 August 1924
43rd Tank Company (Hartford, CT) 1 May 1931
41st Tank Company (Washington State)

Organization

Each of the individual (or Divisional) National Guard tank companies were officially organized under the same table of organization and equipment as the regular Army Tank Company, consisting of three platoons of five tanks each, with a signal tank and nine spare tanks in the company HQ section. Owing to the lack of available tanks, all of these units lacked sufficient tanks to fill out the company and few were given any more than eight of the required twenty-five tanks. The eight tanks represented a full platoon, with its three spare tanks – the same that would have been available to a platoon in a complete company. The National Guard would continue to suffer from lack of equipment until the very eve of World War II.

The American Tanker, 38th Tank Company, Kentucky National Guard, 1932.

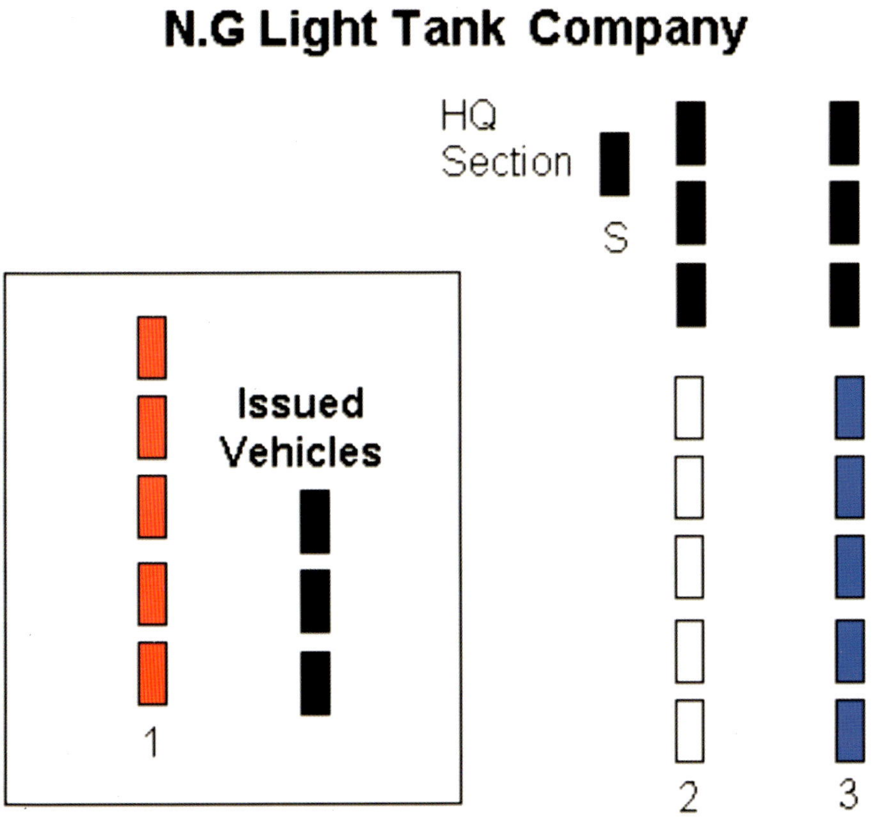

Colors and Markings

As with the regular army vehicles, the National Guard vehicles were painted in Quartermaster olive drab – with either a lusterless or gloss finish. For their first ten years of existence, the National Guard divisional tank companies were not required to mark their vehicles. However, a few units did exercise their options under AR 850-5, and marked their vehicles with some variation of the prescribed marking systems.

As with the Regular Army, the 1931 change to the regulation required the National Guard units to mark their tanks with the new Infantry (Tanks) emblem. It should be pointed out that the regulation was somewhat confusing, as there was no option to mark vehicles with other than regimental markings. In simpler terms, the regulation laid out the markings for regimental vehicles and equipment, but not for individual companies.

M1917 Light Tank of an unknown Tank Company stopped along a city road, circa 1925. The tank is painted in flat olive drab paint with no visible markings.

M1917 Light Tank parked on a busy city street circa 1924. The 37mm gun tank is painted in flat olive drab with no visible markings, typical of National Guard tank companies of the time period.

Another M1917 Light Tank parked along the side of a city street circa 1925. The tank is painted in flat olive drab paint. The white paint on the inside of the turret and hull doors is clearly visible.

In spite of that, some National Guard units did attempt to comply with the new regulation. However, by the early 1930s, the M1917 Light Tanks were beginning to fail because of lack of parts. By 1935 many of the units had already been forced to park some or all of their vehicles.

Units tended to mark their tanks as they thought necessary. Of the two marking systems offered in the army regulations after 1931, photographs of divisional tank companies show that many units used a variation of the first marking system. Under this variation, the markings were painted on the front hull armor taking the form of the divisional patch in color. Underneath was painted the unit designation in white.[1] Most of the National Guard and Regular Army divisional tank companies adopted some variation of the first system, painting the unit markings on the upper front nose plate of their light tanks.[2]

Photographs of tanks during this time period are rare, and written descriptions of markings (outside of the Army Regulations) appear to be almost non-existent. Some units did not adopt a tactical marking system until the late 1930s, and the markings used by National Guard units were discovered by inspection of photographs taken during the period. Markings (or lack thereof) for National Guard units are noted in the following paragraphs.

27th Tank Company

The eight tanks issued to the 27th Tank Company were stenciled in six-inch white letters "27TH/TANK CO" in two lines on each side of the turret. The unit lineal number (1 through 8) was painted in white on the front slope in four-inch numerals.

32nd Tank Company

When the 32nd Tank Company, Wisconsin National Guard, received its eight M1917 Light Tanks in the early 1920s they were marked only with a white, 4-inch tall, lineal number from "1" to "8". These were painted on the nose of the tank, as well as both sides of the turret and on both sides of the engine compartment. Those painted on the engine compartment were located high on the hull.[3] In 1935, the unit was told to store their vehicles and the company was converted to a truck company until newer tanks could be obtained – an event that did not occur until 1937.

Four M1917 Light Tanks assigned to the 32nd Tank Company, Wisconsin National Guard at Camp McCoy, Wisconsin, in July of 1928. The vehicle lineal number is visible high on the side of the engine compartment of the closest vehicle, four-inches tall. This number is also repeated on the front of the hull.

35th Tank Company

The 35th Tank Company, Missouri National Guard marked several of its vehicles with the tricolor armor triangle, which was painted on the upper front nose plate. With the adoption of the new markings regulation in 1931, the 35th Tank Company adopted the second marking system, placing the new Infantry (Tanks) emblem on either side of the turret with "35" below it in three-inch numerals.

Two M1917 light tanks belonging to the 35th Tank Company, one machinegun, one 37mm gun (although the gun is not installed). The vehicles are dust covered, making them appear lighter in color than they actually are. On the front of the closest vehicle can be seen a faint, full color, Tank Corps patch. Photo taken around 1929. (PH)

Tanks of the 35th Tank Company during gunnery practice in 1930. No markings are visible on the sides of the hull or turret. (PH)

38th Tank Company

Issued eight M1917 Light Tanks in the early 1920s, the 38th Tank Company, Kentucky National Guard, did not paint any markings on their vehicles – not even lineal numbers. Their vehicles were painted in flat olive-drab, unlike many other units, which painted their tanks in the gloss paint.

M1917 Light Tank and B Model Liberty Truck of the 38th Tank Company, Kentucky National Guard. The photograph was taken 3 August 1931 at Camp Knox, KY. (PM - McClain)

Group of tanks of the 38th Tank Company, Kentucky National Guard, during training at Camp Knox 3 August 1931. They are all painted in a flat olive-drab paint, making them appear lighter in shade than normally assumed. No markings are visible on sides of the hull or turret. (PM - McClain)

40th Tank Company

As with most of National Guard units, the 40th Tank Company initially did not paint anything on their vehicles. Issued eight tanks in 1923, by 1930 the unit was marking their vehicles by painting a full color 40th Division patch on the front of their tanks with the unit designation below in white. With the adoption of the Infantry (Tanks) emblem in 1931, the 40th Tank Company switched to the new marking convention.

M1917 Light Tank from the 40th Tank Company, California National Guard, on a movie set in Hollywood in the summer of 1930. The movie star, Wallace Beery, was on the set for another movie when this photo opportunity arose. The divisional patch is painted in full color on the nose of the hull, with the company designation below. The vehicle is painted gloss olive-drab. No vehicle lineal number is visible.

An M1917 Light Tank of the 40th Tank Company, California National Guard, climbing a slope on maneuvers in 1933. The tank is properly marked with the new authorized emblem called for by the most recent change to the Army regulations. Vehicle lineal numbers are still not being used by the company, even at this late date. (PM - Icks)

Side view of an M1917 Light Tank assigned to the 45th Tank Company. Interestingly, the tank's serial number is stenciled below the unit marking on the turret. Photo was taken circa 1923.

45th Tank Company

The 45th Tank Company had been issued all eight of its tanks by the end of 1922. The tanks were painted in the regulation olive-drab with the company designation painted on either side of the turret in white 3-inch sans-serif stencils. The tank's serial number was stenciled below. So far, only one photograph of this company has come to light.

5

Infantry (Tanks) Tank Regiments & Battalions 1932-1935

In October of 1932 the U.S. Army's two tank regiments, now both headquartered at Fort Benning, were re-designated as Infantry (Tanks) regiments. The 1st Tank Regiment was renamed the 66th Infantry Regiment (Light Tanks) – with the 1st Battalion stationed at Fort Meade, MD, the 2nd Battalion stationed at Fort Benning, GA, and 3rd Battalion stationed at Fort Devens, MA. The 2nd Tank Regiment became the 67th Infantry Regiment (Heavy Tanks), stationed at Fort Benning. These two regiments would constitute the backbone of the U.S. Army Infantry (tanks) until the activation of the National Guard tank companies in 1940.

The American Tanker, 67th Infantry Regiment (Medium Tanks), 1934.

The only significant "combat" use of tanks by the U.S. Army in this time-frame was the suppression of the Bonus March in late July of 1932, and then only one company of the 1st Battalion, 1st Tank Regiment was utilized for that purpose.

Organization

Light Tank Regiment

The organization for the infantry regiment (Light Tanks) remained the same as it had been before 1931, continuing the wartime organization of twenty-five tanks divided between a Headquarters section and three line platoons. Each of the line platoons was made up of five M1917 Light Tanks, two armed with the 37mm gun and the remainder was armed with a .30 caliber machine-gun. The Headquarters section contained the company's supply of nine reserve tanks (four armed with 37mm guns and five with light machine-guns).

The Light Tank Battalion was made up of three light tank companies, and a headquarters and headquarters company. Unlike the earlier organization, the battalion Headquarters Company had only the single signals tank with no other armor attached. This gave the battalion a total strength of seventy-five light tanks and signal tanks. The light tank regiment contained three tank battalions, each having seventy-three tanks assigned, for a total of 249 tanks.

Heavy Tank Regiment

There was no change in organization from the previous time period. The sole active company was equipped primarily with the Mk.VIII Heavy Tank during this time period, but also was assigned several other types of tanks for evaluation. These tanks included the T1E1 Medium Tank and the T3 Christie Medium Tank. By 1935 the Mark VIII Heavy Tanks had been declared obsolete and were taken completely out of service. In the light of this, the unit was re-designated as a medium tank regiment and was being re-equipped with the T4 series of medium tank.

Colors and Markings

The vehicles were painted in the Quartermaster olive drab in mixed in accordance with Quartermaster specification 3-1. The finish could be either the original lusterless paint, or mixed with spar varnish to give the paint a glossy finish. Those finished in a gloss coat appear to be darker in color than those with the lusterless finish. As was standard with American tanks, the interiors were painted in white – including the engine compartment.

66th Infantry Regiment (Light Tanks)

When the 1st Tank Regiment was re-designated as the 66th Infantry Regiment in late 1932, the tanks were re-marked to reflect the change in unit designation.[1] However, since the unit had been divided between Fort George Meade in Maryland, Fort Devens in Massachusetts, and the Infantry School at Fort Benning, Georgia, there were differences in how the vehicles were marked.

The 1st Battalion of the regiment was stationed at their old home at Fort Meade, MD. Having been formed originally from the 16th Tank Battalion, the unit began using a form of the marking system that had been originally been adopted in the late 1920s. Instead of utilizing the approved Infantry (Tanks)

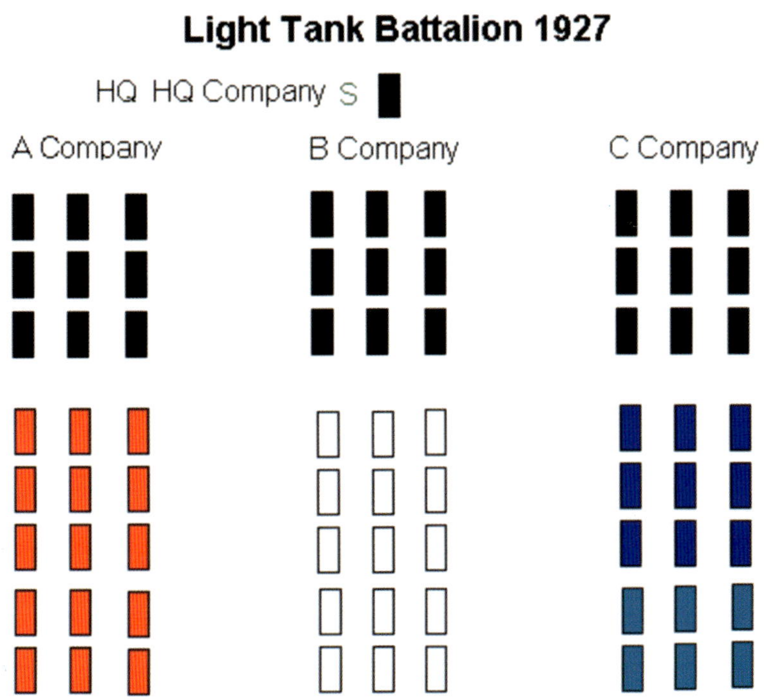

marking, which consisted of the infantry crossed rifles with the silhouette of a Mk VIII heavy tank superimposed, the battalion painted its vehicles with the Infantry crossed rifles. The markings were of the size called for in AR 850-5, and were painted in white with "66" above the emblem and with the company letter below. It would appear that the company letter was applied in the company color.

These colors used by the battalion were red for Company A, yellow for Company B, and blue for Company C. In addition to the branch marking, a three to four inch wide stripe was painted in around the turret tower below the hatch, also in the company color. The tank's lineal company number was applied to the front of the hull in a three-inch color figure, which was also repeated in color on both sides of the engine compartment – twenty-four inches tall. These large numbers were shaded in white for Company C. Headquarters tanks seem to have been marked completely in white, with signal tanks having the entire tower and hatch in that color.

The 2nd and 3rd Battalions, stationed at the Infantry School at Fort Benning, GA, and Fort Devens, MA respectfully, did utilize the regulation Infantry (Tanks) emblem, as called for by Army regulations. Markings were applied in white, with the company lineal number applied in white, three-inch figures on the front slope and on the top armor over the engine compartment.

M1917 Light Tanks assigned to Company A, 1st Battalion, 66th Infantry Regiment (Light Tanks) circa 1933. On both sides of the turret is stenciled the Infantry "crossed rifles" with the regimental number above and the company letter below. The vehicle lineal number painted in large numerals on both sides of the hull in the back in red, the company color, counter-shaded in white. In addition there is a wide red band painted around the cupola tower.

M1917 Light Tanks belonging to Company B, 1st Battalion, 66th Infantry Regiment (Light Tanks) being off-loaded from their transport trucks, Fort Meade, MD 1933. Painted around the cupola tower is a wide yellow stripe, with the lineal number painted in the same color on the sides of the hull. On both sides of the turret is painted the regulation unit insignia.

Scrapyard of the 1st Battalion, 66th Infantry Regiment (Light Tanks) circa 1938. The tanks are painted in a, now faded, olive drab. The tank in the foreground was originally assigned to Company B – recognizable by the yellow numbers on the side of the hull and the wide yellow stripe around the cupola tower. (TLM)

M1917 Light Tank being off-loaded from its Mack Truck transporter. The vehicle is marked for Company C, 66th Infantry Regiment (Light Tanks). The vehicle lineal number is painted in blue on either side of the engine compartment, as well as on the front slope in a smaller figure. (MB)

However, with the introduction of the new M2A1 Light Tank in 1935, the 2nd Battalion adopted an entirely new marking system for these new vehicles. The first light tanks to be given registration numbers, the numbers were painted in four-inch figures on both sides of the turret. Because the tanks were issued to only one of the three companies the markings created were platoon markings – utilizing a hollow square, triangle or circle, depending on the platoon. The vehicle's lineal number was painted at the center in white

67th Infantry Regiment (Heavy Tanks)

Formed from the 2nd Tank Regiment, which was equipped with Mk VIII Heavy Tanks, the 67th Infantry Regiment (Heavy Tanks) consisted of only a single active company and marked its tanks with the unit's crest rather than with the authorized branch insignia. The crest was painted on both sides of the tank on the gun sponsons. It was applied in full color, eighteen to twenty-four inches tall. The vehicle serial number was painted in white, four-inch numbers on both sides near the rear of the

M2A1 Light Tank assigned to the 2nd Battalion, 66th Infantry Regiment (Light Tanks) at Fort Benning, GA in 1935. The vehicle is painted in gloss olive drab with the registration numbers painted on the sides of the turret. Company markings are painted on the front of the sponsons in white.

Rear view of the same M2A1 Light Tank. The position of the rear company marking is clearly visible. The engine hand-crank connection is delineated in two colors – what appears to be a two-inch yellow square outlined in black or red.

vehicle and a ten-inch tall company number was painted on the front triangular plate as well as the vertical sides of the top casemate.

The vehicles themselves were painted a base coat of gloss olive-drab paint, which appears very dark in the period black and white photographs. As the vehicles were used, the dust would cut the glare and make the tanks appear lighter in color.

Throughout the 1930s, the Army continued to experiment with new replacement vehicles for the slow and clumsy light and heavy tanks of the World War period. The Mark VIII Heavy tank was finally declared obsolete in 1935, being replaced by the newly designed, but still experimental, medium tanks – T1E1 Medium Tank and the T3 Christie Convertible Tank being only two of many. None were supplied in great numbers.

Mark VIII Heavy Tanks awaiting destruction at Fort Meade, MD in 1940. These vehicles are painted in a flat shade of olive-drab with most still exhibiting vehicle registration and unit lineal numbers. On many can be seen the full color unit crest of the 67th Infantry Regiment (Heavy Tanks) painted on the sponsons.

Mark VIII Heavy Tank assigned to Company F, 67th Infantry Regiment (Heavy Tanks) circa 1934. The vehicle is painted in a dust colored flat olive-drab paint with its vehicle lineal number (18) painted in white on the cupola. Painted near the rear of both side sponsons is the unit's crest in full color, approximately 14-inches tall.

A Mark VIII Heavy Tank of Company F, 67th Infantry Regiment (Heavy Tanks) being demonstrated for West Point Cadets in 1934. The unit crest is clearly visible on the side of the sponson in full color. The vehicle registration number is painted in white, six to eight-inch tall numerals on the sides of the hull near the rear. Although not visible in this photograph, the vehicle lineal number was painted in white on either side of the cupola.

Mark VIII Heavy Tanks parked in a holding yard at Fort Benning, GA around 1936. Declared obsolete in 1935, it was not until 1940 that the tanks were finally scrapped. This shows a clear view of the vehicle registration number and lineal number on the vehicle in the foreground. The other vehicles have already had the markings removed. Notice also the obsolete M1917 Light Tanks in the background.

T1E1 Heavy Tank assigned to Company F, 67th Infantry Regiment (Heavy Tanks) crossing a pontoon bridge at Fort Benning in 1934. The vehicle is painted in a gloss olive-drab with the regulation pattern insignia painted on either side of the turret. A vehicle name is painted on either side of the hull in four-inch letters, but is unreadable.

Another view of a T1E1 Heavy Tank assigned to Company F, 67th Infantry Regiment (Heavy Tanks) crossing a pontoon bridge at Fort Benning in 1934.

T3 Medium Tank assigned to Company F, 67th Infantry Regiment (Heavy Tanks) circa 1934. Still considered an experimental tank at the time, this particular vehicle stenciled on the front of the hull "MEDIUM T3/CHRISTIE/1" in three lines. It was given the name "Cyclone", which was painted on both sides of the hull in white. The regulation unit insignia is painted in white on either side of the turret, with the unit crest painted in full color in front of it. (SC 34178-3)

T3 Medium Tank Pilot #2, also assigned to Company F of the 67th Infantry Regiment (Heavy Tanks) in 1933. This vehicle was given the nickname "Hurricane." (SC 34178-2)

A view of the three T3 (Christie) Medium Tanks assigned to Company F, 67th Infantry Regiment (Heavy Tanks). Notice the vehicle lineal number painted on the turret cupola and the markings painted in white on the front of the hull.

A closer view of the T3 Medium Tank, Pilot #1.

T3E2 Medium Tank after testing of light machineguns against its armor. An experimental "Christie" pattern medium tank, it was assigned to Company F, 67th Infantry Regiment (Medium Tanks) in 1935. This close-up allows us to see the full color regimental crest and the regulation Infantry insignia. Because of the variety of experimental vehicles assigned to the regiment during the 1930s, they were normally stenciled on both sides with the vehicle designation.

6

Mechanized Cavalry 1931-1936

In early 1931, the Chief of Staff of the Army, LTG Douglas MacArthur, issued a directive to all branches of the service to make their own experiments into mechanization. This directly contributed to the breakup of the experimental Mechanized Force, and lead to the establishment of the mechanized cavalry detachment.[1] When the Mechanized Force officially ceased to exist at Midnight, October 31, 1931, the Detachment, Mechanized Cavalry Regiment came into being, using the same staff, commanding officer and a portion of the cross-assigned units, as well as their equipment.

Created at 12:01am on November 1, 1931, the Detachment, Mechanized Cavalry departed Fort Eustis, where it had been operating as the Mechanized Force, for Camp Knox, Kentucky the next day. It arrived there five days later. In addition to the Detachment Headquarters and Headquarters Detachment, the unit consisted of Troop "A", 2nd Armored Car Squadron, with the 19th Ordnance Company, Company C, 13th Engineer Regiment, and the 28th Mobile Repair Service (MRS) Detachment attached – all veterans of the experimental Mechanized Force. Included in the vehicles retained by the Detachment of Mechanized Cavalry were four Christie Combat Cars – assigned to the Armored Car Troop.

On July 1, 1932, the detachment was officially renamed as the Detachment, 1st Cavalry (Mechanized).[2] In May of 1933 the 13th Engineers were detached and sent back to Fort Eustis. The 19th Ordnance Company and the 28th MRS were assigned to Camp Knox as Post Troops.

As early as November 1931 the 1st Cavalry Regiment had been considered as a candidate for mechanization and in late 1932, after delays by some members of Congress, the 1st Cavalry Regiment was officially selected to be the first cavalry unit to undergo mechanization. At the end of December 1932 the regiment, then located at Camp Marfa, Texas, was stripped of its horses. After transportation arrived from Fort Knox, the 1st Cavalry Regiment began the march to their new home.

The American Mechanized Cavalryman, 1st Cavalry Regiment (Mecz), 1936.

Leaving Camp Marfa on January 2, 1933, it arrived at Fort Knox on the 16th of January 1933, some two weeks later.

Additional troops, in the form of an artillery battalion, an engineer battalion, and other support units, were brought in and, together with the 1st Cavalry, they were organized into the 7th Cavalry Brigade (Mechanized).[3]

Organization

From 1933 until 1935, the 7th Cavalry Brigade (Mechanized) was organized around the 1st Cavalry Regiment (Mechanized). The first armored vehicles transferred to the unit were four T4 Combat Cars (Christie), as well as the various armored cars of the 2nd Armored Car Squadron, and a number of half-tracks. The cavalry regiment itself was divided into A, B, C, and D Troops with a Machinegun (MG) Troop and a Support Troop.

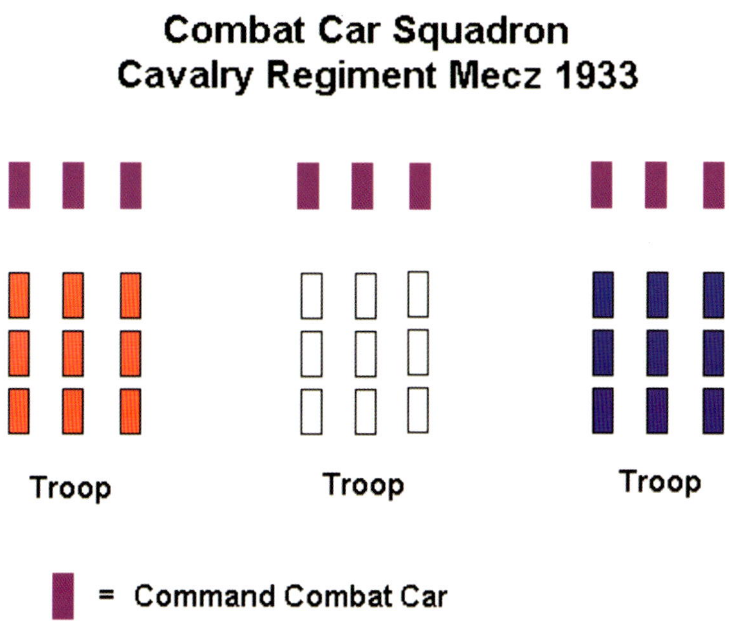

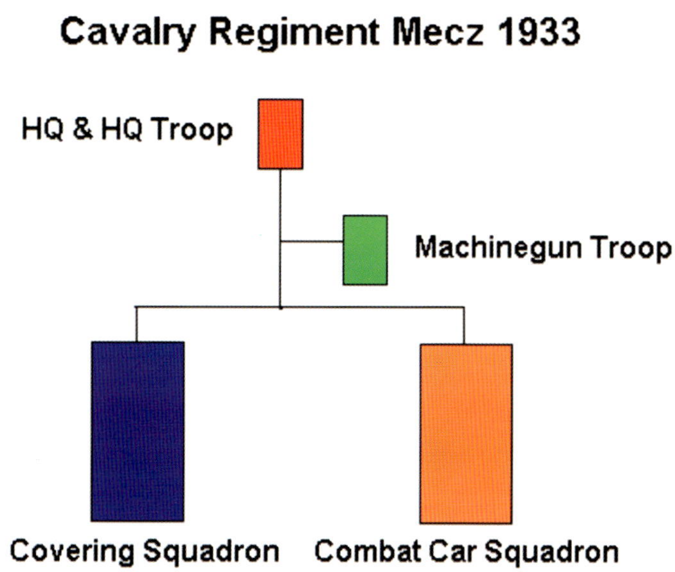

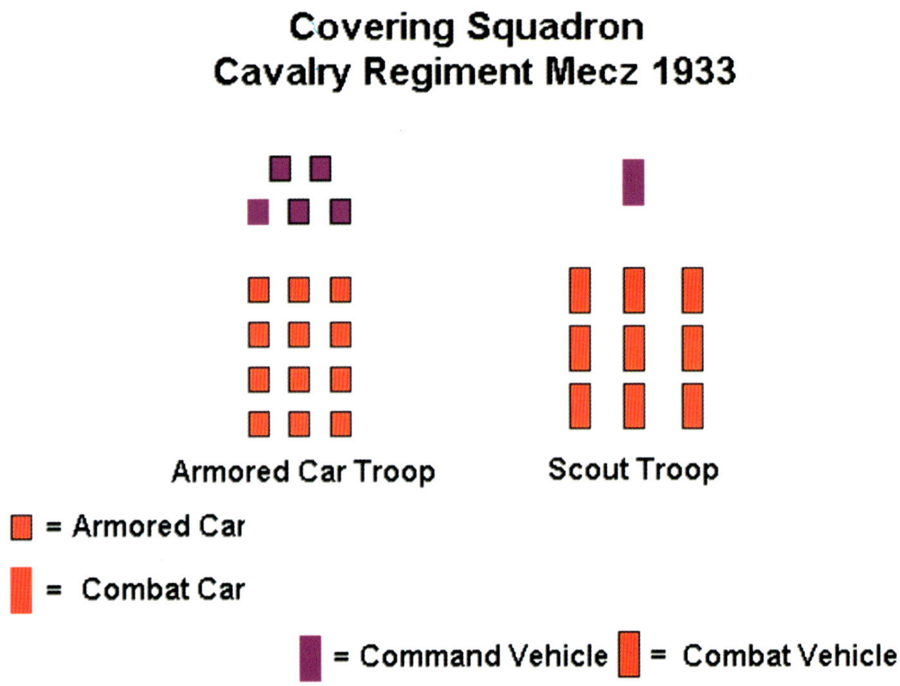

Four T1 Christie Combat Cars assigned to the 1st Cavalry Regiment (Mechanized) in 1934. All four are painted in a gloss olive drab without tactical markings.

Colors and Markings

As with all Ordnance vehicles of this period, the vehicles of cars of the mechanized cavalry were painted in the standard dark olive drab, either in a lusterless or gloss finish. Vehicle registration numbers were painted on either side of the hull in white, 4-inch tall numbers and letters.

1st Cavalry Regiment (Mechanized)

When it was first constituted the 1st Cavalry Regiment lacked much of what it required to perform its mission. Except for the armored cars of the 2nd Armored Car Squadron, the regiment had only the four T4 Christie Combat Cars that had been brought over from the remains of the Mechanized Force.

By the end of 1934, each of the vehicles assigned to the regiment had been marked with the 1st Cavalry Regimental crest in full color. On the T4 Combat Cars, these were eight to ten inches in diameter and painted in full color at the top of the front side plates where they join the roof. In addition, each side of the turret was marked with a yellow crossed saber insignia, approximately eight to ten inches tall and 20 inches wide with "1" stenciled above and "B" below for B troop.

The T4 Christie was the first combat car adopted by the U.S. Army, and when the registration numbers were finally adopted for the vehicles, they were applied in white on either side of the hull – USA 401, 402, 403, and 404.

T1 (Christie) Combat Car assigned to the Company B, 1st Cavalry Regiment (Mecz) in 1934. As required by regulations, the vehicle registration number "401" is crudely stenciled in white on either side of the front hull. Stenciled in flat yellow on either side of the turret is the regulation pattern unit insignia (crossed sabers) with the regimental number at top and company letter at the bottom. The vehicle appears to be painted in a gloss olive-drab, covered in dust. (NIM)

A T1 (Christie) Combat Car of Company C, 1st Cavalry Regiment (Mecz). This shot was taken at Fort Knox, KY in 1934. The vehicle registration number (USA 404) is stenciled on either side of the hull in front. The crossed sabers, with company letter and regimental number are painted in yellow on either side of the turret. By this time the full color unit crest had been added to each of the vehicles.

During the cavalry maneuvers of May 1934 at Fort Riley, KS, the Armored Car Troop painted their vehicles in an experimental camouflage pattern. No written information has surfaced concerning this pattern, and the vehicles were returned to the normal olive drab prior to returning to Fort Knox later in the year.

In 1935, the unit began receiving the new M1 Combat Cars. These vehicles were marked in a way similar to the T4 Combat cars, with the regimental crest remaining a main feature of the marking scheme, painted on either side of the single turret, approximately twelve inches in diameter. In addition, an open rectangle, with a one-half inch border, was painted on the front of the turret above the gun mantlet. This marking was six inches tall and nearly the width of the turret, with the unit designation and the vehicle's lineal number within the troop painted in white inside. A version of the rectangle was also stenciled on the left rear fender, but with the information rearranged to fit the available space. On some vehicles, this was painted on a metal rectangular plate bolted just above the left rear fender. The vehicle's registration number was painted in white three-inch letters and numbers on both sides of the hull. These markings remained in use until 1937.

Armored Car of the 1st Cavalry Regiment (Mecz) at Fort Riley, KS during maneuvers in 1934.The vehicle has been camouflaged in an improvised pattern over the normal olive-drab paint – probably mud.After the maneuvers the camouflage pattern was removed.

M1 Combat Car assigned to Company F, 1st Cavalry Regiment (Mecz) circa 1935.The regimental and company markings are stenciled in white along the top edge of the turret in front and repeated on a metal plate bolted to the left rear of the vehicle above the fender.The regimental crest is painted in full color on either side of the turret. The driver's name is stenciled in yellow on the left sponson in one-inch stencils.

Rear view of the markings of an M1 Combat Car attached to Company C, 1st Cavalry Regiment (Mecz), circa 1935. The rear marking plate is clearly visible at the left. During this period, the vehicle's registration number was painted across the rear of the hull in four-inch numbers and letters. Just visible on either side of the turret are yellow platoon markings that are peculiar only to Company C.

Rear view of an M1 Combat Car assigned to Company F, 1st Cavalry Regiment (Mecz) in 1936. By this time the registration number has been moved to either side of the hull and the unit markings reduced to simply the company letter stenciled on the rear of the engine compartment and on the front of the turret. The regimental crest, although not visible here, continues to be painted on either side of the turret in full color.

M1 Combat Car assigned to Headquarters, 1st Cavalry Regiment (Mecz) in 1935.

Introduction
Chapters 7-9

By 1936, the organization and composition of the Infantry (Tanks) units had begun to change. For a start, the demise of the antiquated Mk VIII heavy tank eliminated, for all practical purposes, the Heavy Tank Battalion and Regiment.[1] In the wake of this action, the 67th Infantry Regiment (Heavy Tanks) was re-designated as a medium tank regiment. That unit continued to suffer from lack of equipment and was equipped, for the most part, with what few experimental medium tanks the U.S. Army possessed. This lack of medium tanks meant that the U.S. Army now had to depend almost entirely on its light tank forces.

The introduction of the M2 series of light tanks, replacing the extremely unreliable M1917 Six-ton Tank, allowed the Army to reduce the number of tanks assigned to the light tank company. Instead of twenty-five tanks, a light tank company now only required seventeen tanks.

The American Tanker, 66th Infantry Regiment (Light Tanks), 1936.

Sign for the Headquarters of the Provisional Tank Brigade during the 1940 Third Army Maneuvers. It was soon after these maneuvers that the Armored Force was created. (PM - Scheller)

As in the previous years, the two tank regiments spent their time in training, and were involved in tank tactics development under the auspices of the Infantry School. In early 1940, as a result of both the 1939 Army maneuvers at Plattsburgh, NY, and the outbreak of war in Europe on September 1, 1939, the Infantry branch was directed to gather their tanks together to form a provisional Tank Brigade. This brigade was made up of the 66th Infantry Regiment (Light Tanks) and the 67th Infantry (Medium Tanks) Regiment, which contained the only medium tanks used during the maneuvers.[2] It also incorporated a newly activated regiment – the 68th Infantry Regiment (Light Tanks), which was formed using seven of the eight divisional tank companies that existed at the time.[3] By mid-January of 1940, most of these units had been gathered at Fort Benning, GA.

Both of the light regiments were armed with combinations of M2A1, M2A2, and M2A3 light tanks, while the sole medium tank company, Co. F, 67th Infantry Regiment (Medium Tanks) was partially armed with the recently introduced M2 Medium tank, as well as a mixture of T4 medium tanks. In May of 1940, the Provisional Tank Brigade participated in the Louisiana Maneuvers along side the 7th Cavalry Brigade (Mechanized) from Fort Knox.

On July 10, 1940, the Armored Force was established, ending armor's long, intimate, association with the Infantry and, conversely signaling the beginning of the end for the Cavalry. The creation of the 1st and 2nd Armored Divisions from the 7th Cavalry Brigade (Mechanized) and the Provisional Tank Brigade ushered in a new era of tactical markings for American tanks.

Colors

In November of 1937, the longstanding Quartermaster olive-drab paint formula was finally updated by the substitution of a new vehicle base to replace the old linseed oil base. The use of a "long-oil" in the paint reduced the its drying time and gave it a finish that both resisted scuffing and wear and gave it an even appearance.[4] The paint was now made available in both lusterless and gloss, the gloss paint appearing darker to the eye. This new formulation gave the appearance of the use of a darker paint in contemporary black and white and color photographs. Both the regulars and the National Guard troops utilized this shade of paint for their vehicles.

7

Infantry (Tanks) Tank Battalions & Regiments 1936-1940

Organization

In 1935, the Light Tank Battalion was reorganized in response to the introduction of a new series of light tanks, the M2. More reliable than the M1917 Light Tank, the M2 light tank allowed for a reduction in the number armored vehicles assigned to tank units. Although the light tank battalion continued to contain three Light Tank Companies, these companies now had only seventeen tanks each, rather than twenty-five. The light tank platoon still consisted of five light tanks, but the Headquarters Platoon for the company was reduced from nine light tanks to only two – and both of these were there specifically for the use of the company commander and staff. The Battalion Headquarters Company was equipped with three tanks, bringing the total for the battalion to fifty-four tanks (as compared to the First World War battalion with seventy-six tanks).[5]

The light tank regiment organization continued to include three light tank battalions, but it was much reduced in size, containing only 162 tanks instead of 225. In any case, the divisional Tank Company remained the predominant light tank organization within the United States Army. The reorganization had no effect at all on the organization of the medium tank units. In actuality, although there was a medium tank regiment in existence, it consisted of only a single company.[6]

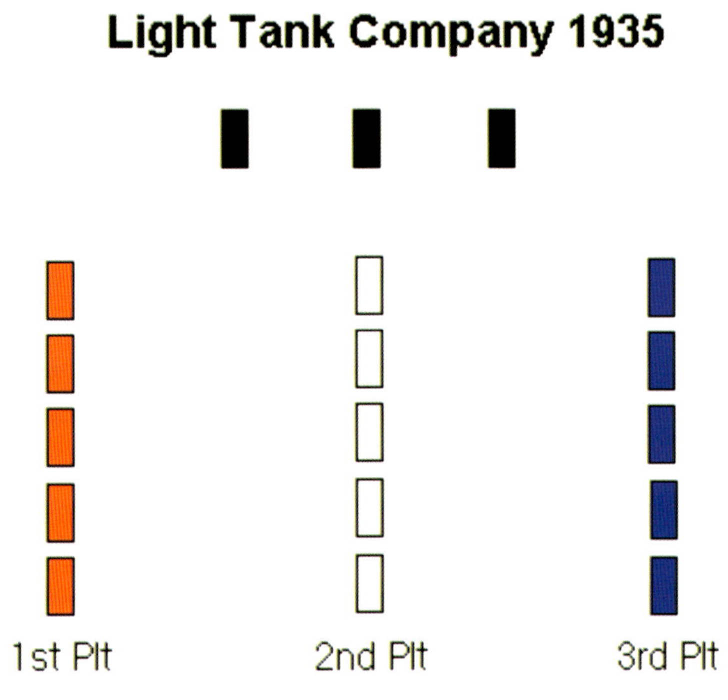

Light Tank Battalion 1935

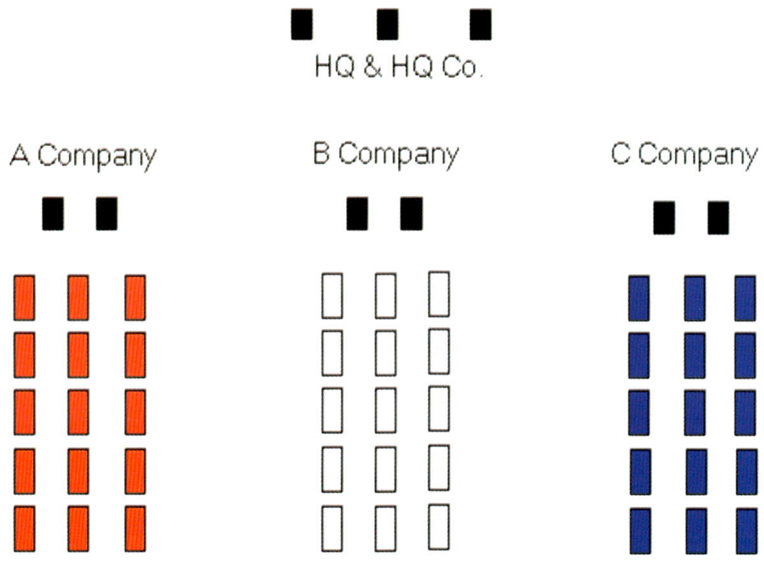

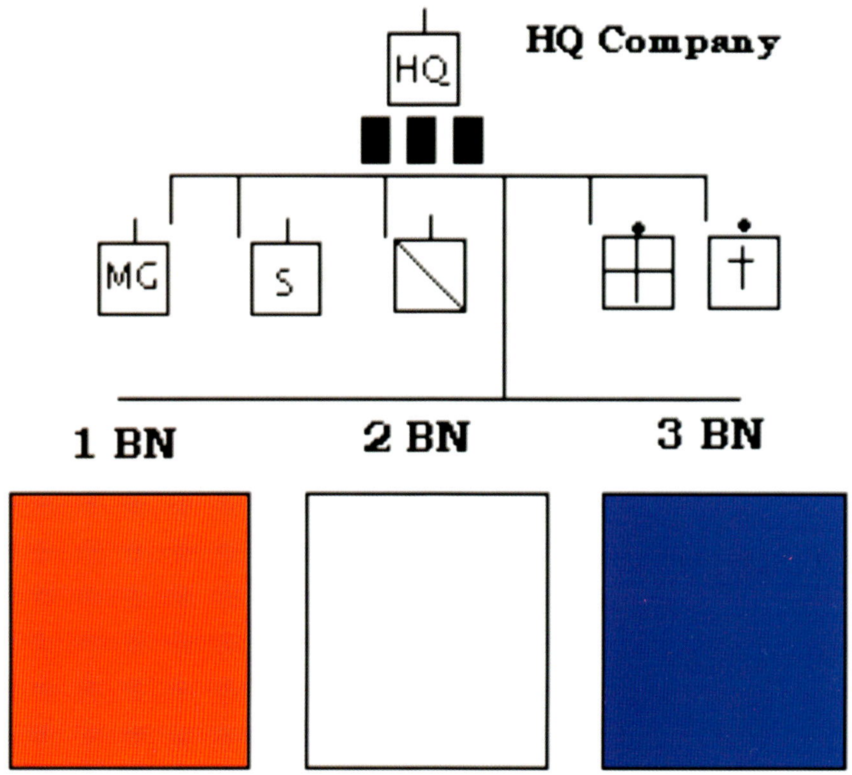

Light Tank Regiment

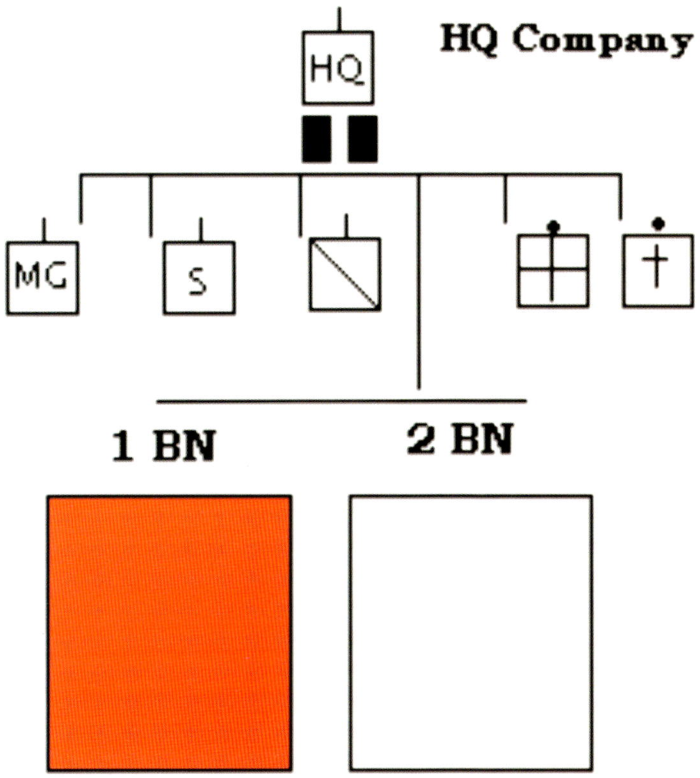

Medium Tank Regiment

A recently issued M2A2 Light Tank belonging to the 2nd Battalion, 66th Infantry Regiment (Light Tanks) being loaded onto a rail car in preparation for the 1936 Third Army Maneuvers. The vehicle is painted olive drab. Newly issued to the unit, the vehicle lacks any markings other than the white registration numbers. (HC)

A recently acquired M2A2 Light Tank assigned to the 1st Battalion, 66th Infantry Regiment (Light Tanks) being demonstrated for the West Point Cadets in 1936. The vehicle is painted gloss olive drab with white registration numbers on either side of the hull. At this point there are no tactical markings applied.

As with the rest of the Infantry (Light Tanks) units, the 66th Infantry Regiment (Light Tanks) was still equipped with M1917 Light Tanks at the beginning of 1935. On 25 November 1935, the refitting of the regiment began in earnest with the delivery of fifty-four experimental light tanks to the 2nd Battalion, stationed at Fort Benning, GA. These new vehicles consisted of nine T2E1 and forty-five T2E2 Light Tanks – soon standardized as the M2A1 and M2A2 Light Tank. By mid-1937, each company within the regiment had been fully equipped with eighteen of the M2 series light tanks.

The 1st and 3rd Battalions initially received only five of the new M2A2 Light Tanks each during 1936, with additional tanks being doled out to them during 1937. By the end of 1937, the 1st Battalion, stationed at Fort George Meade, boasted a total of twenty-nine modern M2A2 Light Tanks. The 3rd Battalion, on the other hand, had thirty-seven modern tanks on hand. The 2nd Battalion, assigned to support the Infantry School, had its full complement of fifty-four M2A1 and M2A2 Light Tanks.

By the end of 1938, both the 1st and 3rd Battalions had been brought up to full strength with the issue of the new M2A3 Light Tanks. The 2nd Battalion was also upgraded with M2A3, receiving fifteen diesel-powered vehicles and giving up its nearly obsolete M2A1 Light Tanks and a few older M2A2s.

Basic markings used by the 66th and 67th Infantry Regiments

Colors and Markings

The M2A1 and its subsequent progeny was a completely different vehicle than the obsolete M1917 Light Tank. Its fielding in 1935 probably contributed to the redesign of regimental and company systems for unit markings.

This new system saw the reappearance of unit tactical markings that utilized the same three basic geometric figures that had been used during the First World War (square, circle, and diamond), but without the card figures. These geometric markings were used to designate the various platoons within the company. Company headquarters tanks were marked with the triangle, the first platoon with a diamond, the second with a disk, and the third platoon with a square. The Army's sole medium tank company also adopted a variation of this geometric system.

It would appear that this new system was initially developed at Fort Benning and then spread to other tank units across the United States. A small number of units continued to use variations of the markings that they had been using for years. The vast majority of units, on the other hand, adopted the new system.

1936 was also the year that tanks were finally added to the U.S. Army vehicle register, being assigned the numerical code of "30." As with all of the other motorized vehicles owned by the army, the numbers were normally applied to the sides of the hull or turret in four-inch tall white figures.[7] Vehicle registration numbers for armored vehicles such as combat cars and armored cars were prefaced with "40" and these markings had been being applied at least since 1931. This registration system survived until the late 1950s and early 1960s, when it was replaced by the Army's present alphanumeric system. The older M1917 light tanks were not included in the registration.

66th Infantry Regiment (Light Tanks)

From its creation in the early 1930s, the 66th Infantry Regiment (Light Tanks) had been split up between three different stations.[8] The entire 1st Battalion, as well as Company I, was stationed at Fort George Meade, MD, the entire 2nd Battalion at Fort Benning, and the Battalion headquarters company and the remaining two companies of the 3rd Battalion posted to Fort Devens, MA. The markings on their vehicles were left to the local battalion commanders and they did not become standardized until 1938.

In 1938, the 2nd Battalion developed a marking system that soon spread to the other two battalions. This new system consisted of two parts. The first part was the platoon marking, something that had already basically been standardized and had been in use by the divisional light tank companies since 1936. Under this system, the two tanks assigned to the company headquarters were designated by a triangle, with either the letter "C" for commander or the letter "S" for staff stenciled inside. The first platoon tanks were marked by a diamond, the second platoon tanks were designated by a disk, and those in the third platoon were marked with a square.

The second part of the system was used to differentiate the companies within the battalion. Unlike the divisional tank companies, which operated alone, the tank battalion needed some way to differentiate between its three companies. The solution was to assign a two-color scheme to each of the companies. The assignment of these colors varied between the battalions, the most common combinations being red and blue, yellow and red, and blue and white. Until January of 1940, there was no reason to differentiate between the battalions within the regiment.

Because the battalions were widely separated they could get by using the same tactical markings and color combinations. The use of identical color combinations was destined to cause problems and, when the regiment was finally gathered together at Fort Benning in the spring of 1940, there was quite a bit of confusion. This resulted in several modifications to the existing markings.

The tactical markings for the M2A2 Light Tanks were painted on the front of each sponson, as well as on the outside of each turret, very near the rear. Marking was also duplicated on the round projection on the rear of the hull. These markings varied in size, with most being around eight to ten inches wide and tall, with the marking on the rear of the hall being just large enough to fit the projection.

The M2A3 light tanks, when they began arriving in mid-1938, were marked in a similar fashion but, because they lacked the rear projection on the hull, they were marked on one or both of the rear engine doors. The vehicle registration numbers were applied to either side of the hull in white, three-inch letters and numbers.

1st Battalion

Initially the 1st Battalion of the 66th Infantry (Light Tanks) marked their new M2A2 light tanks in a manner similar to that used on their M1917 tanks. The design of the new vehicle presented a number of challenges. The more fully sloped front meant that the company lineal number had to be moved to a more visible location – the front side of two sponsons, where it was painted in six-inch tall white numerals. The newly required U.S. Army registration numbers were painted on either side of the hull in four-inch numbers and letters. The vehicle's company lineal number that had been painted on either side of the engine compartment on the earlier vehicles was stenciled in white, six-inch numerals on the circular projection on the rear of the engine compartment. The large air cleaners were also marked with the vehicle lineal number – on the outside and on the rear.

Each of the companies within the battalion continued to be differentiated by a three-inch tall stripe around the turret cupola. Although the M2A2 light tanks had two turrets, only the left turret was equipped with a cupola and that is where the stripe was painted.

The color red continued to designate the first company (Company A), while the second company (Company B) was

Tanks of the 1st Battalion, 66th Infantry Regiment (Light Tanks) and Company I during a pass-in-review at an unknown location in 1938. The vehicle lineal number is visible painted on the front of both sponsons in white. Painted around the cupola of the left turret is the company identification color. The tanks in the foreground are marked in yellow – signifying Company B, while those in the background are marked in red, signifying Company A. (HC)

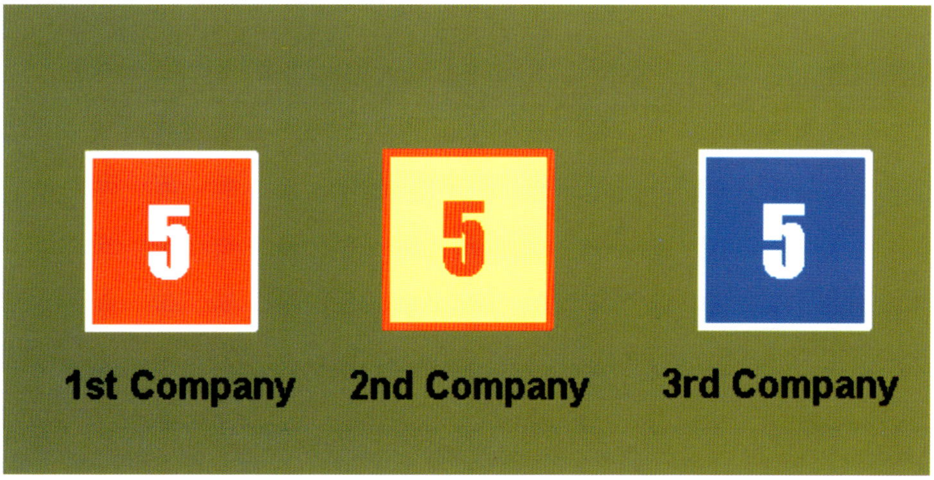

Color Marking scheme of the 1st Battalion, 66th Infantry Regiment (Light Tanks) 1938 to 1940.

M2A2 assigned to Company I, 3rd Battalion, 66th Infantry Regiment (Light Tanks) during maneuvers in 1938. Notice the lineal number painted on the side and rear of the air cleaner in white. (HC)

marked in yellow and the third company (Company C) in medium blue. By the end of 1938, this marking system was replaced by the system developed by the 2nd Battalion, located at the Tank School at Fort Benning, GA.

When the new system was adopted, the battalion assigned the two-color company marking schemes in a manner different than that used by the 2nd Battalion. The 1st company (company A) used red and white, the 2nd company (B) used yellow and red, and the 3rd company used blue and white.

2nd Battalion

Assigned to Fort Benning in support of the Infantry School, the 2nd Battalion was the first unit of the 66th Infantry Regiment (LT) to receive the new M2 series tanks. By the end of 1937, they had come up with a new marking system, which was eventually adopted by the rest of the regiment, as well as by the 67th Infantry Regiment (Medium Tanks), and new 68th Infantry Regiment (Light Tanks).

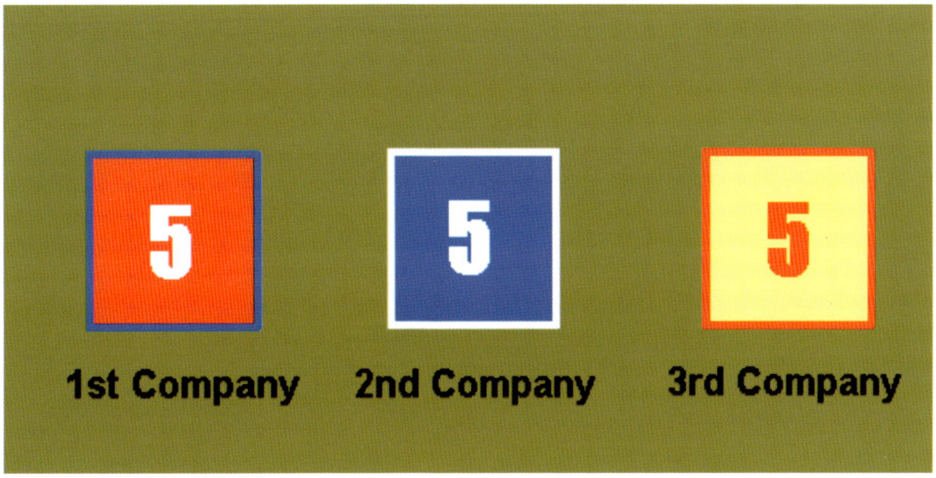

Color marking scheme of the 2nd Battalion, 66th Infantry Regiment (Light Tanks) 1937 to 1940.

Above: Tanks of the Company E, 2nd Battalion, 66th Infantry Regiment passing in review on 14 February 1940 at Fort Benning. The different platoon markings are clearly visible on the rear of the turrets and the hull. There are "repeater" markings to either side of the normal company marking on the rear of the hull in the company's base color – in this case blue. (NIM)

Left: M2A2 Light Tank belonging to the 2nd Battalion, 66th Infantry Regiment during the Third Army maneuvers of 1939. The yellow square with narrow red border and red number at center mark this vehicle as belonging to the 3rd Platoon, Company F. The angle of the lighting makes the square appear white. (HC)

The first company of the battalion (Company D) was given a red background, trimmed in white and marked with white numbers, the second company (Company E), used a blue background trimmed in white and marked with white numbers and the third company – Company F – used a yellow background, trimmed in red with red numbers. When the entire regiment finally adopted the new system the other two battalions adopted the same or similar color combinations– although not always using the same colors for the same companies.

The battalion also placed markings across the front of the cupola of the left turret, as well as the flat front of the top of the right cupola. These took the form of a series of solid figures that duplicated the platoon marking. 1st platoon tanks were marked with wide horizontal rectangles spaced about two-inches apart, the 2nd platoon tanks were marked with a series of three-inch diameter disks, while the 3rd Platoon tanks were marked with vertical rectangles. Headquarters tanks were marked with a series of three-inch triangles. Markings were also painted on rear of the hull – normally on either side of the rear projection. For 1st platoon tanks this was a vertical stripe approximately eighteen inches tall and three-inches wide. 2nd platoon tanks had an eight-inch diameter disk, with the 3rd platoon tanks having an eight-inch square. The headquarters tanks had an eight-inch triangle. The colors of these markings appear to match the base color of the company – blue, red, or yellow.

A company commander's M2A3 Light Tank during the First Army maneuvers of 1939. The yellow triangle with red "C" at the center mark the vehicle as belonging to the second company of the battalion – in this case Company B, 1st Battalion, 66th Infantry Regiment (Light Tanks). The axe is painted with a broad yellow stripe and stenciled in red "66 B". The triangle is bordered in white rather than the normal red color.

Stuck—an M2A2 of the 3rd Platoon, Company E, 66th Infantry Regiment waits for a tow in 1936. The tactical markings, consisting of a blue square with a white lineal vehicle number, are visible on the rear of the hull and near the rear of each turret. Also stenciled on the rear of the hull is a small, three-inch tall white "E". The square appears to be bordered in yellow, but this has not been confirmed. (HC)

Two M2A2 Light Tanks of the 1st Platoon, Company F, 66th Infantry, fording a stream during the Third Army maneuvers at Fort Benning, GA in 1939. The unit markings are visible on the front of the sponsons. The unit crest can just be seen on the front upper hull between the driver and bow machine-gunner. The wide dashed markings on the cupolas of both are additional platoon recognition symbols.

In addition to the new marking system, the tanks of the 2nd battalion also painted the regimental crest of the 66th Infantry Regiment in full color between the driver's and bow machine-gunner's hatch, approximately four inches tall. Only the 2nd Battalion painted this marking on their tanks, and is a very good identification point for their vehicles.

Because of the confusion that resulted from the concentration of the entire regiment at Fort Benning in January of 1940, the tanks of the battalion were given an additional marking. This marking was applied in white, four-inch letters and numbers on either side of the turret – "II/66".

3rd Battalion

Little is known of the markings of the two companies of the 3rd Battalion, 66th Infantry Regiment (Light Tanks) stationed at Fort Devens, MA. Company I of the battalion was stationed at Fort Meade, MD with the 1st Battalion and it followed the marking conventions used by that battalion. The system called for a colored stripe around the left turret cupola and the vehicle lineal number marked in white on the front of each sponson and on the rear of the hull. Because the three main colors – red, yellow, and blue – were already in use, this company was given the color white. In 1938 the 3rd Battalion adopted the new marking system created by the 2nd Battalion.

M2A2 Light Tank assigned to 1st Platoon, Company F, 66th Infantry Regiment (Light Tanks). The yellow diamond with red border and red number identify the company and platoon. The white stenciled "II/66" was applied in the spring of 1940 because of the confusion caused by the concentration of the regiment, and others, at Fort Benning in early 1940. The Infantry-Tank plate, marking the tank as infantry property, is mounted on the side of the turret.

M2A2 Light Tank assigned to the 3rd Platoon, Company E, 66th Infantry Regiment. The 2nd Battalion markings are just visible on the side of the turret, while the repeat marking of white squares can be seen on the cupola. On either side of the marking on the rear of the hull are repeat markings consisting of a blue square on either side. (HC)

The background lit by flares, an M2A3 Light Tank belonging to the commander of Company F sets on the firing line at Fort Benning. The yellow triangle with red border and red "C" is painted on the front of the sponson, while the white repeat markings are painted around the cupola. (HC)

M2A2 Light Tank of the 3rd Platoon, Company E, 66th Infantry Regiment loading onto a train car at Fort Benning in the spring of 1940. The tactical marking is blue with a white border and number. The white stencil on the outside of the turret confirms that the vehicle belongs to the 2nd Battalion of the regiment. The white squares around the cupola of the left turret and on the front face of the right turret are added visual identification features for the platoon. (HC)

M2A2 Light Tank belonging to the 3rd Battalion, 66th Infantry Regiment (Light Tanks) during First Army Maneuvers in 1938. The blue square with white number, both trimmed in red, mark the tank as belonging to the 3rd platoon, H Company, and can be seen on the front of the sponson and side of the turret.

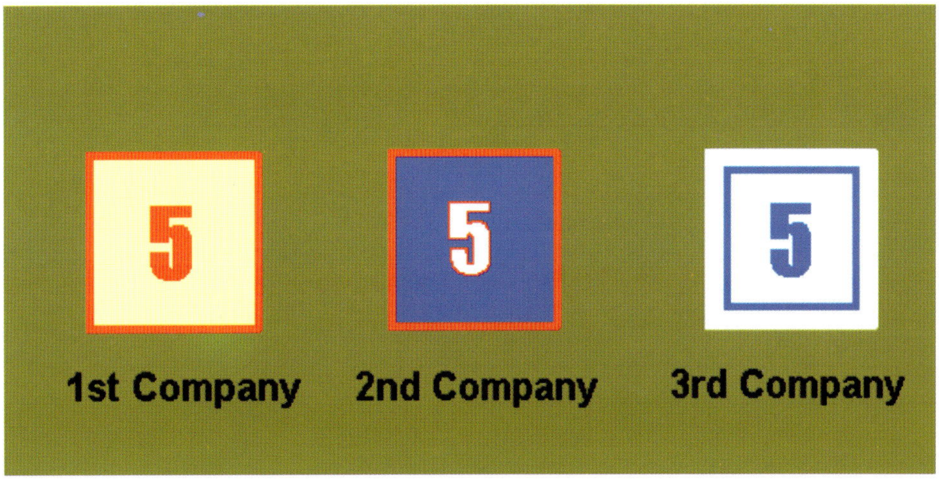

Color marking scheme of the 3rd Battalion, 66th Infantry Regiment (Light Tanks) 1938-1940.

Under this system, Company G used a yellow background with red numbers and red trim. Company H used a blue background with white numbers – with both the figure and the numeral being trimmed in red. Company I, which was assigned to Fort Meade with the 1st Battalion, was given unique markings in order to differentiate it from the other Companies of that battalion. These markings consisted of a white background with an inset blue border and blue numeral.

As was noted in the introduction to this chapter, all three battalions of the regiment adopted the same color combinations for use among their companies. These combinations were a red background with white numbers; a blue background with white numbers, and a yellow background with red numbers. The use of only three sets of colors by each of the battalions had been acceptable as long as the battalions operated separately. However, the concentration of, not only the three battalions of the 66th Infantry in early 1940, but also the two battalions of the newly constituted 68th Infantry, resulted in chaos. As a result of this confusion, the second battalion of the regiment was forced to mark its tanks on the outside of each turret with "II/66" in four inch white numerals.[9]

On 15 July 1940, the 66th Infantry Regiment (Light Tanks) was re-designated as the 66th Armored Regiment (Light), part of the newly formed 2nd Armored Division.

Two light tanks belonging to Company I, 3rd Battalion, 66th Infantry Regiment (Light Tanks) during First Army maneuvers in 1939. The square marking on the turret and sponson mark the tank in the foreground as belonging to the 3rd Platoon. The unique color combination (blue on white) mark it as belonging to Company I. Only this company used the reversed colors of a blue number and border on a white square. (HC)

Tanks of the 66th Infantry Regiment (Light Tanks) pass in review in February of 1940 at Fort Benning. The M2A2 at the center is marked for the Headquarters staff of Company E, 2nd Battalion – the trail vehicle for that battalion. Following behind the vehicle is the entire 3rd Battalion, with their company commander's vehicles leading. (HC)

Tanks of Company E, 2nd Battalion, 66th Infantry Regiment, passing in review during the spring of 1940 at Fort Benning. The closest tank at the right is the last vehicle from the 3rd Platoon, Company D, 2nd Battalion – recognizable by the red square with blue trim and white number. The tank in the left foreground is from Company F. (NIM)

A closer look at the company commanders' tanks of Companies G and H, 3rd Battalion, 66th Infantry Regiment (Light Tanks). The M2A2 to the right is that of H Company, marked with a blue triangle with a white letter "C" all edged in red. The tank to the right, is marked with a yellow triangle edged in red with a red letter "C" at center. Spring 1940. (HC)

A column of light tanks assigned to the 3rd Battalion, 66th Infantry Regiment (Light Tanks). The lead M2A2 belongs to the 2nd platoon, Company G – as evidenced by the yellow and red company markings. The tank in the background is from the 3rd platoon, Company H. (HC)

67th Infantry Regiment (Medium Tanks)

In truth, the 67th Infantry Regiment was a regiment in name only. Since its creation in 1932, the regiment had consisted of only a single company in the 2nd Battalion – Company F. In 1936 the 67th Infantry was completely re-equipped with the experimental T4 Medium Tank – fifteen of the basic T4 and three of the barbette type T4E1 tanks. These tanks would remain in service until they began to be replaced in 1939 by the new M2 series of medium tanks.

As always, the 67th Infantry Regiment (Medium Tanks) took a bit of a different approach to marking its vehicles. Although consisting of only a single company until the eve of World War II, the 67th was the U.S. Army's only regular medium tank unit. Originally part of the 2nd Tank Regiment, F Company had, from the start, marked its vehicles with the unit crest on both sides. When it became a medium tank company in the mid-1930s, its tanks continued to be marked in that fashion, but because of the smaller vehicles, a smaller version

Stuck in the mud. A T4 Christie Medium Tank of Company F, 67th Infantry Regiment at Fort Benning, in 1937. The markings on the rear of the vehicle mark it as belonging to the 1st Platoon. The diamonds are white with yellow trim and black letters and numbers. The small disk is blue with a white "67" at center.

Another view of the same vehicle. In this shot the regimental crest is visible on the side of the turret, as well as the duplicated markings on the side of the hull. The Infantry-Tanks plate, made of brass and nickel, is also visible on the side of the turret.

(twelve to fourteen-inches tall) of the crest came into use. In 1938, the regiment adopted the same geometric marking system as the light tank regiment, even to the point of using the same color combinations.

The regiment, however, used a combination of the standard tactical markings, as well as some homegrown marking. As with the light tank regiment, each platoon within the company was designated by a geometric figure. The first platoon was marked with a diamond, the second with a disk, and the third with a square. Headquarters vehicles were marked with a triangle. Since only the third company (Co.F) of the battalion was the only active unit, its color combination was yellow and red.

In a twist peculiar to the 67th Infantry, the geometric figure was repeated twice on each side of the vehicle, as well as across the rear of the hull, with the left most figure containing the company letter "F", and the right most figure containing the vehicle's linear company number. The background color was yellow, with the numerals and letters in red. This was applied on all four sides of the vehicle. In some cases "67" would also appear on either side of the vehicle near the top in white, three-inch numerals, centered between the two geometric figure markings. In addition, the platoon geometric figure was repeated around the cupola of the turret, in some cases a single color, in others alternating in the two colors assigned to the company. This could be a series of widely separated triangles (for headquarters), disk, squares or diamonds.

Side view of the F Company Commander's T4 Christie Medium Tank. This shot, taken in the spring of 1940, shows that little has changed since the markings were introduced in 1937. The only addition is the duplicated platoon markings around the cupola – in this case triangles – in white.

Another side view of a T4 Medium Tank of 3rd Platoon, Company F, 67th Infantry. The repeated markings are visible on the side of the hull and front of the sponson. The first figure contains the company letter, the second the vehicle's lineal number. The shape of the figure gives you the platoon, while the color designates the company again.

A third side view of a T4 Medium Tank of Company F, 67th Infantry. Again, a tank assigned to the 3rd Platoon, on the turret is visible the regimental crest in full color.

Over the top. A rather unique look at a T4 Medium Tank assigned to the 3rd Platoon, F Company, 67th Infantry Regiment. The regimental crest is clearly visible on turret in this 1938 photograph taken at Fort Benning, GA.

The registration numbers were applied in white, three-inch stencils on either side of the vehicle, while the unit crest was painted between the two geometric figures on either side of the vehicle. The crest was usually only about six to eight inches tall and applied in full color. On one of the T4 Medium Radio Tanks, a series of red and white stripes was painted around the top of the vehicle, each stripe being approximately three-inch wide. The crest continued to be used on tanks assigned to F Company, 67th Tank, until the introduction of the M2 Medium Tank in late 1939.

With the introduction of the M2 series Medium Tank, and the activation of the 1st Battalion, the markings of the regiment were brought into line with that of the two light tank regiments. Most of these new medium tanks were assigned to Company F of the 2nd Battalion and were marked on all four sides of the hull with yellow markings trimmed in red with red numerals. Because only a limited number of medium tanks were available, M2A2 and M2A3 Light Tanks were issued as substitutes – mostly in the 1st Battalion and in the two recently activated companies of the 2nd Battalion (D and E).

Above: A T4E1 Medium Tank assigned to Company F, 67th Infantry Regiment (Medium Tanks) circa 1938. An experimental vehicle, the tank is marked with its vehicle lineal number on the front and back of the hull in large white numbers. These numbers are repeated on the cupola in four places. On the sides of the hull is the regimental crest in full color. Below: Rear view of the same T4E1 Medium Tank. (HC)

M2 Medium Tank assigned to 2nd Platoon, Company F, 67th Infantry Regiment (Medium Tanks) in the spring of 1940. The company and platoon markings are visible on the side and front of the hull – a yellow disk with a red border and red number. The "Infantry-Tank" plate is clearly visible on the side of the hull above the door.

The entire 2nd Platoon of Company F, 67th Infantry Regiment on maneuvers in late spring of 1940. The company and platoon marking is clearly visible. However, the regimental crest is no longer being painted on the vehicles – bringing the regiment into line with the rest of the tank regiments.

Side view of an M2 Medium Tank assigned to 2nd Platoon, Company F, 67th Infantry Regiment (Medium Tanks). The Infantry-Tank plate is clearly visible on the hull These were removed in July of 1940 when the experimental Armored Force was activated.

Shown as an example of the white turret striping, this M2A2 Light Tank is newly assigned to Company D, 192nd Tank Battalion. Drawn from the 69th Armored Regiment, who drew it from the 67th Armored Regiment, the tank remains marked with the broad white stripes around the turrets designating it as a "Medium" tank. On either sponson are the unit markings from the tank company that the vehicle had originally been assigned. At the center of the front armor, between the driver's and machine-gunner's doors is a three-inch tall "D".

For the maneuvers of 1940, the light tanks were marked with wide white stripes around both turrets in order to mark them as substitutes for the missing medium tanks.

As with the 66th Infantry Regiment (Light Tanks), the 67th Infantry was re-designated as the 67th Armored Regiment (Medium) on 15 July 1940, and made part of the 2nd Armored Division.

68th Infantry Regiment (Light Tanks)

Formed by the amalgamation of the various divisional tank companies in January of 1940, this unit first operated as a regiment during the 1940 Louisiana Maneuvers. Although authorized three battalions, initially only two battalions were actually formed – the 1st and 2nd. The vehicles arrived from the various tank companies painted in their own unit markings, but as soon as it could be done these markings were painted out. As with the 66th Infantry (Light Tanks), the companies in this regiment were assigned a set of colors to differentiate between other units within the regiment. In at least one company only the basic shape of the markings were applied in white (triangle, diamond, disk, or square) and were only later fleshed out with color. In addition, the company letter was painted in white on the front of the hull between the two hatches

Unfortunately, these colors were identical to those used by the other two tank regiments in existence, which caused problems when operating with the 66th Infantry Regiment. As a result the tanks belonging to the regiment were soon marked again by simply writing out the unit designation in white between two lines on the outside of each turret. It was not until the Louisiana Maneuvers that the regiment was finally seen outfitted and properly painted and marked.

The 7th Tank Company (Company F) was especially recognizable, containing the whole of the Army's nine M2A1 Light Tanks. Most of its tanks had the regulation Infantry (Tanks) emblem in white on the outside of the turret(s) with a three-inch full-color unit patch below. Some tanks from the 4th Tank

M2A3 Light Tank bearing the colors of the newly activated 68th Infantry Regiment (Light Tanks) during the pass in review of the Provisional Tank Brigade at Fort Benning in spring 1940. The vehicle still bears the tactical markings of the 2nd Tank Company. This vehicle is now in the collection of the Patton Museum at Fort Knox. (NIM)

Tanks of the 68th Infantry Regiment beginning their pass in review in the spring of 1940 at Fort Benning. Tanks from several different units can be seen in this rather long shot, including M2A1 Light Tanks of the 7th Tank Company, identifiable by their rather unique turret markings. (NIM)

Newly repainted vehicles issued to the 68th Infantry Regiment (Light Tanks). The original company markings of the 4th Tank Company have been obliterated and simple platoon markings have been painted on the front of each sponson and the rear of the hull in white. These are assigned to Company C – as evidenced by the small "C" painted between the driver and bow machine-gun position. (PM - Scheller)

An M2A2 Light Tank of the 3rd Platoon, Company C, 1st Battalion, 68th Infantry Regiment. Note that there are crude platoon markings but in white with no lineal number. The company and regimental markings are painted on either side of the turret in white. (PM - Scheller)

Another photograph reveals the name "El Diablo" for a tank of the 3rd Platoon, Company C, 68th Infantry. (PM - Scheller)

El Dorado camped in the woods during the 1940 Maneuvers. The name is barely visible but unreadable on the side of the hull. The turret markings are clear on the outside of the turrets, as is the company letter "C" in white between the driver and bow machine-gunner positions. (PM - Scheller)

Company were transferred to Company C, as the 5th and 6th Companies, which made up company C had little or nothing to offer. In addition, the unit received a number of tanks from the 66th Infantry, still marked for their original units. The 1st Tank Company (Company A) retained its markings, as did the 2nd (Company D).

The Regiment was formed and initially equipped as follows:

1st Battalion
A Company – formed from the 1st Tank Company (10 M2A2, 8 M2A3 tanks)
B Company – formed from the 4th Tank Company (18 M2A2 Tanks)
C Company – formed from the 5th and 6th Tank Companies (Issued 18 M2A2 tanks)

2nd Battalion
D Company – formed from the 2nd Tank Company (10 M2A2, 8 M2A3 Tanks)
E Company – formed from the 3rd Tank Company (14 M2A2, 4 M2A3 Tanks)
F Company – formed from the 7th Tank Company (9 M2A1, 9 M2A2 Tanks)

An M2A2 Light Tank of the 3rd Platoon, Company C, 68th Infantry Regiment crossing a stream during the 1940 Third Army maneuvers. Painted on the front of the sponson is a blue square with white edging and vehicle lineal number. This marking system lasted only a short time ending when the regiment was broken up in 1941. (PM - Scheller)

When the regiment was first fielded, many of the tanks had not been repainted and they retained the turret markings used by the divisional tank companies from which they had been drawn. By May of 1940, at least in the 1st Battalion, the original markings were painted out and replaced with the company letter and "68 INF" in between two parallel lines and separated by a dash.

This combination of units presented quite a sight, which was not fully corrected until the Louisiana Maneuvers and only lasted until the unit was re-designated as an armored regiment on 15 July 1940. It lingered for a while afterwards and then was finally broken up in January of 1941.

8

Infantry (Tanks) Divisional Tank Companies 1936-1941

Organization

As with the Infantry (Tanks) battalions and regiments, the introduction of a new generation of light tanks in 1935 allowed for major changes in the formation of the Light Tank Company. The more reliable M2 Series of light tanks enabled the Army cut the number of vehicles required by a tank company, as well as reduce some of its manpower. The independent (or divisional) Light Tank Company now contained only eighteen tanks instead of twenty-five, with the tanks being divided between three combat platoons and a Headquarters platoon.[1] Each combat platoon of the independent Light Tank Company still consisted of five tanks, but the Headquarters platoon strength was reduced from ten tanks to three.

However, these new tanks were slow in making out to the units. Due to budgetary constraints, only a limited number of tanks were built at Rock Island Arsenal every year, and these had to be shared between, not only the divisional tank companies, but also with the 66th Infantry Regiment (light tanks). Some units eventually received a full complement of tanks, while most received only a portion and at least two companies – the 5th and 6th – received no new tanks at all until ordered to Fort Benning in January of 1940.

Of all of the Regular Army independent Tank Companies, only the 11th Tank Company was not absorbed by the 68th Infantry Regiment (Light Tanks) in early 1940. It was, however, finally relieved from the Hawaiian Division in October of 1941 and in early 1942 was disbanded.

Colors and Markings

In the Regular Army independent or divisional tank companies, a set of geometric figures were used to designate the platoons within the company, and an additional figure, the triangle, was added to designate HQ section vehicles. Tanks of the first platoon in each company were identified by a diamond figure, those of the second platoon by a circle or disk and of the third platoon by a square.

The American Tanker, 2nd Tank Company, 2nd Division, 1935.

Light Tank Company 1935

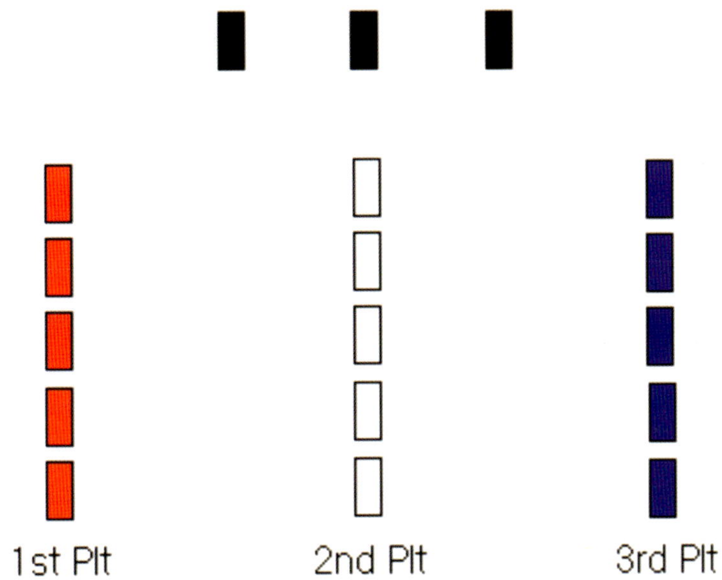

These tactical markings were approximately ten to twelve-inches tall and, as per regulation,[2] were nearly always painted in white solid or hollow figures with the company lineal number (1, 2, 3, 4, or 5) in white or black, eight-inch numerals. Headquarters section vehicles were marked "C" for commander, or "S" for staff, instead of the number, in a white triangle.

The location of the markings was fairly standardized for the M2 series light tanks. Most of the tanks had the markings painted on the front of each side sponson, as well as on the outside rear of the turrets and usually on the rear of the hull. On the M2A1 and M2A2 series of light tanks the rear hull marking was painted on the round projection on the rear of the hull. On the M2A3 Light Tanks the markings were placed on the rear engine access door – sometimes doubled – one on each door.

Sometimes the solid geometric figures were finished with a one half inch black border, while the skeleton figures were left plain. Some units painted these markings on a larger scale, up to eighteen inches square, with the inside markings made proportionally larger.

In addition to these tactical markings, the tanks were still required to be marked with the unit identification markings in accordance with AR 850-5. As described earlier, these markings were painted on the sides of the turret(s) and normally

M2A2 Light Tank assigned to the 1st Tank Company on Staten Island, New York in 1938. The unit marking is clearly visible on both turrets with the shield outlined in white with a red "1" at center. A third 1st Division patch is visible painted between the driver and bow machine-gunner's doors. The platoon marking is barely visible on the front of the sponson. The brass and nickel-plated "Infantry-Tank" plate can be seen attached to the outside of each turret.

Another M2A2 Light Tank assigned to the 1st Tank Company on Staten Island, New York, this time with a view from the left side of the vehicle.

M2A2 Light Tanks of the 1st Tank Company being loaded on a train car for the Third Army Maneuvers of 1940. Although the company markings are not visible from this angle, the platoon markings on the turret and on the rear of the hull can be seen very clearly. (HC)

Unit photograph of the 1st Tank Company in 1938. Three of the unit's eighteen M2A2 Light Tanks are visible in this shot, taken at their home station on Staten Island, New York.

consisted of a painted color rendition of the divisional shoulder sleeve insignia with the company designation stenciled in white three-inch letters on a single line to its right[3] The top and bottom of the markings were bordered by one half inch thick white lines the length of the markings. These were, by far, the most common markings seen on the M2 Series of light tanks. Registration markings were painted (for the most part) on either side of the hull in white, 4-inch letters and numbers.

1st Tank Company

When they received their issue of their first five new M2A2 Light Tanks in mid-1936, the 1st Tank Company adopted the new tactical marking system used by the tank regiments. The unit markings were applied to the outside of each turret according to existing regulations. Previously outlined in black on the M1917 Light Tanks, the full color 1st Division patch was now applied with a white outline – the background being that of the normal olive-drab paint, and the number painted in red. This patch was also applied to space between the driver's and bow machine-gunner's hatches in front. The lettering for the unit designation was in sans serif.

Tactical markings were applied to both the front of each sponson, as well as on the outside back of both turrets and on the round projection on the rear of the engine compartment. These were skeletal markings, approximately twelve inches tall and one-inch thick with the vehicle's lineal number painted inside in white.

In mid-1938, the company began receiving the new M2A3 Light Tanks, eventually getting a total of eight. These were distributed amongst the platoons and painted in the company scheme.

2nd Tank Company

The 2nd Tank Company was issued their first five M2A2 Light Tanks in May of 1936. These were assigned to the 1st platoon. By July of that year the unit was painting its tactical markings in solid figures on the front of both sponsons, repeating it on the round project at the rear of the hull. The vehicle's lineal number was painted in black inside the figure. The 2nd Tank Company painted its unit markings using the regulation pattern, but applied it only on the right side of the .30 caliber (right) turret. The other turret was left unmarked.

By 1937 the company had received enough tanks to fill it out all of its platoons – a total of eighteen. It immediately expanded its existing marking system, adopting a variation of the standard tactical markings. Although the unit continued to paint their company markings on the right side of the .30 caliber (right) turret, the newly equipped platoons within the company were given new tactical emblems. The 1st platoon remained marked with the diamond and the 2nd platoon with the disk, but the 3rd platoon was designated with the triangle.

For its headquarters tanks the 2nd Tank Company used a clipped corner shield instead of the triangle. Instead of using "C" for commander and "S" for staff, the headquarters tanks were simply designated by a number from 1 to 3.

Side view of the markings of an M2A2 Light Tank assigned to the 2nd Tank Company, 2nd Division in Texas. The unit used the regulation company markings on the turret, but only on the right turret – the left turret was left unmarked. On the front of the sponsons and on the rear of the hull is marked the platoon marking – a white diamond with a black lineal number. Photograph was taken in the summer of 1936.

Two M2A2 Light Tanks of the 2nd Tank Company during maneuvers in 1936. The platoon markings are clearly visible on the front of the sponsons but, because of the angle, only the rear tank has a visible company marking on the right turret. The left turret was left unmarked.

Closeup view of the company markings of the 2nd Tank Company. The 2nd Division patch is painted in full color. Also visible is the brass and nickel "Infantry-Tank" plate that is attached to the outside of each turret.

A new M2A3 Light Tank assigned to the headquarters platoon, 2nd Tank Company being demonstrated for West Point Cadets in late 1939. Although the company markings have not changed, the platoon markings are now marked, not only on the sponsons, but also in the area between the road wheels on the lower hull. This particular vehicle is now in the collection of the Patton Museum of Cavalry and Armor at Fort Knox. (HC)

Another M2A3 Light Tank of the 2nd Tank Company, 3rd platoon, during a demonstration for West Point Cadets in 1939. (HC)

Above: The 2nd Tank Company stationed at Fort Sam Houston, TX in October of 1937. The vehicles are all painted in high gloss olive drab paint with their platoon markings in white and black. The company markings are painted only on the outside of the .30 caliber (right) turret.

Left: A demonstration for the West Point cadets by an M2A2 Light Tank of the 1st platoon, 2nd Tank Company, in 1939.

The platoon markings were painted on the outside of each turret (near the rear), on the front of each sponson, on the rear of the hull on the engine door, and on either side of the lower hull between the road wheel sets. These markings continued in use until the company was absorbed by the 68th Infantry Regiment in 1940.

3rd Tank Company

The 3rd Tank Company was initially supplied with only five of the new M2A2 Light Tanks in 1936. In mid-1938 it received an additional eight light tanks, four new from the factory and four reconditioned light tanks which had originally been issued to the 2nd Battalion, 66th Infantry. This gave the company a total of thirteen M2 series light tanks. In the winter and spring of 1940, the company participated in operational maneuvers with the 3rd Division at Camp Ord, California. By July of 1940, the entire company had been transferred to Fort Benning and absorbed by the 68th Infantry Regiment (Light Tanks).

In marking these new tanks, the company utilized the standard platoon markings used by the other tank companies. Having only the five tanks, the tanks were initially all issued to the 1st platoon, and were marked with an open white diamond with the lineal number at the center. These were placed on the fronts of the sponsons, as well as the rear of the hull on the round projection. In addition, each of the tanks was given a name, which was painted in four-inch white letters on the outside of each turret.

In 1938, with the receipt of enough tanks to begin outfitting the other two platoons in the company, the markings were modified. In addition to the standard platoon markings, the cupola of the left turret was marked with three-inch tall, solid white copies of the platoon marking. These were evenly spaced around cupola so that they would be visible from all directions. The tanks continued to be named as before.

M2A2 Light Tank of the 3rd Tank Company jumping an obstacle during a demonstration in 1937. The vehicle name (Cyclone) is visible on the turret, although the platoon markings are not visible due to the angle of the photograph.

3rd Tank Company commander's tank (Sweeney) knocking down at tree at Camp Ord, California in April of 1940. This is one of the new M2A3 light tanks that had been assigned to the company in 1939. The triangle marking with the "C" inside can be seen on the front of the sponson and the rear of the turret. Smaller solid white triangles circle the cupola.

3rd Tank Company parked during maneuvers at Camp Ord in early April 1940. All thirteen tanks of the company are present. The markings around the turret cupola are clearly visible.

Oooh! that has to have hurt. An M2A2 Light Tank of the 2nd platoon, 3rd Tank Company speeding out of a ditch during a demonstration at Camp Ord in 1940.

M2A2 Light Tank assigned to the 3rd Platoon of the 4th Tank Company. The vehicle is marked with an open square with a simple number stenciled at the center. Taken circa 1939. (PM - Scheller)

4th Tank Company
The 4th Tank Company was initially supplied with only five of the new M2A2 Light Tanks in 1936, with an additional two reconditioned light tanks being received by the middle of 1938. By the end of 1938, the company had been equipped with its full complement of 18 light tanks. Few photographs have come to light of this company. However in the one available shot of a tank from 3rd Platoon, it shows a white, open figure with the vehicle lineal number inside in white painted on the side of the turret. These markings are probably duplicated on the front of the sponson, as well as the rear of the hull. In January of 1940, the company was absorbed by the 68th Infantry Regiment (Light Tanks).

5th Tank Company
According to available information, the 5th Tank Company was not issued any of the new M2 Series light tanks – so when its M1917 Light Tanks were placed in mothballs, the unit was basically left with nothing until it was ordered to report to Fort Benning, GA in January of 1940

6th Tank Company
The 6th Tank Company shared the fate of the 5th Tank Company – having been left out in the cold without tanks, the unit languished until ordered to Fort Benning, GA in January of 1940, where it supplied personnel for the creation of the 68th Infantry Regiment (Light Tanks).

An M2A1 Light Tank assigned to the 7th Tank Company. Unlike most of the other tank companies, the 7th used an alternate marking system – painting the Infantry (tanks) emblem on both sides of the turret. In addition to the white "7" below, it was also marked with full color 7th Division unit patch centered above. The platoon marking is visible on the front of the sponson in white outline. This photograph was taken at Fort Benning in January or February 1940.

Rear view of a second M2A1 Light Tank assigned to the 7th Tank Company. The platoon marking is clearly visible painted in white on the rear of the hull. These tanks were painted in a gloss olive-drab finish – hence the dark appearance of the paint. (HC)

7th Tank Company

Like many of the Regular Army units, the 7th Tank Company initially received only enough tanks to fill a single platoon. The 7th Tank Company had to make due with its M1917 Light Tanks until enough of the new M2 series became available. Originally slated to receive new M2A2 Light Tanks in 1938, it was instead issued nine reconditioned M2A1 Light Tanks that had been originally issued to the 66th Infantry. Upon receipt, the unit immediately painted its new tanks using a variation of the first marking system allowed by regulation. This involved painting a solid white version of the Infantry (Tanks) emblem on the both sides of the turret, with the company number painted in white underneath and a three-inch diameter, full color 7th Division patch above.

The unit applied its tactical markings in skeletal white figures, approximately twelve-inches tall, with the vehicle number painted in white inside. These were painted on the front of each sponson, as well as the round projection on the rear of the hull.[4] The USA registration numbers were applied in the normal fashion on either side of the vehicle in white, three-inch letters and numerals.

The 7th Tank Company, along with nearly every other Regular Army tank company, was absorbed by the 68th Infantry Regiment (Light Tanks) in January of 1940.

11th Tank Company

When the new M2A2 Light Tanks became available in 1936, the 11th Tank Company was immediately issued its full compliment of eighteen. Assigned to the Hawaiian Department, far from the center of authority, the company took some liberties in the marking of its tanks. Painted on each front of each sponson was the Infantry (Tanks) emblem in white, which were then detailed in black paint. On the outside of each turret was painted a white, fourteen- inch wide diagonal stripe. On it was painted a twelve-inch tall lineal vehicle number in black as well as an eight-inch diameter, full color Hawaiian Division unit patch outlined in black. This same marking was duplicated in miniature on the round projection at the rear of the hull.

Some of the unit's tanks also had the driver's name and rank stenciled in one-inch white letters on the front slope in front of the driver's hatch. Unlike all of the other Regular Army light tank companies, the company remained in Hawaii during the Maneuvers of 1940. The 11th Tank Company was relieved from assignment to the Hawaiian Division on 1 October 1941 and finally disbanded on 23 April 1942.

Company line of M2A2 Light Tanks belonging to the 11th Tank Company, Hawaiian Division at Schofield Barracks in 1940. The unique markings of this company are clearly visible on the outside of the turret. On the second tank in, the Infantry-Tank emblem can just be seen painted in white on the front of the sponson. (TLM)

Front view of an M2A2 Light Tank assigned to the 11th Tank Company. The unit marking on the front of the sponson can be clearly seen. Unlike other regular tank companies, the unit lineal marking is stenciled on the turret.

Front view of another M2A2 Light Tank assigned to the 11th Tank Company. The unit marking on the front of the right sponson can be clearly seen. On this particular vehicle, the driver's name is painted in yellow on the front of the hull. (Corporal Loudermilk).

Left side view of an M2A2 Light Tank, 11th Tank Company taken in 1940. Notice that the numeral on this vehicle is visibly smaller than that of some of the previous photographs. The full color Hawaiian Division patch is very clear.

Detail photograph of the turret markings for the 11th Tank Company.

9

Infantry (Tanks)
National Guard Divisional Tank Companies
1936-1940

On the whole, prior to World War II National Guard divisional tank companies were never fully equipped with tanks. While in the previous ten years or so they had been issued with eight M1917 Light Tanks, the appearance of the new M2 series actually resulted in a reduction in their share of vehicles. The depression had cut deeply into the defense budget and by the mid-1930s, many units had been forced to park their old 6-ton tanks due to lack of repair parts. When the new M2 series of light tanks finally became available, most of National Guard units received only two of the vehicles for training purposes. Since many of these units did not get these new tanks until 1937 or 1938, that meant that some had been without operational tanks for nearly three years. By mid-1937 most had received their new tanks

Three additional National Guard divisions had been formed during the intervening years, along with their tank companies – boosting the total of National Guard Tank Companies to eighteen. The three additional units were:

34th Tank Company (Brainard, MN) 10 June 1936
36th Tank Company (Houston, TX) 19 April 1937
44th Tank Company (NJ) 21 September 1939

The declaration of a National Emergency by President Roosevelt in 1940 resulted in the call up of nearly all of the National Guard tank companies. Only the 28th, 41st, and 44th Tank Companies were not called up. Of these, the 28th Tank Company was re-designated as D Troop, Cavalry Reconnaissance Mechanized – part of the 2nd Squadron, 104th Cavalry Regiment (Mechanized). Re-equipped with Scout Cars, the unit was forced to relinquish its tanks. The 44th Tank Company suffered a similar fate. The fate of the 41st Tank Company remains a mystery at the time of publication. The rest of the National Guard tank companies were incorporated into the four GHQ Reserve Tank Battalions.

National Guard Tanker, 28th Tank Company, 1938.

Organization

The official organization of the National Guard Tank Company mirrored that of the Regular Army units. However, the National Guard companies were usually only issued two of the newer M2 Light Tanks, as they became available. When activated for yearly training, the National Guard Tank Company would take their two tanks to the training area and, occasionally, then be supplied with additional tanks by a Regular Army Tank Company stationed nearby.

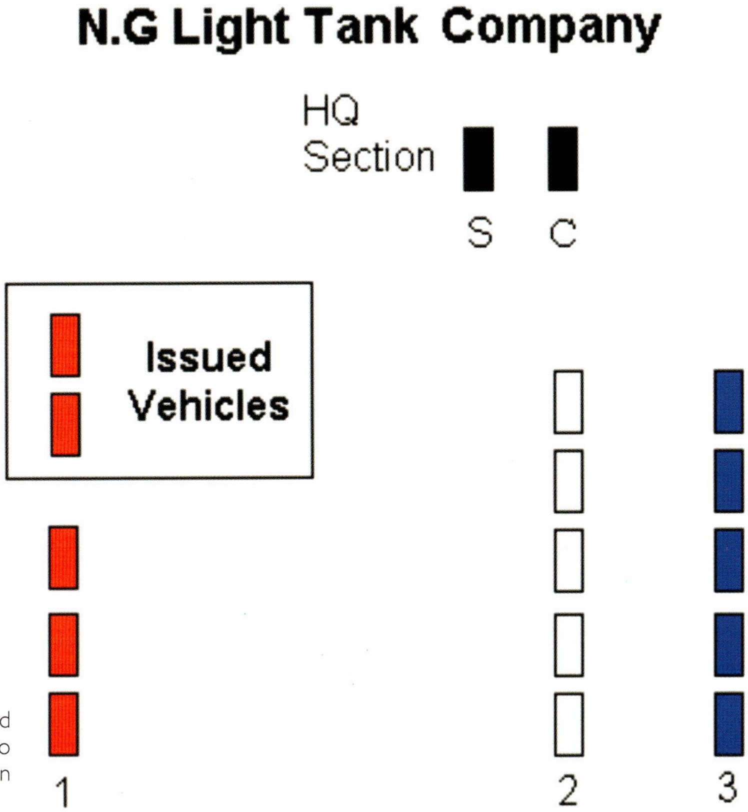

Organization of a National Guard Tank Company. Usually only two of the authorized seventeen vehicles were ever issued.

Colors and Markings

As with the Regular Army divisional tank companies, many of the National Guard tank companies adopted the geometric figures used to designate the platoons within the company. However, since all of the National Guard tank companies were equipped with only enough tanks to partially fill one platoon, the most common geometric figure is the Diamond – designating the 1st Platoon. These tactical markings were from ten to twelve-inches tall and were nearly always painted in white with the tank number (1, 2, 3, 4, or 5) in black, six-inch numerals.

The main difference between the Regular Army and National Guard companies came in the unit markings used on the vehicle. As required by regulation, vehicle registration numbers were painted on either side of the hull in white, 4-inch tall numbers and letters.

The following are units whose markings have been identified and confirmed.

26th Tank Company

The 26th Tank Company was given two M2A2 Light Tanks in 1938. The only known photographs of the company show their two tanks in the distance. The only visible markings are a full color Tank Corps triangle, approximately four-inches tall, on the outside of each turret near the front.

27th Tank Company

The company was issued at two M2A2 Light Tanks in 1938. Only a single photograph one of the company's tanks has come to light, and it was misidentified as an M2A3. In the picture it is painted in a gloss olive-drab paint with the company's distinctive insignia was painted on the outside of left turret in full color. No other markings, except for the vehicle's white registration number, were applied.

An M2A2 Light Tank of the 27th Tank Company (New York National Guard) during a parade in New York in 1938. Painted a gloss olive drab, the company crest – the gold colored ship of Henry Hudson on a blue shield with a blue and orange ribbon below – is painted on the left turret in full color.

Two light tanks of the 28th Tank Company in 1938. The center tank is marked for the company commander with the triangle and "C". The "28" stenciled in white between the two front hatches is clearly visible in the tank to the right. (OC)

28th Tank Company

The 28th Tank Company was an exception among the National Guard tank companies in that it was ultimately issued four M2A2 Light Tanks in 1938. Three of the tanks were each assigned to a platoon, with the fourth tank being marked for the company headquarters. In addition to the white outline tactical markings, each of the tanks was marked "28" in white between the driver's and bow machine-gunner's hatches in one-inch numerals. In 1939, the unit gave up at least one of their tanks to help outfit the 44th Tank Company (New Jersey National Guard).

29th Tank Company

This unit marked its two tanks on the outside of each turret with the regulation unit markings – the unit patch between two lines and "29th Tank Company". In addition is painted "VA" above and "N.G." below. The tactical marking is a skeletal diamond painted on the front of each sponson with the lineal number painted in white. This marking is duplicated on the rear hull projection.

One of the four M2A2 Light Tanks assigned to the 28th Tank Company in 1938. (OC)

Two additional M2A2 Light Tanks of the 28th Tank Company in 1938. Painted between the driver's and bow machine-gunner's positions is stenciled "28" in white, 2-inch tall stencils. (OC)

M2A2 Light Tank belonging to the 29th Tank Company (Virginia National Guard) in operation during the Second Army Maneuvers in 1938. The divisional patch is in gray and blue, while the rest of the stenciling is in white. It is not known whether the markings are duplicated on the right turret. (HC)

Two M2A2 Light Tanks assigned to the 32nd Tank Company (Wisconsin National Guard) circa 1939. Notice the full color unit patch on the side of the turret with the divisional designation written out below and on the side of the sponson in white. Although the turret markings are nearly identical, the markings are the both sides of the hull are unique to the individual vehicles. It is not clear exactly what the first and last lines are, but the centerline reads "32d DIVISION." Barely visible on the right front fender of the front tank is another red painted division patch, with "32d" in white on the left fender

Marking of the 32nd Tank Company, Wisconsin National Guard, circa 1938.

32nd Tank Company

The 32nd Tank Company received its two M2A2 Light Tanks in February of 1937. Markings were not immediately added, but by 1939 the tanks had been marked on the forward, outside portion of each turret with the divisional insignia in red (a long red arrow piercing a line) and the number "32" in white underneath the symbol close to the front. The insignia was about twelve to fourteen inches long and set at an upward angle. The crew names were added to the hull in white stencils. On one vehicle the names and ranks were added to the side of the hull at the very front of the sponson. On the other, the names and ranks were added to the very front edge of the sponson. By the time of the unit was ordered to active duty, the divisional insignia had been further added to the front fenders – with the arrow pointing upwards and inwards in red, and "32" in white at the upper and outer portion of each front fender.

33rd Tank Company

The 33rd Tank Company's last few M1917 Light Tanks finally wore out during their maneuvers in 1936. Fortunately, it received two new M2A2 Light Tanks in early 1937. Within a couple of months, both tanks had been painted with unit markings, but not identically. M2A2 Light Tank, registration number 30199, was marked on the outside of each turret cupola with "33RD DIVISION" in white, two-inch letters and numbers. Registration number 30200 was marked on the forward portion of the outside of each turret with the division patch – a twelve-inch diameter black disk with a four-inch wide golden yellow cross at the center.

A light tank of the 33rd Tank Battalion on the move. The black and yellow divisional patch is clearly visible on the outside of the turret. (ISM)

A bit more distant view of the right side of one of the M2A2 Light Tanks of the 33rd Tank Company in 1938. Only two tanks were assigned to the company and both were painted differently. (ISM)

The other M2A2 Light Tank belonging to the 33rd Tank Company. On this vehicle it is identified by a simple stencil at the top edge of each turret on the outside in white. This shot was taken in 1938. (ISM)

Another view of the M2A2 Light Tank from the 33rd Tank Company. (ISM)

M2A2 Light tanks belonging to the 34th Tank Company, Minnesota National Guard in 1938. These vehicles have no markings other than the vehicle registration numbers painted on either side of the hull.

34th Tank Company
Like most National Guard tank companies, the 34th was issued two M2A2 light tanks around 1937. The unit did not bother to mark either of their tanks with unit markings.

35th Tank Company
This unit was issued at least two M2 series light tanks around 1937. As with the 33rd Tank Company, the tanks were not marked in an identical manner. One of the tanks was neatly marked on the outside of each turret with the divisional patch. The 35th Division was one of a small number of divisions that customized its unit patch for each subordinate unit. This differentiation was reflected by the colors used in the creation of the patch. In the case of the tank company, which was part of the special troops attached to the division headquarters, the upper left and lower right quarters were in light blue while the upper right quarter was in yellow and the lower left quarter in red. In late 1940, the company was federalized in Missouri and then sent to Fort Lewis, Washington as Company B, 194th Tank Battalion.

An M2A2 Light Tank of the 35th Tank Company on the first day of the Fourth Army Maneuvers at Fort Riley, KS in August 1937. While much of the patch on the side of the turret is light blue, the upper right quarter is in yellow and the lower left quadrant in red. The tank at the rear is of the same company and marked in a similar manner.

36th Tank Company

The 36th Tank Company was issued two M2A2 Light Tanks when it was activated in 1937. Unlike most of the National Guard tank companies, the 36th maintained two platoons – giving each a single tank. As a result one tank was marked with an open white diamond with a white "1" at the center, while the other was marked with an open white disk with a white "1" at the center. The markings were painted on the front of each sponson, as well as on the round projection at the back of the hull. By 1940 the 36th Division unit patch had been painted on the outside of each turret, to the left of a white stenciled marking "36TH TANK COMPANY" between two white lines.[1]

37th Tank Company

The one known photograph of the 37th Tank Company, taken in 1939, shows no markings on their M2A2 Light Tanks except for the registration number – painted in white four-inch numerals on either side of the hull.

Both M2A2 Light Tanks newly assigned to the 37th Tank Company, Illinois National Guard taken in 1938. You will notice the lack of tactical markings.

M2A2 Light Tank of the 37th Tank Company during maneuvers in 1939. The vehicle still lacks any unit markings even at this late date. Identification was done by the vehicle's registration number USA W-30220. (HC)

An M2A2 Light Tank assigned to the 41st Tank Company on maneuvers in 1939. Notice the small, full color divisional patch on the side of the turret near the front, as well as the white painted divisional name down the side of the hull. (WNM)

M2A2 Light Tank assigned to the 43rd Tank Company during the First Army maneuvers in 1938. The platoon marking is in red with the lineal number (1) in white. (HC)

The other light tank assigned to the 43rd Tank Company during the 1938 maneuvers. The red solid triangle, and the articulated Tank Corps patch centered low on the outside of the right turret are good identification points for this company. (HC)

41st Tank Company

The 41st Tank Company received its two M2A2 Light Tanks in mid-1937. As with many of the National Guard Tank Companies, it did not make use of tactical markings on its tanks. It did, however, mark its tank with unit markings. On the forward outside edge of each turret was painted a full color rendition of the divisional patch for the 41st Division (approximately 2 inches tall by three inches wide). Painted on either side of the hull, above the brush guard and close to the rear, was "41st TANK CO." in three-inch white letters. Directly below the brush guard was painted the tank's registration number. On the front of each sponson was painted either "1" or "2" in six-inch numeral. This number was repeated on the right lower front hull and left rear hull.

43rd Tank Company

The company received their two M2A2 Light Tanks in 1938 and marked them with a red diamond on both sponsons and on the rear of the hull on the projection of the engine compartment. The vehicle lineal number, either a 1 or 2, was stenciled in white at the center. Low on the turret, underneath the Infantry (tank) emblem was stenciled an articulated Tank Corps emblem in full color.

44th Tank Company

A short time after activation in September of 1939, the 44th Tank Company received at single M2A3 Light Tank from the 28th Tank Company. Although it made no use of tactical markings, it did paint a two-inch diameter full color 44th Division patch on the outside of the right turret with "44TH TANK CO" in white, three-inch lettering to the right of the patch. The left turret was apparently left unpainted. The original 28th Tank Company markings had been completely painted out. The unit was disbanded within the year.

A 44th Tank Company M2A2 Light Tank during maneuvers in 1939. This tank was drawn from the 26th Tank Company just months before and this would be the first and last maneuver this company would participate in. Notice the very small, full color unit patch to the left of the company markings on the turret. (HC)

10

Mechanized Cavalry 1936-1940

In 1936 the existing mechanized cavalry regiment at Fort Knox was a joined by a second, the 13th Cavalry. The arrival of this second cavalry regiment completed the basic structure of the 7th Cavalry Brigade (Mechanized). The year of 1936 was also when the T4 Combat Cars (Christie) were finally dropped from the army inventory and replaced completely by the M1 Series Combat Car.[1] The structure of the 7th Cavalry Brigade (Mechanized) would remain unchanged until July of 1940, when the brigade was re-organized as the 1st Armored Division.

Cavalryman, 1st Cavalry Regiment (Mecz), 1939.

Organization

The organization of both regiments was basically identical and remained unchanged from the 1933 model. Each of the cavalry regiments was divided into two squadrons, with each squadron having two troops. The troop strength varied somewhat through the life of the Brigade, especially in the number of vehicles assigned.

By 1938 each of the cavalry regiments were equipped with fifty-four M1 and M1A1 Combat Cars divided between a Headquarters troop, and two squadrons (first and second). Each of the squadrons contained two combat car troops, each with thirteen combat cars and one additional combat car in the squadron HQ troop for a total of twenty-seven. In the Regimental HQ troop was an additional two combat cars. This gave the brigade a total of one hundred and eight combat cars.

1939 (Tentative) Brigade HQ
- 2 Cavalry Regiments
  - HQ & HQ Troop (T/O 424)
    - 1 - Combat Car (Assigned to Communication Platoon)
    - 2 - Armored Cars (Assigned to Communication Platoon)
    - 1 - Half-track (Assigned to Troop HQ)
  - Service Troop (T/O 425)
    - No Armored Vehicles
  - Machinegun Troop (T/O 430)
    - 1 - Combat Car (Attached to Troop HQ)
    - 22 - Half-tracks (5 per machinegun Platoon {3} - 2 per section, 1 in the Platoon HQ)
    - (5 - attached to Rifle Platoon - 2 per section, 1 in Platoon HQ)
  - (2 - attached to Troop HQ)
  - Armored Car Troop TO 414
    - 17 - Armored Cars (1 - attached to Troop HQ, 4 in each of the 4 Armored Car Platoon)
  - Combat Car Squadron (T/O 426) Two per Regiment
    - 27 - Combat Cars per Squadron (1 attached to Squadron HQ)
    - (13 per troop - 3 per platoon {4} 1 per Troop HQ)
  - Field Artillery Battalion (Attached)
    - 4 - batteries of four guns (75mm How) each with ten half-tracks
      - (1 per gun and 2 per Battery HQ, 2 in maintenance section, 2 in 5th Section
  - Attached Medical
  - Attached Chaplain

Colors and Markings 1936-1937

1st Cavalry Regiment (Mechanized)

During this first part of this period, combat cars assigned to the regiment continued to be marked in white at the center of the turret above the gun mantlet, with a line across the top and bottom. This marking was repeated on a plate mounted above the left rear fender. As always, the regimental crest was painted in color on both sides of turret.

On the combat cars assigned to B and C troops, 1st Squadron, additional platoon designators were painted in dark yellow between the machinegun mounts and as well as centered on the rear of the turret. Painted in six to eight inch tall figures, these designated the platoon to which the vehicle belonged.

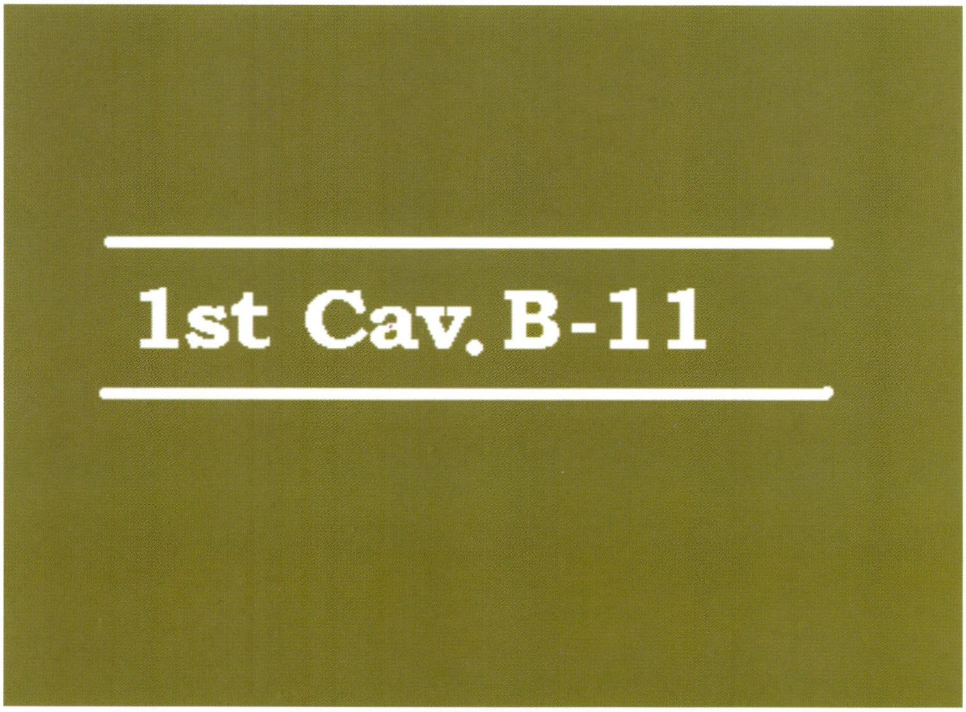

Example of the turret markings used by 1st Cavalry from 1935-1936, and by the 13th Cavalry in 1936.

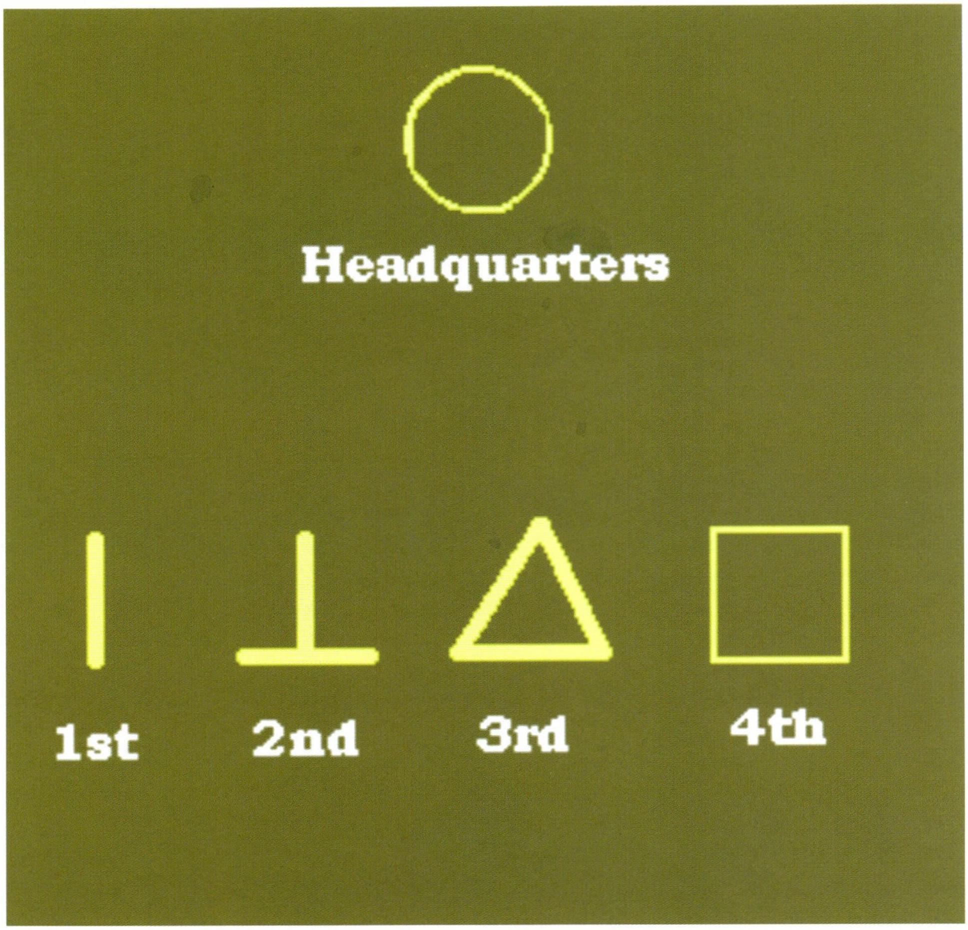

Platoon Markings of the 1st Cavalry Regiment.

M1 Combat Car assigned as the commander's vehicle for the 1st Squadron, 13th Cavalry Regiment (Mecz). The vehicle number "1-1" is visible on the front of the turret with the commander's metal guidon attached to either side. Circa 1936.

Troop headquarters vehicles were marked with a cut stenciled circle, while the 1st Platoon was marked with a single vertical line, about one-inch thick. An upside-down "T" designated 2nd Platoon combat cars, while an open triangle designated those from the 3rd Platoon. An open square designated the 4th Platoon. By 1938, only B troop was still renewing these stencils, and a reorganization of the troops had eliminated the 3rd and 4th platoons.

In addition to the painted markings, the regiment made use of painted metal guidons – which designated the various command combat cars within the regiment and the squadrons. These were painted in red and white with the regimental number and squadron number countercharged.

13th Cavalry Regiment (Mechanized)

Mechanized and assigned to the 7th Cavalry Brigade in 1936, the 13th Cavalry Regiment did not begin to receive its combat cars or other armored vehicles until 1937. When they were finally received, the vehicles were marked in a similar manner as the 1st Cavalry Regiment. Stenciled on each side of the turret was a full color 13th Cavalry crest, approximately twelve inches in diameter. Other markings are similar to 1st Cavalry on front of turret and on left rear fender.

M1 Combat car assigned to F Troop, 1st Cavalry Regiment (Mecz) at Fort Knox, KY in 1935. The white stenciled unit and vehicle identification is painted on the front of the turret above the guns, with the full color unit crest painted on either side of the turret. On the left sponson is painted the driver's name and rank in yellow, 1-inch stencils. The vehicle is painted in a gloss olive-drab paint. It is interesting to note that the vehicle registration number is not visible, having been painted on the very back of the tank.

Rear view of an M1 Combat Car assigned to the C Troop, 1st Cavalry Regiment (Mecz) at Fort Knox in 1935. Notice the black on white stenciled identification plate attached to the left rear fender, as well as the white stenciled registration number painted across the rear of the hull. On the either side of the rear of the turret is painted a yellow vertical stripe, marking the vehicle as belonging to the 1st platoon. (HC)

Unified Marking System, 1938

In 1938, the markings used by the two regiments forming the 7th Cavalry Brigade had become standardized. For the troop combat cars, the regimental crest was stenciled in full color on either side of the turret. Because of the difference in turret shape between the M1 and M1A1, the location of the crest was not in the same location on the vehicles.

On the late model M1A1 combat cars, the crest was painted on the flat areas near the rear of the turret. For the early "horseshoe" pattern turret of the M1, these were painted on flat area near the front of the turret. The troop letter was stenciled above and between the guns in front in white, eight to ten-inch letters and numbers. For the Regimental HQ tanks, either "HQ" or "Hq" was marked above and between the guns in white.

Side view of an M1 Combat Car of the C Troop, 1st Cavalry Regiment (Mecz) on maneuvers at Fort Knox in 1936. Note by now that the registration numbers had been moved to the sides of the hull. The unit crest is painted in full color on both sides of the turret. Just visible behind the Lister bag hanging on the turret is an upside-down yellow "T", marking the vehicle as belonging to the 2nd platoon. Another interesting treatment is the yellow strips of paint on the shovel and axe.

C Troop command combat car. In addition to the unit markings, the Headquarters marking of an open circle is also painted on the front of the turret. The red and white metal guidon is attached to the side of the turret – the mark of the troop commander. This photograph was taken in 1937.

M1 Combat Cars ofTroop B, 1st Cavalry Regiment (Mecz) on parade at Fort Knox in the spring of 1937.The unit markings are clear on the front of the turret, along with the yellow platoon markings.

Detail of M1 and M1A1 Combat Cars of the 1st Cavalry Regiment during maneuvers at Fort Riley, KS in 1938. (PM - Scheller)

M1 Combat Cars of C Troop, 1st Cavalry Regiment (Mecz) fueling along the side of the road at Fort Knox in 1938. By this time the old pattern of markings, painted in a single line across the front of the turret, had been replaced by a white, eight-inch tall company letter painted on the front of the turret and on the rear projection on the hull. The yellow platoon markings are not visible on these vehicles. The unit crests are also not visible due to the angle of the shot.

Troop and squadron HQ tanks were identified by the mounting of 1/2 scale painted metal guidons that were bolted to either side of the turret, near the front. The guidons were painted in the proper red and white colors, with the Regimental number and Troop letter or Squadron number countercharged, and measured approximately 14-inches tall and 24-inches. The guidon for the regimental HQ tank was painted solid yellow rather than red and white, and had a full color rendition of the regimental crest painted at the center.

Soldiers of C Troop, 1st Cavalry Regiment (Mecz) changing track on an M1 Combat Car at Fort Riley during the spring of 1938. (PM - Scheller)

Combat cars of the 13th Cavalry Regiment (Mecz), driving along Wilson Road at Fort Knox in 1938. The full color unit crest is visible on the side of the turret. Like the 1st Cavalry, the 13th marked its vehicles with the company letter on the front of the turret and the rear of the hull. The vehicles are painted in a gloss olive drab.

Problems with identification – It belongs to Troop C, but the angle of this photograph prevents you from knowing whether this Combat Car is from the 1st or 13th Cavalry Regiment. Taken in May 1938. Because of this problem, the regimental number was added to the markings in 1939.

M1 Combat Cars of E Troop, 1st Cavalry Regiment (Mecz) refueling on their way back from Fort Riley in 1938. The company commander's vehicle is visible in the foreground with its metal red and white guidon. Notice the large five-gallon fuel cans secured on the front fender. The troop letter is stenciled in white on the front of the turret.

Painted in a high-gloss olive-drab paint, this is the command vehicle for the regimental commander of the 13th Cavalry. The metal guidons are attached to either side of the turret and are painted yellow with the regimental crest in full color. The "HQ" marking with no regimental number mark this as being taken prior to 1939.

LTC Andrus, 1st Squadron Commander of the 1st Cavalry Regiment (Mecz), stands smiling in the turret of his M1A1 Combat Car in 1938. The squadron number can be seen on the back of the hull – this was repeated on the front of the turret. The unit crest can be seen at either side of the turret. Barely visible is the detachable, red and white metal guidon designating the vehicle as the belonging the squadron commander. (PM - Andrus)

Close up view of the command M1 Combat Car for C Troop, 1st Cavalry Regiment (Mecz). The yellow open circle is clearly visible on the front of the turret below the white company letter. The metal guidon, painted in red and white, can be seen attached to the side of the turret. The cavalry plate is also clearly visible. (PM - Andrus)

M1A1 Combat Car belonging to the commander of the 2nd Squadron, 13th Cavalry Regiment. The numeral "2" is visible on the front of the turret, with the commander's red and white metal guidon attached to the turret side – obscuring the regimental crest. 1938.

Example of a troop commander's guidon attached to an M1A1 Combat Car. This belongs to the E Troop commander – evident by the "E" painted on the guidon and on the front of the vehicle. 1938.

Unified Marking System, 1939

Apparently some confusion arose from the lack of the regimental number visible on the front or rear of the combat cars, so in 1939 the regimental number was added below the troop letter on the front of the turret and on the rear of the hull. The markings on the rear of the hull were painted in six to eight-inch tall figures – the company letter to the left side of the hull and the regimental number to the right. These markings continued in use until the conversion of the brigade to the 1st Armored Division in July of 1940.

During the maneuvers of 1939, two vehicles were marked with a large (up to thirty-six inches) "2" or "3" as an air recognition marking. The exact meaning of the markings is, as yet, unknown – but the marking was visible with or without the driver's hatch being open.

M1 and M1A1 Combat Cars of the 1st Cavalry during the 1939 First Army Maneuvers. Because of the confusion caused by the use of only a company letter on the vehicles, the regimental number was added to the front of the turret and back of the hull. (PM - Scheller)

Winter camouflage on M1 Combat Cars of the 1st Cavalry Regiment at Fort Knox in 1939. This is the same vehicle as in the previous picture with, not only the tank, but also the metal guidon, painted over in a thin whitewash. The unit markings are barely visible through the coat.

Vehicle park of the 13th Cavalry Regiment during the First Army maneuvers in 1939.

Complete layout of equipment for an M1A1 Combat Car. This particular vehicle belongs to the 2nd Squadron Commander, 13th Cavalry Regiment (Mecz). The guidon plate is rather interesting in that there has been a square hole cut into it so that the pistol port can be opened. The "2" is painted directly onto the turret. Circa 1938.

M1 Combat Car belonging to the E Troop Commander, 1st Cavalry Regiment during the First Army maneuvers in New York during 1939. In addition to the normal painted markings and the commander's metal guidon, there is a large white "3" painted on the front hull. This marking is probably a air recognition marking adopted for the maneuvers. Another vehicle of the regiment has been identified with the numeral "2" also.

Vehicles as assigned in 1938:

13th Cavalry Regiment. Totals: 45 Scout Cars, 3 C&R Cars, 72 Combat Cars (44)
- HQ - 4 Combat Cars, 6 Scout Cars, 3 C&R Cars, plus motorcycles
- 1st Squadron (HQ - 2 combat Cars)
  - A Troop 17 Scout Cars (
  - B Troop: 14 Combat Cars (9)
  - C Troop: 11 Combat Cars (11)
- 2nd Squadron (HQ - 2 Combat Cars)
  - MG Troop: 22 Scout Cars (D Troop)
  - E Troop: 11 Combat Cars (7)
  - F Troop: 11 Combat Cars (9)

1st Cavalry Regiment. Totals: 36 Scout Cars, 33 Combat Cars
- 1st Squadron (HQ 3 Combat Cars)
  - A Troop: 16 Scout Cars
  - B Troop: 7 Combat Cars
  - C Troop: 8 Combat Cars
- 2nd Squadron (1 Combat Car)
  - MG Troop: 20 Scout Cars
  - E Troop: 7 Combat Cars
  - F Troop: 7 Combat Cars

Brigade Troops:
- Headquarters
  - 6 Scout Cars
- 68th Field Artillery
  - 8 Guns
  - 8 Howitzers
  - 20 Scout Cars
  - 20 Half-tracks
  - 9 Trucks
- Armored Car Troop
  - 13 Armored Cars

11

The Armored Force GHQ Reserve Tank Battalions & Separate Tank Battalions 1940-1941

The eruption of war in Europe in 1940 gave impetus to the activation of several American National Guard units for advanced combat training. In conjunction with the creation of the Armored Force on July 10, 1940, plans for the creation of a number of independent tank battalions had also been made. The General Headquarters (GHQ) Reserve tank battalions were designed to be Army and Corps level assets, to be used wherever needed on the battlefield.

The first GHQ Tank Battalions were formed, for the most part, by the consolidation of the existing National Guard Divisional light tank companies. An additional Regular Army battalion, the 70th GHQ (Reserve) Tank Battalion (Medium) was also created in 1940. By early 1941, the GHQ (Reserve) tank battalions had been re-designated as Separate Tank Battalions and the term "GHQ (Reserve)" was dropped from their designations.

On the 1st of January 1941 an additional ten separate Regular Army tank battalions were created. These battalions, five light tank and five medium tank, were originally numbered from 71st to the 80th, but in early May of 1941 they were renumbered the 751st through 760th Tank Battalions, to fall into line with the Army's new numbering system. All ten were ultimately activated on 1 June 1941.

General Adna Chaffee, Chief of Armor wrote to the Army Deputy Chief of Staff on October 6, 1940:

"*The main concern which I have right now is the prompt formation of efficient GHQ reserve tank battalions (light) out of the 18 scattered National Guard Companies, which will come into the federal service. I deem it of primary importance that these battalions be whipped into shape with the utmost rapidity in order that they may be available as task forces to meet the demand of the Green and Rainbow plans and thus save the disruption and loss of a great deal of training which has been accomplished in the armored divisions.*" (Author's italics).[1]

National Guard Tanker, 192nd Tank Battalion, Fort Knox, KY, Spring 1941.

The initial four National Guard GHQ Reserve Tank Battalions were officially activated on the 1st of September 1940, although the actual activation and organization was spread out over a 6-month period. The battalions were organized by Army Area – the 191st in the First Army area, the 192nd in the Second Army area, the 193rd in the Third Army area and the 194th in the Fourth Army area.

Organization

With the exception of the 194th (which was short one line company), each of the National Guard GHQ Reserve Tank Battalions (Light) was initially made up of four line tank companies, but there was no battalion headquarters company. This ad-hoc organization was necessary due to the fact that the units composing these battalions hailed from different states and no provisions had been made to form a headquarters company. This oversight was finally corrected by early-1941. Under the existing Table of Organization and Equipment (TO&E), each of the line companies was supposed to have seventeen light tanks (five in each platoon, and two in the HQ platoon), giving each battalion a strength of fifty-one light tanks. When they were called to activation, each of the National Guard Companies was instructed to bring both of their tanks with them to the activation station.[2]

The 70th GHQ Tank Battalion, being a regular army unit, was the only GHQ Reserve tank battalion that had been organized from the start with a headquarters company and therefore had the extra three Battalion headquarters tanks, giving it a strength of fifty-four light tanks. By mid-1941, all of the National Guard battalions had been re-organized with a headquarters company made up of personnel drawn from each of the individual companies. The units were then filled out with draftees to bring them up to full strength. The ten additional Regular Army separate tank battalions were all organized along the same lines as the 70th Tank Battalion.

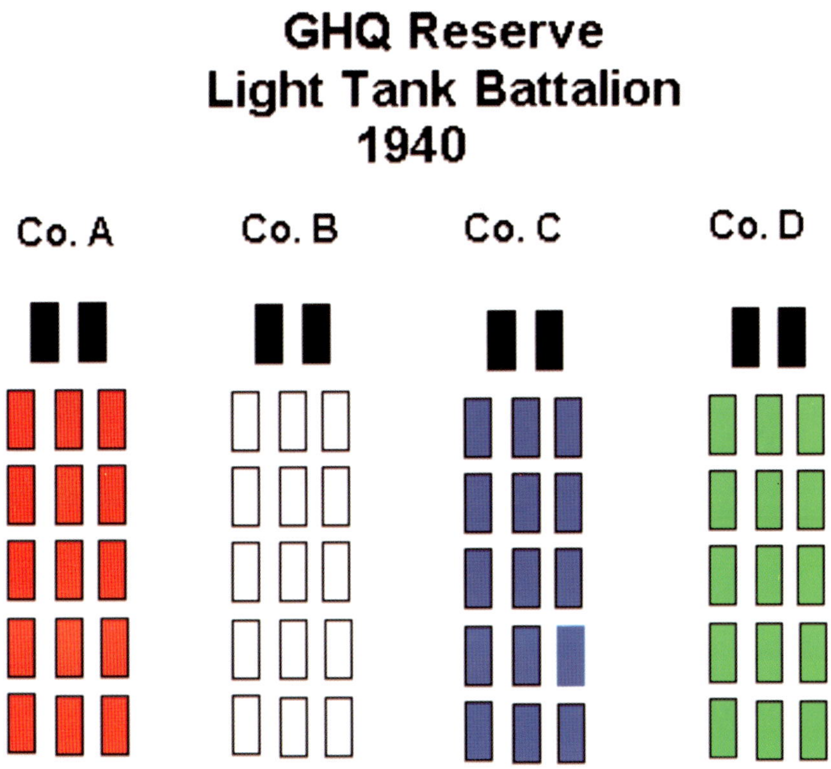

Organization of the GHQ Reserve Tank Battalion – 1940.

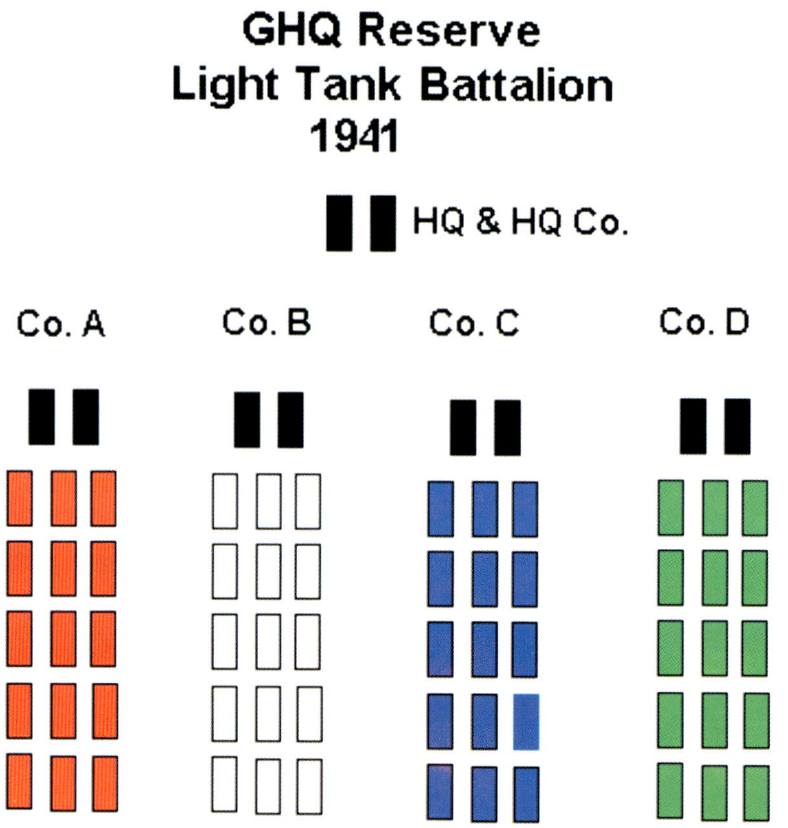

Organization of the GHQ Reserve Tank Battalion – 1941.

191st GHQ (Reserve) Tank Battalion (Light)
The First Army area, comprising the heavily populated Northeastern United States, had six National Guard light tank companies available. Since the organization of the 191st Tank Battalion only required four of those companies, the 28th and 44th Tank Companies was inactivated or otherwise converted and their tanks turned over to the new battalion. The companies that ultimately formed the 191st Tank Battalion were activated at their home stations on the 3rd of February 1941 and were shipped to Fort George G. Meade for training and final organization later that month.

A Company – 27th Tank Company (New York National Guard)
B Company – 26th Tank Company (Massachusetts National Guard)
C Company – 29th Tank Company (Virginia National Guard)
D Company – 43rd Tank Company (Connecticut National Guard)

192nd GHQ (Reserve) Tank Battalion (Light)
The 192nd Tank Battalion was organized and trained at Fort Knox in the late fall of 1940, with the tank companies drawn from the four National Guard divisions assigned to the Second Army area. These units were activated and inducted into Federal Service between May and November of 1940 at their home stations.

A Company – 32nd Tank Company (Wisconsin National Guard)
B Company – 33rd Tank Company (Illinois National Guard)
C Company – 37th Tank Company (Ohio National Guard)
D Company – 38th Tank Company (Kentucky National Guard)

193rd GHQ (Reserve) Tank Battalion (Light)
The 193rd Tank Battalion was created from the four National Guard tank companies assigned to the Third Army area, and was inducted into Federal Service on January 20, 1941 at Fort Benning, GA.

A Company – 30th Tank Company (Georgia National Guard)
B Company – 31st Tank Company (Alabama National Guard)
C Company – 36th Tank Company (Texas National Guard)
D Company – 45th Tank Company (Colorado National Guard)

194th GHQ (Reserve) Tank Battalion (Light)

The last battalion, the 194th, was incomplete even though the Fourth Army area had four tank companies assigned. Nevertheless, the separate companies of the battalion (A, B, and C Companies) were inducted into Federal Service between December 1940 and March 1941 at their home stations. The abbreviated battalion was finally organized at Fort Lewis, WA on 12 March 1941.

A Company – 34th Tank Company (Minnesota National Guard)
B Company – 35th Tank Company (Missouri National Guard)
C Company – 40th Tank Company (California National Guard)

After months of training, the 191st, 192nd, and 193rd all participated in the Third Army maneuvers in Louisiana in September of 1941. The 194th had been divided up and ordered to the Philippine Islands and to Alaska as part of the "Orange" Plan in early September. By the second phase of the maneuvers in November, only the 191st was still available to take part. This was due to the fact that the 192nd Tank Battalion had been ordered to re-enforce the 194th Tank Battalion in the Philippines, leaving San Francisco in late October, while the 193rd had been ordered to prepare to go to the Hawaiian Islands.

The history of these battalions is of great importance to understanding the conduct of American military policy in the pre-war period. As part of the "Orange" Plan, two of these GHQ battalions (192nd and 194th) were sent to the Philippine Islands in September and November 1941, where they surrendered to the Japanese Fourteen Army in April of 1942. Only two companies of the 194th were sent to the Philippines, with the third company being sent to Alaska.

The 191st Tank Battalion saw action in the European Theater of Operations in Italy and Northern Europe, while the 193rd spent its time in the Pacific Theater. The sole surviving company of the 194th Tank Battalion, which had been sent to Alaska in September of 1941, was re-designated as the 602nd Separate Tank Company after the demise of the rest of the battalion.

Regular Army and National Army GHQ Tank Battalions

70th GHQ Reserve Tank Battalion (Medium)

The 70th GHQ Tank Battalion (Medium), was the sole regular Army battalion activated in 1940 Brought into being 15 July 1940 at Fort George G. Meade, it was created using the personnel from the 1st Battalion, 66th Infantry Regiment (Light Tanks). Because of the lack of medium tanks, it was initially equipped as a light tank battalion – a situation that would not change until well into 1942. It saw action in the European Theater of Operations during World War II.

HQ & HQ Company - HQ & HQ Company, 1st Battalion, 66th Infantry (Light Tanks)
A Company – A Company, 66th Infantry (Light Tanks)
B Company – B Company, 66th Infantry (Light Tanks)
C Company – C Company, 66th Infantry (Light Tanks)
D Company – Newly created

71st Tank Battalion (Medium) – 751st Tank Battalion (Medium)

Activated at Fort Benning, GA on the 1st of June 1941 as the 751st Tank Battalion (Medium) the unit was initially manned using a cadre from the 2nd Armored Division, then filled out with newly enlisted or drafted personnel. Like most of these first separate battalions, the 751st was initially equipped with a small number of M2 series light tanks, used for training. It did not receive a full complement of tanks until well into the spring of 1942. For administrative purposes, it was assigned to the 2nd Provisional Tank Group.

72nd Tank Battalion (Medium) – 752nd Tank Battalion (Medium)

Activated at Fort Lewis, WA as the 752nd Tank Battalion (Medium) on 1 June 1941, the unit was not even issued tanks until February of 1942. For administrative purposes it was assigned to the 2nd Provisional Tank Group.

73rd Tank Battalion (Medium) – 753rd Tank Battalion (Medium)

Activated at Fort Benning, GA on the 1st of June 1941 as the 753rd Tank Battalion (Medium). The unit was initially formed using a small cadre of troops from the 2nd Armored Division, but did not receive any tanks until early 1942. The initial issue consisted of recycled M2A2/A3 and M2A4 Light Tanks.

74th Tank Battalion (Medium) – 754th Tank Battalion (Medium)

The 754th Tank Battalion (Medium) was activated at Fort Knox KY on the 1st of June 1941.

75th Tank Battalion (Medium) – 755th Tank Battalion (Medium)

The 755th Tank Battalion (Medium) was activated on 1 June 1941 at Camp Bowie, TX. The unit was issued twelve obsolete M2A2/A3 light tanks in September of 1941 for training use. For administrative purposes, the battalion was assigned to the 3rd Provisional Tank Group.

76th Tank Battalion (Light) – 756th Tank Battalion (Light)
Activated at Fort Lewis, WA on 1 June 1941, the unit was not even issued tanks until early 1942. For administrative purposes the unit was assigned to the 2nd Provisional Tank Group.

77th Tank Battalion (Light) – 757th Tank Battalion (Light)
The 757th Tank Battalion was activated at Fort Ord, CA on 1 June 1941. It received its first tanks, a mixture of M2A2, M2A3, and M2A4 Light Tanks from Fort Knox in early September of 1941. It was assigned to the 2nd Provisional Tank Group for administrative purposes.

78th Tank Battalion (Light) (Cld) – 758th Tank Battalion (Light) (Cld)
Activated at Fort Knox on 1 June 1941, the 758th Tank Battalion was the first black tank battalion to be created by the United States Army. It did not receive any tanks until early in 1942.

79th Tank Battalion (Light) – 759th Tank Battalion (Light)
The 759th Tank Battalion (Light) was activated at Fort Knox, KY, on 1 June 1941. It was assigned to the 3rd Provisional Tank Group for administrative purposes.

80th Tank Battalion (Light) – 760th Tank Battalion (Light)
Activated at Camp Bowie, TX on 1 June 1941, this battalion had been issued twelve M2A2, M2A3 and M2A4 Light tanks in September of 1941. By the end of November, it had received another nine M3 Medium Tanks. It was assigned to the 3rd Provisional Tank Group for administrative purposes

Colors and Markings

The exterior color for this period remained the regulation olive-drab of the mid- to late-1930s, with some vehicles still being painted in the pre-war gloss finish. The declaration of a national emergency in 1939 resulted in the repainting of many of the vehicles into the wartime flat olive drab. The Army registration markings for armored vehicles were applied in white during the first year of the Armored Force existence but, in July of 1941, the color was changed from white to a lusterless blue,[3] apparently as a result of low visibility testing by the Corps of Engineers.

National Guard GHQ Reserve Battalions

The formation of these new battalions heralded the introduction, however brief, of new tactical markings to aid in identifying the units and the vehicles within those units. The geometric figures that had been in use to designate platoons within the regimental and independent companies were retained, but were modified instead to designate the individual companies within the newly formed battalion.

The triangle marking was now strictly used to designate vehicles of the battalion headquarters company, with "A" company being marked with a red diamond, "B" company with a white disk, and "C" company with a blue square. For "D" company, a new figure, a green spade, was introduced. A lineal vehicle number was painted in black or white at the center of the geometric figure. The figures "C" or "S" were still used to designate the Commander's or the Staff tank in the HQ Company. All of the figures were outlined with a one-inch thick orange border.

The National Guard GHQ Reserve Tank Battalions were, for the most part, issued with the castoffs from the two newly formed armored divisions.[4] These tanks, in conjunction with the two tanks that each National Guard tank company was supposed to have brought with them on activation, constituted the whole of their strength until late 1941. This resulted in a very mixed appearance, as the companies were equipped with a mixture of M2A2 and M2A3 "Mae West" Light Tanks, as well as M1 series Light Tanks for most of their initial training. Information on the GHQ (Reserve) Tank Battalions is somewhat sketchy, but the organization and marking system used by the three battalions which took part in the 1941 North Carolina Maneuvers is documented in both photographs and in written descriptions.[5]

From what information that is available, it is evident that by the middle of 1941 three of the four tank battalions were using the exact same markings and colors for their unit tactical markings, with the only difference being the colored stripe markings around the base of the turret(s). Each of the individual markings were outlined in a one inch orange border with the company unit lineal number (1-17) painted inside in either black or white, depending upon the background color.[6] The

Striped turret markings used to designate the individual GHQ (Reserve) Tank Battalions. The 194th was never fully organized and, because it never operated with the other battalions it was never given its own battalion marking.

Above left: Tactical marking for the Headquarters Company tanks of GHQ (Reserve) Tank Battalions. The "C" designates the Company Commander's tank Above right: Tactical marking for tanks of Company A in a GHQ (Reserve) Tank Battalion. Below left: Tactical marking for tanks of Company B in a GHQ (Reserve) Tank Battalion. Below right: Tactical marking for tanks of Company C in a GHQ (Reserve) Tank Battalion. Right: Tactical marking for tanks of Company D in a GHQ (Reserve) Tank Battalion.

An M2A2 Light Tank of the 191st Tank Battalion crossing a stream during the maneuvers of 1941. One of the few existing color photographs taken of any of the battalions, you can see 3-inch wide orange-red band around the base of each turret, as well as the orange edged, dark green "spade" painted on the outside of each turret. This marks the vehicle as belonging to Company D. By this time, the registration number for the vehicle was applied in lusterless blue. (HC)

M2 series light tanks under repair during the Tennessee Maneuvers of 1941. The two closest vehicles are assigned to the 191st Tank Battalion; both marked with a 3-inch orange-red stripe around the base of the turrets. The M2A4 Light Tank in the background appears to be one assigned to the 2nd Armored Division, although the numbering system does not appear to be consistent with their marking system. It is possible that it is one assigned to the 70th Tank Battalion.

numbers and letters were generally eight to ten inches tall, depending on the size of the geometric figure.

This new marking system was simply an expansion of the old tank company marking system. The triangle marking was now reserved for battalion headquarters tanks, but as most of the GHQ Tank Battalions initially had no battalion headquarters company assigned, it was not used at first. When the headquarters companies were finally organized in September of 1940 the triangle mark, with its accompanying "S" and "C" markings,[7] came into use by the GHQ Tank Battalions.

Under this new geometric marking system, the diamond now designated "A" Company; the disk – "B" Company, and the square – "C" Company. An additional geometric figure, the spade, was introduced to designate "D" Company. Unlike the old company system, which placed the geometric markings on the front of each sponson and on the rear of the hull, this new system placed the tactical markings on the outside of each turret, as well as on either side of the back of the hull. The number placed at the center of the figure denoted the vehicle's linear number within the company (1-17).[8] Only the 194th Tank Battalion seems to have not used this marking system. The addition of a stripe or dashes around the base of the turrets differentiated between the battalions.

191st Tank Battalion

The 191st Tank Battalion was organized and trained at Fort George Meade in early 1941 with tanks from, not only the four National Guard tank companies comprising the battalion, but also from the two inactivated companies assigned to First Army. Additional tanks were transferred in from other sources, such as the 2nd Armored Division, to fill out the battalion. As with the other battalions, the unit's tanks carried a mixture of markings until the adoption of standardized markings in the middle of 1941. By the time of the 1941 Maneuvers all of the tanks had been painted in the standard GHQ Tank Battalion markings, with a single orange stripe, three inches tall, painted around the base of each turret. The tactical markings were, of course, identical to that of the 191st and 193rd Battalions. It is interesting to note that of the four GHQ Reserve Tank Battalions, only the 191st remained in the continental United States after December 1941.

192nd Tank Battalion

The 192nd Tank Battalion was organized and trained at Fort Knox with tanks brought by the individual tank companies, and filled out with light tanks drawn from the 69th Armored

M2A2 Light Tank newly assigned to Company D, 192nd Tank Battalion in early 1941. The vehicle was transferred from the 69th Armored Regiment, who had gotten the vehicle from the 2nd Armored Division only months before. The broad white stripes had marked the vehicle as filling in as a "Medium" tank. The 192nd Tank Battalion temporarily marked its vehicles with a one-inch white stencil on the front of the right sponson "CO. D 192". A three-inch white "D" is also stenciled on the center of the front armor between the two front doors.

An M2A2 Light Tank assigned to the 192nd Tank Battalion, Company C at Fort Knox in 1940 – although the company designation is not visible in this photograph. The wide stripe around the turret mark this vehicle as having been drawn from one of the medium tank regiments.

Regiment, 1st Armored Division – who had gotten their tanks from the 68th Armored Regiment at Fort Benning. For the first few months this was quite confusing, because many of the tanks retained their original markings. On some of the tanks, men of the new unit simply stenciled the company and battalion designation in one-inch numbers and letters somewhere on the front of the tank. For example, the photograph of one vehicle shows a stenciled "Co. B 192 BN" in white above the tactical marking on the tank's right sponson.

Because of their close connection with the 1st Armored Division, the unit marked its tanks with tactical markings similar to that of the division to aid in identification. In order to differentiate their tanks from those of the 1st Armored Division, the battalion painted a two-color scheme of red and blue dashes around the base of the turrets. When this marking was first introduced in the spring of 1941, the company letter and linear number were stenciled in white on the front of the turret cupola, as well as on the rear of the hull. However, by mid-1941, the new marking system was adopted which incorporated the geometric markings, but also retained the dashed stripes around the turrets.

Light Tanks assigned to the 192nd Tank Battalion at Fort Knox. By late spring of 1941, the battalion was using a set of colored dashed markings around the base of the turret(s) in a manner similar to the 1st Armored Division. The colors were red and medium blue. The company letter and number were stenciled on the front of the cupola of the left turret in white. Registration numbers were painted in four-inch white letters and numbers on either side of the hull.

M2A2 Light Tank assigned to a Headquarters platoon of the 192nd Tank Battalion. The vehicle lineal number is clearly visible on the cupola of the left turret. Taken at Fort Knox during training in 1941. (JR)

Pair of M2A2 Light Tanks assigned to Company B, 192nd Tank Battalion. These two vehicles are painted in the first pattern scheme adopted by the battalion, with the two color dashed markings and the company letter and vehicle number on the cupola in white. Taken in early 1941.

Right side view of an M2A2 Light Tank assigned to headquarters platoon of the 192nd Tank Battalion in early 1941. (JR)

According to some accounts, the 192nd Tank Battalion never received a full complement of light tanks until just before it was shipped out for the Philippines in October-November 1941. The number mentioned is twenty-four M2A2 or M2A3 Light tanks, enough for 6 per company.[9] However, a photograph taken of D Company's tanks in October of 1941, shows a complete complement of light tanks for that unit. Just prior to being loaded out for California, the unit was re-equipped with fifty-four M3 Light Tanks, most of them drawn from other units. The vehicles that they were issued were marked solely with the blue registration numbers and no effort was made to place any unit markings onto the vehicles. When the war came to the Philippines on the 8th of December 1941, the first American manned tanks to go into combat were from the 192nd and 194th Tank Battalions – both of them National Guard units. The tanks themselves went into combat with no tactical markings or unit markings applied. Several survivors from the Bataan death march stated that some of the tanks had been stenciled in white with names on the turret sides, such as LULU BELLE and HELEN, but that no other markings had been added.

M2A2 Light Tank passing by a cameraman during training at Fort Knox. The markings around the turret mark this vehicle for the 192nd Tank Battalion, while the tactical marking show that it is part of Company C. Notice the absence of the Infantry-Tank plate that was originally placed on the outside of each turret. In addition, the side tool storage and accompanying brush guards have been removed and the bolt holes filled. This vehicle's registration numbers have also been repainted in the lusterless blue paint.

Above: M2A2 Light Tanks of Company B, 192nd Tank Battalion moving through a smokescreen during the Tennessee Maneuvers in September 1941. The blue and red dashed markings are clearly visible around the base of the turrets.

Right: Pair of M2A2 Light Tanks assigned to Company B, 192nd Tank Battalion crossing an open field during the Tennessee Maneuvers in the late summer of 1941. The battalion and company markings are clear on both turrets.

M2A2 Light Tank of Company B, 192nd Tank Battalion during the Tennessee Maneuvers of 1941. Note the doubled unit tactical markings on the rear of the hull. These are white with black numbers and an orange border.

Mixed column of light tanks from the 192nd Tank Battalion in September 1941. The red and blue tactical markings are clearly visible around the base of the turrets.

Tank park of Company D, 192nd Tank Battalion near the end of the Third Army maneuvers of 1941. The orange outline of the green spade appears white in this black and white photograph, but helps to identify the alternating dashes as being red and blue. The vehicle registration numbers are barely visible in lusterless blue. These tanks all seem to retain the original tool storage and brush guards, but also have had the Infantry-Tank plate removed from the turrets.

193rd Tank Battalion

The 193rd Tank Battalion was activated at Fort Benning, GA and was initially equipped and trained using tanks from the 66th Armored Regiment (Light), 2nd Armored Division. In a manner similar to the 192nd Battalion, the unit painted a series of white and blue dashed markings around the base of their tank turrets. Given the black and white photography of the period, it is sometimes very difficult to differentiate between the two units. The unit moved by train to San Francisco in mid-December, 1941 in reaction to the attacks at Pearl Harbor. There, the unit was re-equipped with M3 Light Tanks and shipped off to Hawaii, where they arrived in early January 1942. The tanks

M2A2 Light Tank assigned to Company C, 193rd Tank Battalion. It is sometimes difficult to differentiate between tanks assigned to the 192nd and the 193rd Battalions because they both utilize a dashed marking system around the turret. The 193rd was assigned the colors blue and white as opposed to the blue and red assigned to the 192nd. The markings for the companies, on the other hand, were identical.

Whoops – A tank from Company C, 193rd Tank Battalion after it rolled during maneuvers in the fall of 1941. The "X" marks SGT James Leach, a member of the 36th Tank Company, Texas National Guard. SGT Leach was commissioned in 1942 and commanded Company B, 37th Tank Battalion, 4th Armored Division under LTC Crieghton Abrams. As a full colonel, he commanded the 11th Armored Cavalry Regiment in Vietnam. (HC)

were apparently received in the dark olive drab with lusterless blue registration numbers and the only markings applied to the tanks were a lineal number painted on either side of the turret in eight-inch tall numbers between 1 and 71.

194th Tank Battalion

The last unit to be organized, the 194th Tank Battalion was brought together as at unit at Fort Lewis, Washington and consisted of only three companies rather than the standard four. They were equipped with the same eclectic mixture of light tanks as the other battalions – with the same attendant problems. As war approached in the Far East, it was decided to activate part of the "Orange" Plan and the battalion was split. The Headquarters Company, Company A and Company C were re-equipped with M3 Light Tanks and then ordered to the Philippines in early September of 1941, arriving there on the 26th of September. The M3 Light Tanks issued to the unit were painted in a basic dark olive-drab with the registration numbers applied in lusterless blue. Apparently, no tactical markings were applied prior to departure from the United States. Although only staffed for two companies, the battalion was issued the full fifty-four light tanks of a complete battalion. The 194th, along with the 192nd Tank Battalion, was totally destroyed in April of 1942 by the Japanese 15th Army.

The sole remaining company, Company B, had been equipped with M1 and M1A1 Light Tanks. Painted in dark olive drab with the lusterless blue registration numbers, these vehicles were drawn mostly from the 1st Armored Regiment, 1st Armored Division. The company, after being split away from the battalion, was sent to Fort Richardson, Alaska in September of 1941 as part of the "Orange" Plan.

Soon after arriving in Alaska, B Company's light tanks were painted in an overall white camouflage, obscuring whatever markings they may have had. With the surrender of the main portion of the battalion to the Japanese in April 1942, B Company was re-designated as the 602nd Separate Tank Company. Soon afterwards, it received a number of newer tanks, including at least one T14 and one T16 Light Tank built by

M1 Light Tank (M1 Combat Car) assigned to Company B, 194th Tank Battalion being off-loaded in Alaska in September of 1941. The company and battalion designation can barely be seen chalked onto the side of the hull. (PH)

"It could be worse!" Soldiers of Company B, 194th Tank Battalion and their M1 Light Tanks at Fort Richardson, Alaska, in December of 1941. (PH)

Marmon-Herrington. These arrived painted in a dark olive drab, with a broad white stripe around the turret and a single white star on either side. The T16 had a "33" hand painted in white, three inch numerals, on the front of the hull above the machineguns. The T14 was marked in a similar manner with "86". These could very well be the serial number of the vehicle, but at present it is not known. The vehicles were not marked with registration numbers.

The entry of the United States into World War II marked the end of the brief, but colorful, history of the National Guard GHQ Reserve Tank Battalions.

70th GHQ Tank Battalion (Medium)

Photographs of this battalion are rare prior to 1942, but it can be assumed that their initial look would have been the same as the 1st Battalion, 66th Infantry Regiment until they had an opportunity to repaint their vehicles. Although called a medium tank battalion, the unit did not receive any medium tanks until well into 1942. In February of 1942, C Company was dispatched to Iceland. Now equipped with M3 Light Tanks, the tanks were painted in the light olive drab then being used. Registration numbers were painted in lusterless blue paint on each side of the hull. Painted on either side of the turret was the vehicle's lineal number in white, ten-inch numbers between two short diagonal stripes, two inches thick. These stripes were painted in yellow. It can probably be safely assumed that the other companies of the battalion used different colors for designation – blue, red, and white.

751st through 760th Tank Battalions

Most of these battalions did not even receive their tanks until early 1942, and few photographs identified to these units have surfaced. One small photograph of the 757th Tank Battalion in September-November of 1941 revealed no unit markings.

Introduction Chapters 12-15 Armored Divisions 1940-1941

On 10 July 1940, nearly twenty years after the demise of the Tank Corps and after years of struggle and experimentation, the day of vindication for American armor and mechanization finally arrived. With the stroke of a pen the Armored Force was established and, with it, the 1st and 2nd Armored Divisions came into being. This laid the groundwork for the rapid expansion of the Armored Force into a powerful, and permanent, arm of the American Army. By the end of 1941, a total of five armored divisions had been activated, the 1st and 5th Armored Divisions at Fort Knox, the 2nd Armored Division at Fort Benning, the 3rd Armored Division at Camp Beauregard, Louisiana, and the 4th Armored Division at Pine Camp, New York.[1]

The American Tanker, 2nd Armored Division, Fall, 1940.

Organization

The first, provisional, organization of the armored division was built around the armored brigade, which contained the division's three armored regiments – two regiments of light tanks, and one regiment of medium tanks. The brigade also included an artillery regiment, and an engineer battalion for support. The rest of the division was rounded out with an Infantry regiment, a Quartermaster battalion, a Reconnaissance battalion, a Signal Corps company, an Ordnance company (Heavy Maintenance), and a Medical battalion – all reporting directly to the Division Commander. Of all of these various components, only the tank regiments in the armored brigade, and the reconnaissance battalion, were equipped with tanks.

The provisional arrangement did not last long and a more permanent Table of Organization, T/O 17-10, was adopted on 15 November 1940. This removed the engineer battalion from the armor brigade and placed it directly under the division commander. Another change was the attachment of a medical detachment to the armor brigade.

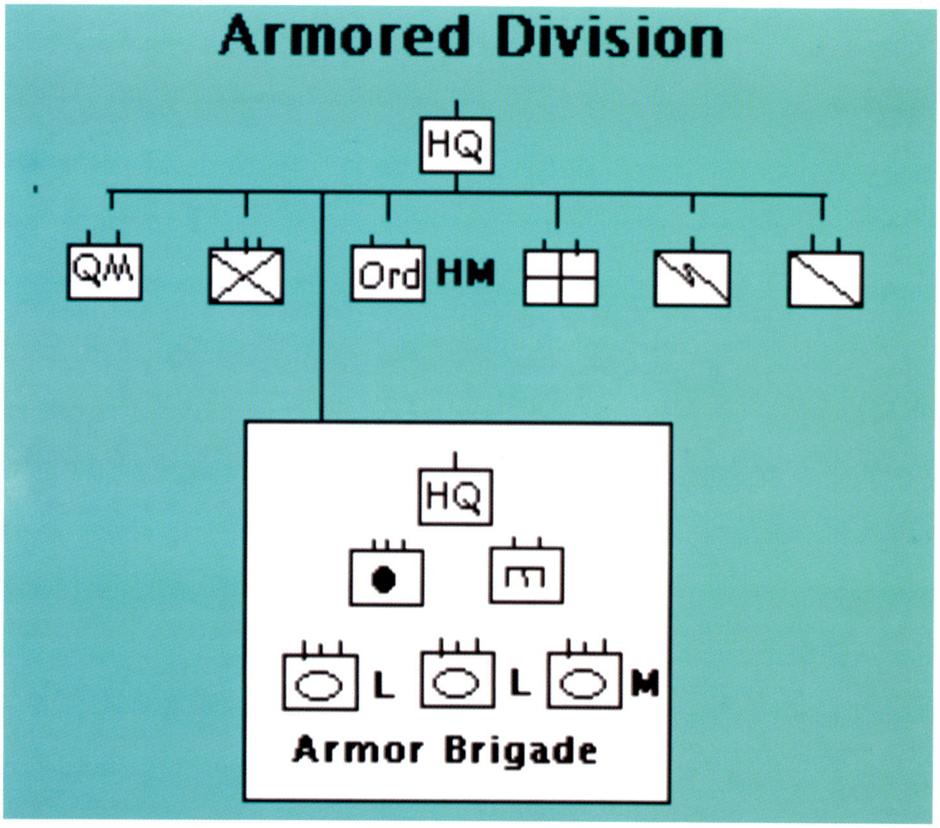

Provisional organization of the Armored Division, July 10, 1940.

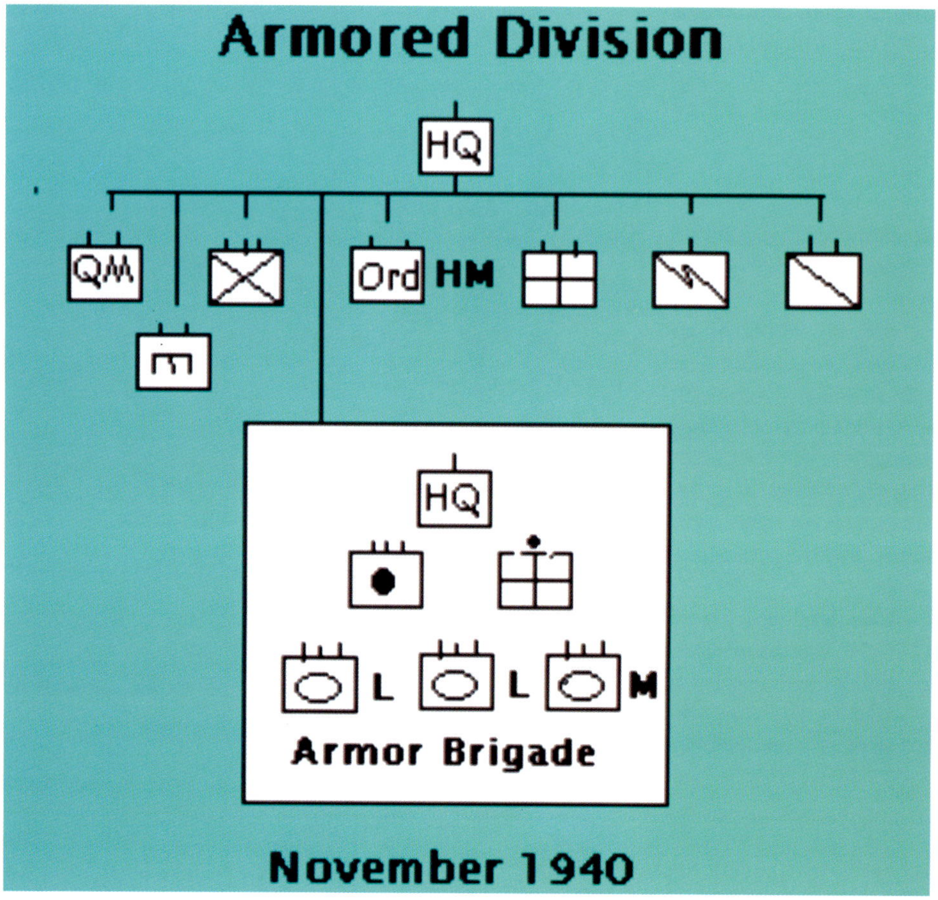

Organization of the Armored Division as of November 1940.

Colors and Markings

These first few years, from 1940 to the end of 1941, were a transition period for both armor organization and for the colors and markings used on U.S. Army vehicles. The dark olive drab of the mid to late 1930s was still in use, but near the end of 1941, the formula for olive drab was involuntarily modified due to shortages caused by the war and these replacement pigments had lightened the shade. By 1942 this lighter shade became the unintentional standard color for U.S. Army vehicles for much of the war period.

Unit markings and registration numbers at the start of this period continued to be painted in white, in accordance to Army Regulation 850-5, but in July of 1941 the color for registration numbers was changed to a dark, lusterless blue, and they remained that color until late in 1944.[2]

Initially, 2nd Armored Division and, to some extent, the 1st Armored Division, continued to use the marking system originally established in the early 1930s and used by the Infantry (tanks) regiments. It was based on the company – with each company within a battalion being given a set of colors for their use. The system utilized four basic figures, the triangle – for HQ vehicles, the diamond – 1st platoon, the disk – 2nd platoon, and the square – 3rd platoon within each company.

Light Tank Regiment

The Light Tank Regiment was organized under Table of Organization T/O 17-11, adopted on 15 November 1940. In this T/O, each of the light tank regiments contained a Headquarters & Headquarters Company, a service company, a machine-gun company, a reconnaissance company, and three light tank battalions. Also included were medical and chaplain detachments. The Headquarters Company was supplied primarily with half-tracks, motorcycles, and trucks, as well as three light tanks. The Service Company contained little or no armor, being mostly comprised of light trucks. The Reconnaissance Company was heavily equipped with half-tracks and motorcycles, as was the Machinegun Company.

Under the 15 November 1940 Table of Organization, the Regimental HQ company retained three light tanks, and each of the three tank battalions was equipped with forty-two light tanks for a total of one hundred twenty-nine for the regiment.

Each of the battalions was made up of three line companies – each having thirteen tanks, three for each of the four platoons and one as a HQ tank. The battalion HQ retained 3 tanks. This basic T/O would be superceded by T/O 17-11 dated March 1, 1942 Armored Regiment.

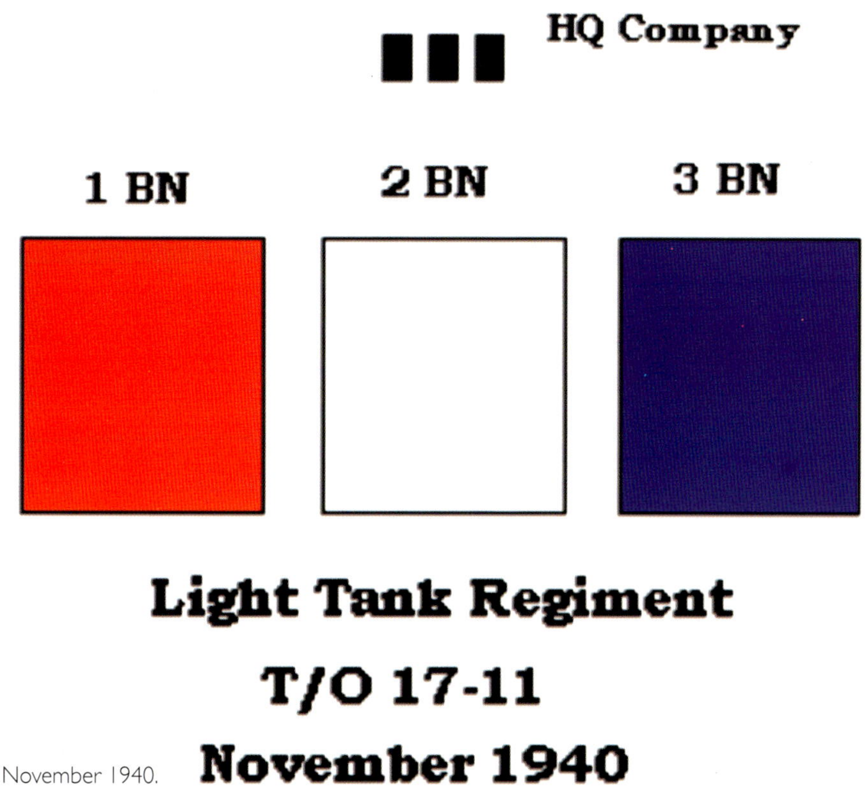

Light Tank Regiment of November 1940.

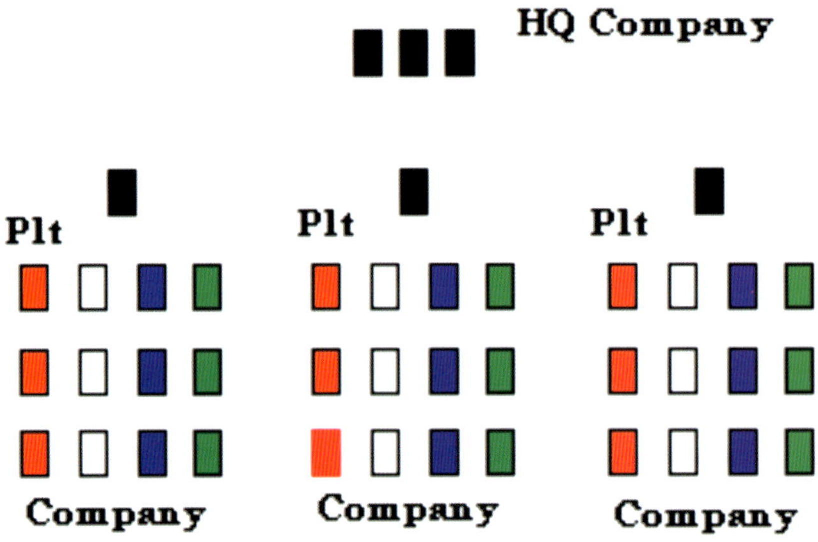

Light Tank Battalion

November 1940

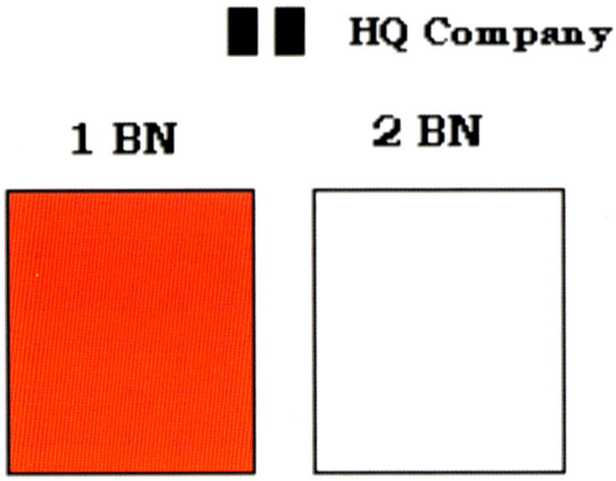

Medium Tank Regiment
T/O 17-21

November 1940

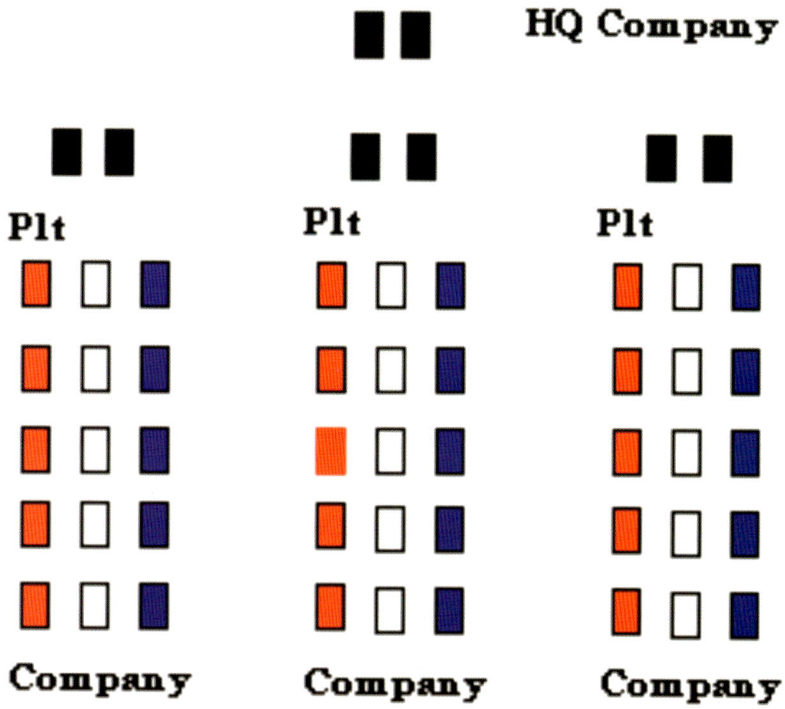

Medium Tank Battalion
November 1940

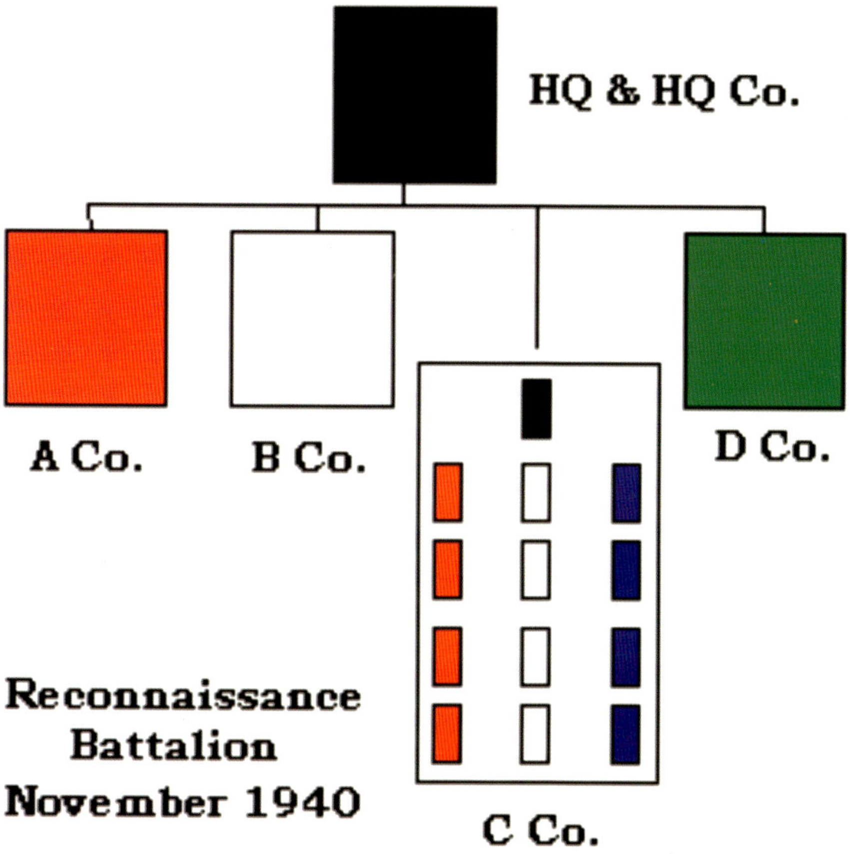

Reconnaissance Battalion
November 1940

Medium Tank Regiment

Under T/O 17-21 adopted 15 November 1940, the medium tank regiment had the same support units as the light regiment, but contained only two medium tank battalions. The third battalion, originally intended for activation with the Infantry regiment (Medium Tanks) configuration, was dropped. The regimental headquarters retained only two tanks instead of the three seen in the light regiment. However, the two medium tank battalions each had fifty-three tanks. Broken down, this meant that each of the three companies of the medium battalion had seventeen tanks – two in the headquarters and five in each of the three platoons. The Battalion headquarters had two medium tanks assigned to it.

Both the light and medium tank battalions contained a battalion headquarters & headquarters detachment, and three tank companies. This basic T/O would be not change until after the entry of the United States into World War II. In March of 1942, this Table of Organization would be superceded by T/O 17-11 Armored Regiment dated March 1, 1942

Armored Reconnaissance Battalion

The armored reconnaissance battalion consisted of four line companies, and a headquarters and headquarters company. "A" and "B" companies consisted of cavalry troops equipped with scout cars. "C" company was equipped with light tanks (initially cavalry combat cars) and "D" company was the infantry component of the unit and was equipped with half-tracks.[3] A total of thirteen light tanks or combat cars was assigned to "C" Company, four in each of the three tank platoons and one in the company Headquarters.

12

The Armored Force
The 1st Armored Division
1940-1942

The 7th Cavalry Brigade (Mechanized) was re-designated as the 1st Armored Division on 10 July 1940 at its home station at Fort Knox Kentucky. The division was based around the 1st Armored Brigade, which contained the 1st Armored Regiment (Light), the 13th Armored Regiment (Light), the newly organized 69th Armored Regiment (Medium), the 68th Armored Field Artillery Regiment, and the 16th Armored Engineer Battalion. The rest of the division was made up of the 6th Infantry Regiment; the 27th Armored Field Artillery Battalion; the 1st Armored Reconnaissance Battalion; the 13th Armored Quartermaster Battalion; the 19th Armored Ordnance Company (Heavy Maintenance); the 47th Armored Signal Company, and the 47th Armored Medical Battalion.[4]

Formed from the two mechanized cavalry regiments, the 1st and 13th Armored Regiments (Light) were initially equipped with the M1 and M1A1 Combat Cars (M1 Light Tanks), but these tanks were quickly replaced by M2 Series Light Tanks as they became available. These were in turn, replaced by M3 Light Tanks in mid- to late-1941. The sole medium tank regiment, the 69th Armored Regiment (Medium), had been formed from one battalion of the 67th Infantry (Tanks) Regiment and was initially outfitted with a mixture of M2 series Medium Tanks and M2A2 and M2A3 light tanks. By late 1941 nearly all of the vehicles had been replaced by the M3 Medium Tank.[5]

M2A4 Light Tanks of the 1st Armored Regiment at Fort Knox, in late 1940. Several of the tanks are still marked with the regimental crest on either side of the turret, while on others these markings have been painted out or never applied. The company letters and numbers are visible stenciled in four-inch letters and numbers on the front of the vehicle sponsons.

Above: M2A4 Light Tanks of the 1st Armored Regiment at Fort Knox on the move. in late 1940. Some of the tanks are still marked with the regimental crest on either side of the turret, while on others these markings have been painted out or never applied. The company letters and numbers are visible stenciled in four-inch letters and numbers on the front of the vehicle sponsons.

Left: M3 Light Tank rolling off a rail car during the start of the Tennessee Maneuvers in August of 1941. The red dashed markings of the 1st Armored Regiment; and the company markings, "D-1" are visible in white on either sponson. These markings were also repeated at the back of the hull.

Colors and Markings

When first organized, the 1st Armored Division took some time to regularize its organization and to integrate both its new units and new vehicles. This meant that, initially, many of the tanks and other vehicles assigned to the division retained their old markings until they could be repainted. The vehicles were painted in the regulation dark olive-drab color, in a flat finish. The registration numbers continued to be applied in white.

In a holdover from their cavalry days, the two light tank regiments continued to designate their command tanks by the use of painted metal guidons, which were bolted into the pistol ports at either side of the turret near the front. The metal guidons used on the battalion headquarters tanks were painted to resemble a cavalry squadron guidon, red above and white below with the regimental number on top and squadron (battalion) number below, countercharged.

The metal guidons for a company commander's tank had the regimental number above and company letter below. The guidons for the regimental commander's tank were painted yellow overall and had a full color rendition of the unit crest painted at the center. At least one example of the unit guidon being painted directly onto the turret is known where the squadron/battalion number was painted onto the armored side cover for the turret.

By January of 1941, the three armored divisions in existence at the time adopted a new, standardized marking system. This new system allowed for the differentiation of tanks belonging to each regiment within a division, including those assigned to the reconnaissance battalion, by means of stripes around the base of the turret. This stripe served to identify the division and the armored regiments or reconnaissance battalion to which the tank belonged.[6] Three of the four armored divisions that had been fully activated before December 7th 1941 adopted the system.

Each regiment was color-coded – red for the 1st regiment, white for the second regiment, and blue for the third regiment. The reconnaissance battalion tanks were marked with the color yellow. The 1st Armored Division used dashed stripes, the dashes being approximately six inches long, separated by a six-inch space. A major change from previous systems was the identification of individual tanks by company letter and vehicle number. Both the 1st, 2nd and 3rd Armored Divisions adopted the system, which identified their tanks through the use of either a solid or dashed stripe around the base of the turret(s).

In preparation for the 1941 Maneuvers, all of the vehicles belonging to the division were marked with a large, 18-inch tall, 1st Armored Division unit insignia painted in full color on

Colonel Alexander D. Surles and his M1 Light Tank in 1941. As commander of the 1st Armored Regiment, his tank is marked with a yellow metal guidon with the crest of the regiment in full color. The regimental color – red – appears as dashes around the base of the turret. "HQ 1" is painted in white on the front of the turret in two lines.

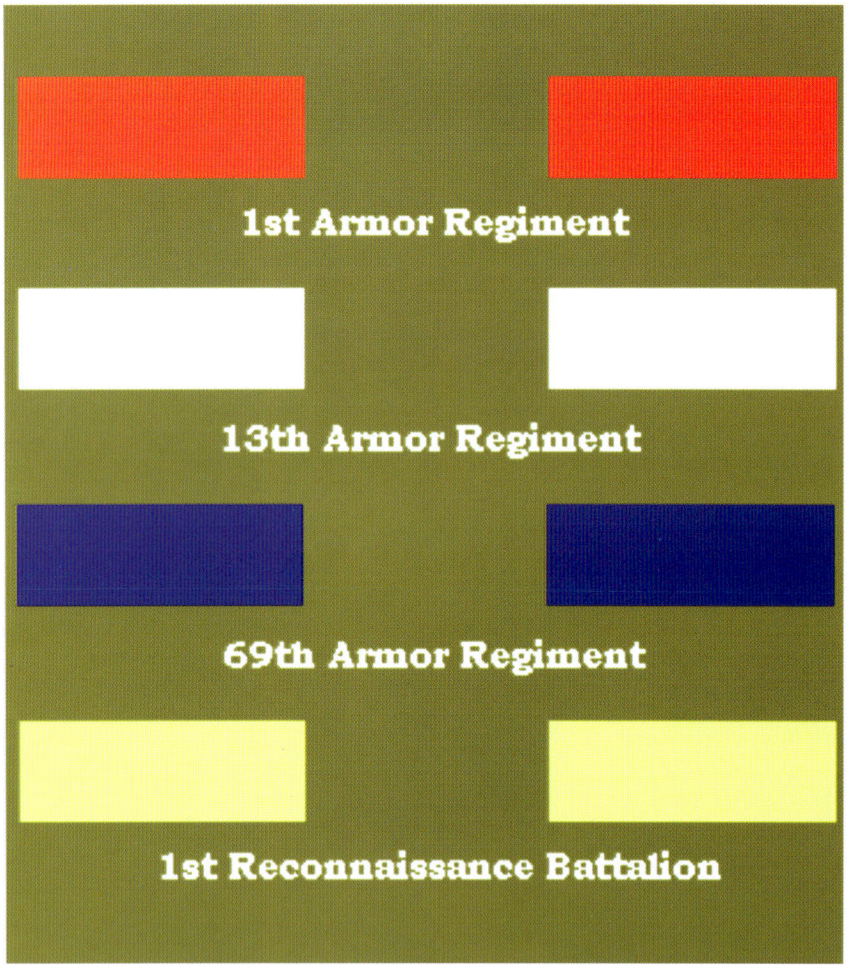

Turret markings for the various armored units within the 1st Armored Division – 1941.

the front of the vehicle, with a smaller version painted on the rear of the vehicle. For both the light and medium tanks, this patch was painted centered on the front slope.[7]

By the September of 1941, the light tank regiments had been fully equipped with the M2A4 Light Tank and new replacements, in the form of the M3 Light Tank, had begun to arrive. In the medium tank regiment most of the M2 and M2A1 Medium Tanks had already been replaced by M3 Medium Tanks. The M3 Mediums, although marked in a manner similar to the M2s, had been delivered in the lighter, modified shade of olive drab.[8] The outbreak of war in December of 1941 marked the beginning of the end of this system of tactical markings

1st Armored Regiment (Light)

For at least the first few months, the combat cars of the two light tank regiments remained painted as they had been when they were Cavalry vehicles. The regiment was filled out with an influx of older M2A2 and M2A3 light tanks, but soon began to receive the new M2A4 tanks. Unmarked when they arrived, these new tanks received new markings within a few months. This consisted of painting a full color regimental crest on either side of the turret(s) and painting the company letter and lineal number on the front of the sponson and across the rear of the hull in six-inch numbers and letters.

In January of 1941, the new standardized division marking system was put into place. The regimental crests were painted over and the assigned regimental color – red - was applied as a series of three-inch tall dashed markings around the base of the turret(s) of the unit's light tanks. As a company identification a six-inch tall white company letter was stenciled on the front of the right sponson, while a six-inch tall white company lineal number was painted to the front of the left sponson. The number was repeated on the back of the hull with a dash separating them. It should be noted that when they were initially organized, each light tank company in the regiment was initially equipped with only 14 light tanks.[9] This was not to change until the end of 1941 with the adoption of a new TO&E. The size of these markings, as well as the exact location, tended to vary between battalions, but they were always painted in white in accordance with Army regulations.[10] Battalion headquarters vehicles substituted the battalion number for the company letter.

M2A4 Light Tank of the 1st Armored Regiment during the Tennessee Maneuvers in August of 1941. The red cloth wrapped around the turret marks the tank as belonging to the "Red" Army. The red dashed markings around the base of the turret are clearly visible, as are the lusterless blue US Army registration numbers along the side of the hull. The company letter is not visible due to the angle, but the vehicle lineal number on the front of the sponson is. Painted on the center of the front hull slope is a full color 1st Armored Division unit patch.

13th Armored Regiment M2A4 light tank cruising across Fort Knox in early 1941. The white dashed markings are clearly visible around the base of the turret. This vehicle was assigned to Company I, lineal number 12. The US Army registration, being stenciled in lusterless blue paint, is not visible on the side of the hull.

M3 Light Tank assigned to Company B, 13th Armored Regiment, at Fort Knox during the late spring of 1941. The dashed white markings and white company markings are clearly visible.

Camouflaged M3 Light Tank of the 13th Armored Regiment speeding along a Tennessee highway in the summer of 1941. The white dashed marking around the turret is clearly visible. The vehicle lineal number is visible, although the company letter is not. The vehicle's US Army registration number is barely visible under a coating of dust. The red cloth stretched around the turret marks the vehicle as part of the "Red" Army during the maneuvers. Barely visible on the front slope of the hull is a full color 1st Armored Division patch. Due to a lack of weapons, the main gun and mantlet have been replaced by a plate and steel pipe. (HC)

In preparation for the 1941 Third Army maneuvers, the entire division was directed to paint a full color rendition of the 1st Armored Division patch on the front of the hull, measuring twenty-four-inches tall and twenty-four-inches wide.

13th Armored Regiment (Light)

Creation of the 13th Armored Regiment paralleled that of the 1st Armored Regiment. It too retained the markings previously used when it was a mechanized cavalry regiment and when its new replacement vehicles arrived, they were painted with a full color regimental crest on either side. This continued until January of 1941, with the adoption of the standardized divisional marking system. The 13th Armored Regiment was assigned the color white as its identifying color – otherwise its markings were identical to that of the 1st Armored Regiment. For the maneuvers of 1941, the regiment also complied with the divisional order to apply a standard sized divisional patch on the front slope of their light tanks.

M3 Light Tank belonging to headquarters, 2nd Battalion, 13th Armored Regiment during the maneuvers of 1941. The patch of the 1st Armored Division is visible on the front slope of the tank.

M2A4 Light Tank assigned to headquarters company, 3rd Battalion, 13th Armored Regiment. The regimental color (white dashes) is visible around the base of the turret – with the battalion marking on the right sponson and vehicle lineal number of the left. 1941.

Rear view of the same M2A4 Light Tank. The battalion number is visible to the left, with the lineal number just barely visible at the right. The white dashed marking show it belonging to the 13th Armored Regiment. 1941.

Hodge-podge collection of vehicles assigned to the 69th Armored Regiment upon its creation in 1940. Many of the vehicles are still painted in the markings of their former units. Those light tanks with the white bands around the turret(s) were transferred from the 67th Armored Regiment of the 2nd Armored Division. The M2 and M2A1 Medium Tanks were also transferred in from the 67th. The rest of the vehicles were transferred from other units. The white bands marked the light tanks as being "Medium Tanks."

69th Armored Regiment (Medium)

The creation of the 1st Armored Division required the activation of a medium tank battalion to bring it up to TO&E strength. Initially it was formed by the re-designation of the 3rd Battalion, 67th Armored Regiment as the 1st Battalion, 69th Armored Regiment. The second battalion was created of whole cloth, using new personnel and equipment. The entire regiment was activated on 15 July 1940. The re-designation was actually quite deceiving, as the 3rd Battalion of the 67th Armored Regiment was, in reality, the 1st Battalion of the 68th Armored Regiment – which had previously been re-designated only months before.

In any case, the first battalion arrived at Fort Knox equipped with the vehicles they had been using at Fort Benning. Only nine medium tanks had been assigned to the unit before its transfer to the 1st Armored Division, so the battalion had been given an additional thirty-four M2A2 and M2A3 light tanks to fill out the table of organization.

The medium tanks transferred to the 2nd battalion initially retained the markings of the 67th Armored Regiment – but these were quickly painted over with markings for the new regiment. The light tanks were also remarked for the 69th Armored Regiment but, because they were supposed to represent the missing medium tanks, they were painted with a ten-inch tall stripe around each of the turrets.

At least one of the M2 Medium Tanks arrived painted with the Army Air Corps version of the national emblem painted on the front slope and both sides: a blue disk with a white star with a smaller red disk superimposed.[11] This was apparently a precursor to the markings ultimately adopted by the 2nd Armored Division just prior to the 3rd Army Maneuvers of 1941.

Being brand new with no traditional markings to fall back on, the unit apparently left its vehicles marked however they arrived. Medium tanks of the regiment had their company letters and linear number painted in white, eight-inch, figures, separated by a dash, centered on the front slope and also centered on the engine access doors at the rear of the hull.[12] The M2A2 and M2A3 light tanks assigned to the unit were marked on the front of the cupola on the left turret and at the rear of the hull.[13] These light tanks were also marked with a ten-inch tall

M3 Medium Tanks of the 69th Armored Regiment entrained in Tennessee at the start of the 1941 Maneuvers. The 1st Armored Division patch is clearly visible on the front slope of the tank, as is the Company letter and lineal number. The dashed blue regimental marking around the base of the turret is barely visible. (HC)

M3 Medium Tanks of Company B, 69th Armored Regiment during the Third Army maneuvers of 1941.

white stripe around both turrets so that they would be recognized as acting as "medium" tanks.

Under the new standardized divisional marking system adopted in January of 1941, the 69th Armored Regiment was given the color blue for the marking of its vehicles. Under this system, the medium tanks, both the M2 Series and M3 Series, were marked with a series of three-inch tall dash markings around the base of the turret. The company letter and lineal number continued to be painted in white eight-inch figures on the front slope of the hull and across the rear of the hull. For the 1941 Third Army maneuvers, a full color 1st Division patch was painted on the front of the hull.

1st Reconnaissance Battalion (81st Reconnaissance Battalion)

In contrast to the light armored regiments, the newly organized 1st Reconnaissance Battalion had immediately repainted their assigned combat cars to reflect their new status, with the previous unit markings on the turret being removed and a new troop letter and linear number painted in. (C troop).[14] The regimental markings of the 1st and 13th Cavalry regiments were painted out. Like the cavalry regiments, from which it was drawn, the headquarters tank of the battalion used a pair of metal guidons to designate the C Troop (light tank troop) commander's tank; blue and white with the blue field on top. Centered in the blue field was "1-R" in white with the company letter (C) in blue on the white field.[15]

When the standardized divisional marking system was adopted, the 1st Reconnaissance Battalion (re-designated as the 81st Reconnaissance Battalion in May 1941)[16] was painted with yellow dashed stripes around the base of the turret.

As new tanks rolled off the assembly line at American Car and Foundry and at Rock Island Arsenal, the old combat cars and early model light tanks being used by the armored regiments were quickly replaced by new M2A4 Light Tanks and M2A1 Medium Tanks. At one point during this transition, the 1st Armored Division had a mixture of six different types of light tanks and two of medium tanks, as well as several obsolete armored cars.[17]

M1A1 Light Tank of the 1st Reconnaissance Battalion, 1st Armored Division. The battalion was initially equipped with half-tracks and recycled M1 series combat cars, re-designated as M1 and M1A1 light tanks. The guidon, painted on either side of the turret, mark this vehicle as belonging to C company headquarters. The guidon is medium blue and white with countered charged numbers and letters. The registration numbers are painted in a gray-blue lusterless paint for low visibility.

Another M1A1 Light Tank (C-3) of the 1st Reconnaissance Battalion, 1st Armored Division driving down the Salt River during maneuvers at Fort Knox, 1941.

General Notes for the Standardized Divisional Marking System

The other vehicles within the division were initially marked on the front bumper with white unit markings, and further marked on the both sides of the vehicle with a white lineal number. The letters on the left side of the front or rear of the vehicle designated the company or platoon within the unit, the number at the right designating the regiment or battalion.

Left Side (as viewed from the front of the vehicle)

1st Armored Division	1DIV
1st Armored Regiment	1
6th Armored Infantry Battalion	6
12th Observation Squadron	12
13th Armored Regiment	13
13th Quartermaster Battalion (Armored)	13QM
16th Armored Engineer Battalion	16
19th Ordnance Battalion (armored)	19
27th Armored Field Artillery	27
A = A battery	
B = B Battery	
C = C Battery	
47th Armored Medical Battalion	47
47th Signal Company (Armored)	47SIG
68th Armored Field Artillery	68
A = A battery	
B = B Battery	
C = C Battery	
69th Armored Regiment	69
81st Reconnaissance Battalion	81
Anti-tank Platoon	AT
Machinegun Platoon	MG
Military Police	MP
Maintenance	MAINT
Supply	S
1st Battalion HQ	1st Bn
2nd Battalion HQ	2nd Bn
3rd Battalion HQ	3rd Bn
Division Headquarters	HQ

13

The Armored Force 2nd Armored Division 1940-1941

With the official establishment of the Armored Force on 10 July 1940 the ad hoc Provisional Tank Brigade, which had been brought together by the Infantry Branch for the 1940 Third Army Maneuvers, was officially re-designated as the 2nd Armored Brigade, 2nd Armored Division. Activated at Fort Benning, Georgia on the 15th of July 1940, the division was rounded out by the addition of several units. These included the 2nd Reconnaissance Battalion, 14th Armored Field Artillery Regiment, 78th Field Artillery Battalion, 41st Armored Infantry Regiment, 17th Armored Engineer Battalion, 14th Armored Quartermaster Battalion, 48th Armored Medical Battalion, 48th Armored Signal Company, and the 17th Ordnance Company (Heavy Maintenance).

Organization

The 1940 armored division was organized around an armored brigade, which controlled nearly all of the tanks assigned to the division and which consisted of three armored regiments and added artillery support. For the 2nd Armored Division these armored regiments were the 66th, 67th, and 68th, with the 66th and 68th Armored Regiments being equipped with light tanks, and the 67th being the solitary medium tank regiment within the brigade. This weighted the division towards light tanks and reflected the armor policy of that period. This policy would, however, change drastically after Pearl Harbor.

Each of the light tank regiments contained three battalions of tanks, as well as a headquarters and headquarters company. When first formed, the light tank regiments were organized under the Table of Organization and Equipment (TO&E) for the Infantry (Tanks) and under this TO&E, each light tank battalion was supposed to contain three light tanks companies. A light tank company was equipped with seventeen light tanks, broken down into three platoons of five tanks each, with two additional tanks assigned to the company headquarters. This gave the battalion a strength of fifty-four light tanks.[1] However, in August of 1940 a new table of organization was developed for the armored brigade and division.[2]

The proposed light tank battalion now had only forty-four light tanks in its inventory. The regiment continued to be divided into three battalions of three companies each, but the internal arrangement of the companies was modified. The company headquarters platoon retained its two light tanks, but now, instead of three platoons of five tanks each, the company was divided into four platoons of three tanks each. This gave the company a total of fourteen light tanks. This, combined with the two light tanks assigned to the battalion headquarters gave the battalion a total of forty-four light tanks. By the fall of 1940, this Table of Organization and Equipment (TO&E) was adopted as standard.[3]

The 66th Armor Regiment (Light) was completely reorganized under the new TO&E by the winter of 1940-41. However the 68th Armor Regiment (Light), which had been formed by amalgamating the various independent light tank companies, never actually became fully formed. It was broken up in January of 1942 and its component parts used by the other two regiments when they were again reorganized under a new TO&E.[4]

The medium armored regiment, on the other hand, was not reorganized. The 67th Armor Regiment, which had been re-designated from the 67th Infantry Regiment (Medium Tanks), was made up of only two battalions, each containing three medium tank companies. Each of these companies contained seventeen medium tanks, two in the company headquarters and the other fifteen split evenly between three platoons. This, in combination with the three medium tanks assigned to the battalion headquarters gave the medium tank battalion a strength of fifty-seven medium tanks.

At one point during 1941 an attempt was made to "add" a battalion to the medium tank regiment. In order to accomplish this, a company was withdrawn from each of the two existing battalions to form a third battalion, with each battalion having only two companies. This experiment lasted only a short time.[5]

During this period before Pearl Harbor, the division was equipped with a variety of tanks. In the Light Armored Regiments, the M2A4 Light Tank was quickly replacing the older M2A1, A2, and A3 light tanks and by the late spring of 1941 this transition had been completed. By the fall of 1941, the M2A4 tanks were themselves being replaced by the newly introduced M3 Light Tank. These were also issued as the Division and Brigade command headquarters light tanks. As with the M2 light tanks, these were replaced with newer vehicles by the end of 1941.

The medium tank regiment was initially armed with a mixture of M2 and M2A1 medium tanks, as well as a mix of M2 series light tanks. As the end of 1941 approached the M2 Medium Tank was rapidly being replaced by the M3 "Lee" Medium Tank.

Colors and Markings

U.S. Army combat vehicles of the late 1930s were painted in a dark olive drab, similar to that used after World War II and through the Korean War period.[6] Because of changes to the paint caused by shortages of pigment the, now familiar, light shade of olive drab had begun to be used by the middle of 1941. Most vehicles received after the fall of 1941 were arriving from the factory in this lighter shade and the older vehicles were only changed over when repainting was necessary. The U.S. Army registration number was painted on either side of the hull in white, four-inch tall stencils.[7]

Because the 2nd Armored Division had been formed by the amalgamation of Regular Army divisional tank companies and the two existing infantry (Tanks) regiments the initial appearance of the division was somewhat mixed. This was because all of the tanks within the division initially retained the original unit markings of their previous units.

The "old" tactical marking system utilizing the square, diamond, circle and triangle, applied in the individual company color combinations, was initially left in place. However by January of 1941, a new system of tactical markings had been designed and adopted by all three armored divisions in existence at that point.

The 2nd Armored Division used a solid, 3" thick stripe painted around the base of the turret or turrets to mark its tanks, and company markings were added to the vehicle in white so as to be visible from front, rear, and sides.[8] The new system allowed for the differentiation of tanks belonging to each regi-

Turret markings for the various armored units within the 2nd Armored Division – 1941.

Experimental aerial recognition marking used by the 2nd and 3rd Armored Divisions in 1941. The colors are the reverse of the Army Air Corps marking, with a red background rather than blue.

ment within the division, including those assigned to the reconnaissance battalion by means of stripes around the base of the turret. Each regiment was color-coded – red for the first regiment, white for the second regiment, and blue for the third regiment. The reconnaissance battalion tanks were marked with the color yellow. Combinations of these colors were also used by several of the Brigade and Division level headquarters tanks. The 2nd Armored Brigade headquarters tanks were marked with stacked stripes of red, white, and blue to represent the three regiments in the brigade. The Divisional headquarters tanks were marked with four stripes red, white, blue, and yellow.[9]

A major change from previous systems was the identification of individual tanks by company letter and vehicle number. Company markings on tanks were relatively standard between the different regiments within the division. Location of the markings depended mainly upon the type of vehicle being marked. Under the new marking system, the base of the turret(s) was painted with a 3" tall stripe of color representing the regiment. Company letters and numbers were then added so as to be visible from all sides. In the case of the M2A4 Light Tank, the numbers were stenciled on either side of the turret, close to the front, in twelve to fourteen-inch figures, separated by a three by two-inch dash. This was repeated on the back of the turret. The company letter was also painted on the left rear of the hull armor, with the vehicle number painted on the right rear. These were in six to eight-inch tall stencils.

In April and May of 1941 the vehicles of the 2nd Armored Division were marked with experimental aerial identification markings, which were painted in color on the hulls and turrets of the tanks and on the front and rear of the wheeled vehicles. This marking consisted of a red disk with a white, five pointed star at center with a small blue disk superimposed at the center of the star. The size of this emblem depended on its location and the type of vehicle to which it was applied. Tanks issued to the unit after the Third Army maneuvers did not receive these markings – for example M3 Medium tanks received after the GHQ Maneuvers of 1941 (September to October) were not marked with the air recognition star.

An interesting feature, seen only on tanks used during the 1940 Third Army maneuvers, is a large white square painted on the rear of both engine air cleaners, apparently for visibility and safety purposes.[11] The squares measured approximately twelve by twelve-inches.

The lessons learned during the Third Army maneuvers of 1941 indicated that the present makeup of the Armored Division was not perfect and on the 22nd of December 1941 a new TO&E was adopted. It took affect on 1 January 1942 and didn't arrive a moment too soon. Although the old tactical marking

M1A2 Light Tank assigned to the Divisional Commander of the 2nd Armored Division. Metal guidons attached to the front fenders mark the rank and the command of its occupant. The solid stripes around base of the turret represent the armored units he commands. Louisiana Maneuvers, 1941.

MG George S. Patton and his command tank in color. Louisiana Maneuvers, 1941.

system then in use lingered for another two months, the attack at Pearl Harbor triggered a change in the way U.S. vehicles would be marked for the next forty years.

66th Armored Regiment (Light Tanks)

The tactical markings of the tanks assigned to the 66th Armored Regiment originally remained unchanged despite the shift from infantry to armor. With the adoption of the new marking system, all of the regimental tanks were repainted. The M2A2 and A3 light tanks were painted with a three-inch tall medium red stripe around the base of both turrets, with the company letter and lineal number separated by a four-inch dash painted on the outside of each turret and across the rear of the hull. The registration numbers remained painted on either side of the hull in four-inch numbers and letters. The M2A4, and later the M3 light tanks, were marked in a similar manner, with some vehicles having the rear markings placed on the back of the turret instead.

In preparation for the 1941 Third Army maneuvers, the 2nd Armored Division adopted an experimental air recognition emblem, which was painted on the top and rear of the turrent, and on the front of the hull overlapping between the two upper front hull doors (approximately six-inches in diameter). At least two companies of the 66th Armored Regiment (Companies C & D) also painted the device on top of their turrets offset to the right and approximately fourteen-inches in diameter. In many cases the marking on the rear of the turret is painted directly over the pre-existing company letter and number stencil, almost completely obscuring them.

M2A4 Light Tank assigned to Company L, 66th Armored Regiment, around November of 1940. The red stripe marking is visible around the base of the turret and the white painted company marking is visible on either side of the turret. Company L existed only for a short time in November – December 1940 as part of an experimental expansion of the Armored Regiments.

M2A4 Light Tanks assigned to the, 2nd Armored Division in early 1941at Fort Benning, GA. The three-inch tall red stripe painted around the base of the turret mark the tanks as belonging to the 66th Armor Regiment. The date of early 1941 can be established by the following observations. The small rectangular spot on the side of the turret is where the "Infantry-Tank" plate was removed when the Armored Force was established in July of 1940, while the white registration numbers show that the tanks were delivered prior to April of 1941, when the blue registration numbers were adopted.

An M2A4 light tank of Company F, 66th Armored Regiment, speeds along a road in Tennessee during the 3rd Army Maneuvers in the late summer 1941. The red painted stripe around the base of the turret is barely visible. The red does not show up well in the black and white film of the time period. What is interesting is that this tank does not have the air recognition markings that were normally applied on 2nd Armored Division tanks during the maneuvers. This tank is lacking its main armament. (SC-41-14297)

M3 Light Tank of Company I, 66th Armored Regiment, 2nd Armored Division during the Tennessee Maneuvers in September 1941. A red stripe can be seen around the base of the turret. For the purposes of the maneuvers a blue paper label was glued to either side of the turret to mark the vehicle as part of the "Blue Army." The red, white, and blue air recognition marking is clearly visible at the rear of the turret. The company markings are in white on the sides of the turret and back of the hull.

Sized for each location, the device consisted of a red disk background, with a single white, five-pointed star at the center. Superimposed at the center of the star was a medium blue disk. In appearance, it was a reversed color version of the Army Air Corps marking.

Also used during the Third Army maneuvers were a set of temporary markings used to indicate the army to which the division was assigned. Units for the maneuvers belonged to either the Blue Army or the Red Army. Vehicles of units belonging to either army were required to be marked with the color of that army. While assigned to the Blue Army, the tanks of the division were marked with a medium blue paper label glued to either side of the turret, measuring approximately six by eight-inches. When the division was transferred to the Red Army, a red fabric sheet was wrapped around the base of the turret. When the cloth proved to be too short, it was often locked into the pistol port at either side of the light tank turret and stretched across the front of the turret over the mantlet.

M2A4 Light Tank assigned to Company H, 66th Armored Regiment during the Tennessee Maneuvers, September 1941. The red stripe of the 66th Armored Regiment is visible at the base of the turret, with the company markings painted on the sides of the turret. A blue paper label is glued to either side of the turret to mark the vehicle as part of the "Blue Army." The red, white, and blue air recognition emblem is visible at the back of the turret.

An M2A4 light tank drives past farm buildings during the Tennessee Maneuvers, 14 September 1941. Assigned to H Company, 66th Armored Regiment, the tank has a red stripe painted around the base of the turret and the red, white, and blue air recognition marking is visible between the front doors. Remnants of a blue paper label adhere to the side of the turret and a blue painted steel plate is wired to the right front headlight guard – both marking the tank as belonging to the "Blue Army."

In the 66th Armored Regiment, at least during the maneuver time period, the individual company commander's tanks were also marked with a small painted metal banner mounted to the left front fender parallel to the track. Measuring approximately six by twelve-inches, the rectangular placard was divided equally horizontally: red uppermost with yellow below. The wording "66 AR" was painted in yellow on the red and the company letter was painted in red on the yellow. It was attached by a single metal pole, which was bolted to the left front light guard.[12]

Recently arrived light tanks of the 66th Armored Regiment in Tennessee for the maneuvers of 1941. Each tank carries the three-inch red stripe for the 66th Armored Regiment around the base of its turret. The red, white, and blue air recognition emblem is visible on all of the vehicles, both on the top and front. Vehicles from nearly all nine companies, most notably B, C, D, E, F, G, H, and I companies, are visible.

A newly re-marked M2A2 Light Tank assigned to the headquarters of the 2nd Battalion, 67th Armored Regiment at Fort Benning, GA in the summer of 1940. The red, white and blue marking on the turret are from the, as yet unidentified, unit from which the vehicle was drawn. The broad white stripes around the turret and the white numerals identify this as vehicle number 1 of the headquarters. The previous unit also marked the vehicle number between the two front hatches.

67th Armored Regiment (Medium Tanks)

The 67th Armored Regiment, despite being a medium tank unit, was initially armed predominately with light tanks. This problem was not solved until the fall of 1941, when a sufficient number of M3 medium tanks became available. Like the 66th Armored, the tanks of 67th Armored Regiment initially remained marked in their old paint scheme and the new vehicles they received from other units arrived in their old unit markings. The light tanks were painted with broad white stripes around their turrets to show that they were filling the spot of a medium tank. In January of 1941, the new marking scheme came into use. The company letter and lineal number were stenciled on either side of the turret, as well as across the back of the hull, in fourteen-inch tall white numbers and letters.

Trainload of M2 series light tanks assigned to Company C, 67th Armored Regiment (Medium). The white "M" painted on the front of each sponson marks the vehicles as stand-ins for medium tanks, which the Army sadly lacked during the 1941 maneuvers. The white regimental stripe is visible around both turrets.

M2A3 Light Tank assigned to the 67th Armored Regiment at the start of the Tennessee Maneuvers of 1941. The lack of medium tanks forced the army to substitute light tanks in its medium armored regiments. The red, white, and blue air recognition marking can be seen on the rear of the right turret. No company markings are visible, but the white stripe designating the 67th Armored Regiment is painted around the base of both turrets. Although not visible, a large white "M" (for medium tank) is painted on the front of each sponson.

During the Third Army maneuvers of 1941, the regiment still lacked sufficient medium tanks. The new light tanks being received were marked with a large white "M" on the front of the sponson instead of the broad white stripes previously used. In addition, the assumed size of the main gun was hand painted at the top of the 37mm gun shield – for example "75MM". These vehicles were marked for the individual Armies of the maneuvers in the same manner as those of the 66th Armored Regiment.

For the 1941 maneuvers, the regiment applied the experimental air recognition marking to all of its tanks. For the light tanks assigned to the unit, these were marked in the same manner as those assigned to the 66th Armored Regiment. For the M2 medium tanks, the device was applied to the front of the hull and on the rear of the turret. The size, in both cases, appears to have been about twelve inches in diameter. Movie footage of an M3 Medium Tank assigned to the 67th Armored Regiment has also been observed with these markings, but the front

Column of light tanks assigned to the 67th Armored Regiment awaiting orders during the Tennessee Maneuvers, September 1941. Because of the lack of sufficient medium tanks for the Army, these M2A4 light tanks have been marked with a large white "M" on the front of both sponsons to mark them as substitutes. Hand painted over the gun mantlet is the designated size of the gun the vehicle is supposed to represent – in this case "75mm." The white stripe of the 67th Armored Regiment is visible around the base of the turret, partially covered by a blue cloth used to designate elements of the "Blue Army." (HC)

A new M3 Medium Tank assigned to Company I, 67th Armored Regiment moving down a road during maneuvers on 27 February 1942. The white regimental stripe is clearly painted around the turret and the air recognition insignia is painted on the side of the hull and rear of the turret. The company letter and vehicle lineal number is on the rear of the hull. Vehicle registration numbers are painted in blue and are virtually invisible. (HC)

marking was nearly twenty four-inches in diameter. As with other units in the regiment, the tanks were temporarily marked for the Army to which the division was assigned during portions of the maneuvers. For the M2 Series light tanks, these markings normally consisted of a blue paper rectangle pasted to either side of the turret representing the "Blue" army, or a length of red cloth wrapped around the turret, representing the "Red" army. These rectangles were also placed on the M2 and M3 Medium tanks, but were affixed in several spots around the circumference of the turret. Also painted on the lower front of the hull of the medium tanks is painted a white equal arm cross, approximately twelve by twelve-inches, with two-inch thick arms.

Another M3 Medium Tank on maneuvers on 27 February 1942. The air recognition marking locations are clear, as is the white unit markings on the side of the turret in white. (HC)

A column of M3 Medium Tanks crosses a pontoon bridge during the Third Army maneuvers on 18 December 1941. The two lead vehicles have their air recognition insignia painted with the star pointing down, while those in the distance have the point up. The lead vehicle is the company commander's tank, having a blue metal guidon attached to a pole affixed to the tank's left front fender. It is marked with a white "67 AR/C" in two lines. (HC)

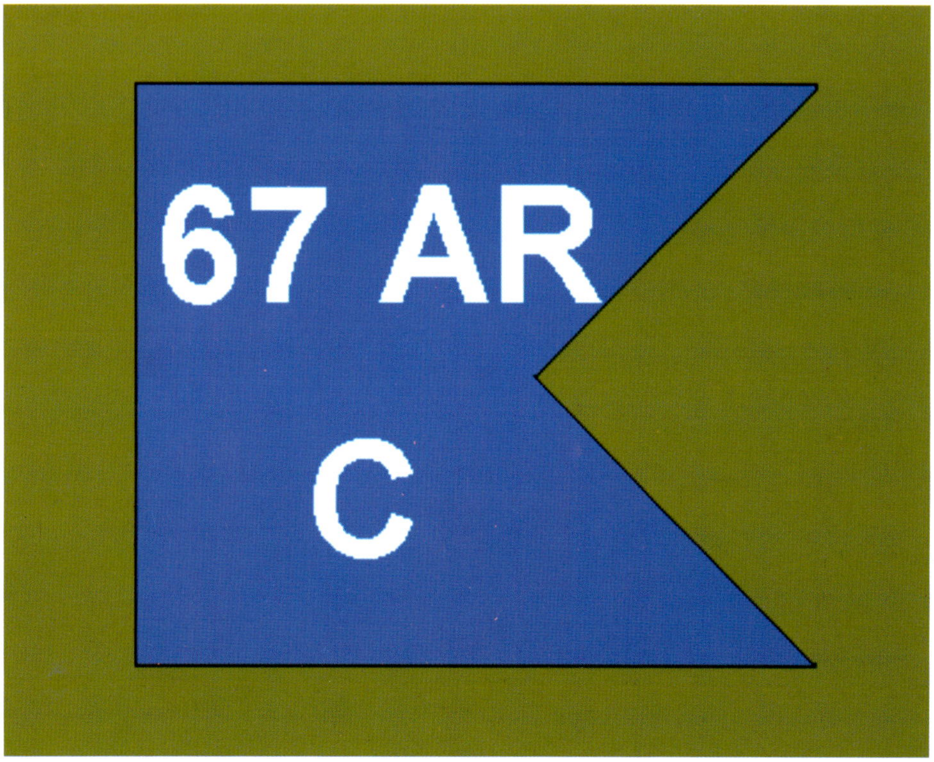

Commander's guidon for Company C, 1st Battalion, 67th Armored Regiment (Medium Tanks) December 1941.

68th Armored Regiment (Light Tanks)

The newly formed 68th Armored Regiment contained a collection of light tanks from the various Regular Army independent tank companies, each retaining the markings from their former units. It was evident that this conglomeration of markings was too confusing, and by January of 1941 both the 1st and 2nd Armored Divisions, as well as the newly organized 3rd Armored Division, adopted a new tactical marking system, which was used by all three units until the outbreak of hostilities.

Photographs and existing film footage from the 1940 Third Army maneuvers indicate that each of the light tank companies assigned to both the newly formed 68th Infantry Regiment (Light Tanks), as well as those assigned to fill out the 67th Armored Regiment, had retained the two-color combination for their company markings. In addition, some of the recently assigned independent tank companies still retained their company markings, most notably the 7th Tank Company, which retained its Infantry (Tanks) marking on their tank turrets.

In this late period the tactical markings on the light tanks were painted on the front of both sponsons and on the outside rear of each turret, as well as centered on the rear of the lower hull. The medium tanks were marked in a similar fashion with the markings painted on the front of the hull, just below the driver's window, on the access doors at either side of the hull, and on the rear of the hull superstructure. The unit markings, mandated by regulations, do not appear on the tanks used during the 1940 maneuvers, probably as a deception measure.

The new tactical marking system, adopted after the maneuvers, was a cooperative venture worked out between the three armored divisions. It involved the use of striping around the base of the tank turret to identify both the division, and the regiment or battalion to which the tank belonged also.

Members of the 68th Armored Regiment gather around an M2A4 Light Tank from Company A of that regiment in the spring of 1941. The stripe around the turret is a light-medium blue with the company letter and number in white. The registration numbers are in white, four-inch numerals on both sides of the hull. The vehicle's brush guards have been removed, but the fixed idler wheel is clearly visible at the rear of the hull.

On the firing line at Fort Benning. M2A4 light tanks of Company D, 68th Armored Regiment firing sub-caliber ammunition at targets in the spring of 1941. The medium blue stripe is barely visible around the base of the turret, with the company letter and number on the rear of the turret. These numbers are also duplicated on either side of the turret.

Side view of an M2A4 of Company C, 68th Armored Regiment on the sub-caliber firing range during the spring of 1941. The medium blue stripe and company markings are clearly visible. Unlike Company D, Company C did not use a dash in its tactical markings.

Close-up of an M2A4 Light Tank assigned to Company D, 68th Armored Regiment in the spring of 1941.

A column of M2A4 Light Tanks speeding along a road during the Tennessee Maneuvers during August of 1941. These vehicles are from the 68th Armored Regiment, identifiable by the medium blue stripe around the base of the turret. A red cloth is wrapped around the front of the turret, identifying the vehicle as part of the Red Army for this part of the maneuvers. The red, white and blue air recognition emblem is visible between the two front hull doors. The company letter and number are painted on both sides of the turret in white.

M3 light tank Company G, 68th Armored Regiment parked outside of a country home in Tennessee, September 1941. The blue identifying stripe is clearly visible around the base of the turret, while the blue registration numbers practically disappear against the olive-drab background. The company markings can be seen on the side of the turret and the rear of the hull. A blue cloth is draped across the front of the turret, marking the vehicle as part of the "Blue Army". Remnants of a rectangular blue paper tag adhere to the side of the turret, apparently it fell off to be replaced by the blue cloth.

Rare photograph of M1A1 Light Tanks assigned to the 82nd Reconnaissance Battalion, 2nd Armored Division at Fort Benning in early 1941. Painted in the regulation olive drab, each of these tanks has a yellow stripe around the base of its turret and white company markings on the front of the turret. Only C Company was equipped with tanks. The vehicle's registration numbers are not visible, having been repainted in the lusterless medium blue. (SC-41366-1)

Under this system tanks of the 68th Armor Regiment were marked with a blue stripe. These vehicles were marked for the individual Armies of the maneuvers in the same manner as those of the 66th Armored Regiment.

2nd Reconnaissance Battalion (82nd Reconnaissance Battalion)

The divisional reconnaissance battalion had been issued the older M1 and M2 Cavalry Combat Cars, which had been re-designated as the M1A1 and M1A2 Light Tanks in August of 1940.[13] These vehicles, like the tanks issued to the armored regiments, were marked with a solid yellow stripe around the base of the turret.

Because the companies were divided into four platoons, the vehicles were marked with the company letter, the platoon number and then a vehicle number from 1 to 3.

14

The Armored Force 3rd Armored Division 1941

Organization

The 3rd Armored Division was activated at Camp Beauregard on 15 April 1941. As with the first two armored divisions, the heart of the unit was the 3rd Armored Brigade, which contained the 2nd and 3rd Armored Regiments (Light Tanks) and the 4th Armored Regiment (Medium Tanks).

The 2nd Armored Regiment had been formed around a cadre of soldiers drawn from the 66th Armored Regiment (Light Tanks), while the 3rd was organized using cadre from the 68th Armored Regiment (Light Tanks) and various units from the 1st Armored Division. These three regiments were re-designated as the 32nd, 33rd, and 40th regiments respectably on 12 May 1941. The rest of the division was rounded out with the following units:

54th	Armored Field Artillery Battalion
67th	Armored Field Artillery Regiment (later a Battalion in 1942)
23rd	Armored Engineer Battalion
36th	Armored Infantry Regiment.
3rd	Reconnaissance Battalion (83rd as of May 12, 41)
18th	Armored Ordnance Battalion
15th	Armored Quartermaster Battalion
45th	Armored Medical Battalion.
46th	Signal Company (renumbered 143rd Armored Signal on 5 SEP 41)

Colors and Markings

Upon activation, the division had available only twenty tanks available for issue – and these were all cast-off from the 2nd Armored Division. By the end of July 1941 the armored vehicles assigned to the 3rd Armored Division were marked with the same red, white and blue national markings that was being used by the 2nd Armored Division. On the all of the division's medium tanks, these markings were generally about 16" in diameter on rear and top of the turret, as well as on front slope above the final drive and on either side of the hull on or near the side doors. On the light tanks the markings were applied on the front of hull – about 5-inches in diameter on the vertical armor between the driver and bow machine-gunner's hatches, as well as on the top and rear of the turret (about 12 to 14-inches in diameter).

On both light and medium tanks a full color, four-inch tall Tank Corps patch was painted on the side of the hull near the rear of both the left and right sponson, just above the fenders. This marking was also painted on both sides of the final drive in front. On the medium tanks the company letter and lineal number was painted in white, 12-inch letters and numbers on both sides of turret, the back of cupola (6-inch tall), and front of hull above driver's front hatch. Instead of a dash between the letter and number, they were divided with a color armor triangle (3-inches tall). The light tanks were painted in a simi-

Example of turret marking for 3rd Armored Division tanks late 1941.

M3 Medium Tank of Company G, 40th Armored Regiment in November 1941. Although marked nearly identically to the 2nd Armored Division, the only real difference is the use of the full color armor triangle on the four fenders and as a replacement for the dash between the company letter and vehicle lineal number.

lar fashion, with slightly shorter numbers and letters, on each side of the turret and across the upper portion of the rear hull. Battalion Headquarters tanks were marked with the battalion number and a lineal number.

In the exact same manner as the 2nd Armored Division, this division made use of a 3" thick colored stripe around the base of the turret on its tanks to differentiate between the three armored regiments. The colors used were the same red, white, blue, and yellow, as that used by the 1st and 2nd Armored Divisions.

The 32nd Armored Regiment (Light) was given red, the 33rd Armored Regiment (Light) – white, and the 40th Armored Regiment (Medium) – blue. Tanks assigned to the 3rd Armored Reconnaissance Squadron (later re-designated the 83rd Reconnaissance Battalion) were marked with a yellow stripe. On all of the vehicles, the registration numbers were painted in four-inch blue numbers.

The Bayou Blitz demonstrating its name. An M3 Light Tank assigned to Company D, 35th Armored Regiment speeds along a road during training in late 1941. The color band around the base of the turret is barely visible, but the color armor triangles on the fenders can be seen.

15

The Armored Force
4th Armored Division
1941

Organization

The 4th Armored Division was activated at Pine Camp, New York on 15 April 1941. The Division was organized around the 4th Armored Brigade that was composed of the 5th Armored Regiment (Light), 7th Armored Regiment (Light) and the 8th Armored Regiment (Medium). On the 8th of May 1941 the two light tank regiments were re-designated as the 35th and 37th Armored Regiments (Light) respectably, while the medium was re-designated the 80th Armored Regiment. The rest of the division included:

51st	Armored Infantry Regiment
22nd	Armored Field Artillery Regiment
94th	Armored Field Artillery Regiment
24th	Armored Engineer Battalion
5th	Reconnaissance Battalion (Mecz) – re-designated 25th Cavalry Reconnaissance Battalion
126th	Armored Ordnance Battalion
144th	Armored Signal Company
4th	Armored Medical Battalion

Colors and Markings

While the base color used by the division were of the adopted shade, the markings used on 4th Armored Division tanks were quite different than those used on the other three divisions. The earliest markings for the tanks of this armored division appear, at first, to be a variation of the geometric system that was used by the tank companies and battalions during the 1930s. But that is where the resemblance ends.

Instead of utilizing different geometric figures for each battalion, company, or platoon, as previous systems had, the 4th Armored Division used only the open triangle and square. Under this system, the triangle designated headquarters tanks, while the square designated tanks belonging to the line platoons in each company. It was the color of the figure that identified the regiment. The letter placed at the center of the figure identified the company.

As with the other three armored divisions, the colors red, white, blue, and yellow were used to differentiate the various armored regiments and reconnaissance battalion assigned to the division. Oddly enough there seemed to have been no attempt to further identify the vehicles with a lineal number, as had been the habit of previous units.

Example color turret markings for the 35th Armored Regiment, late 1941.

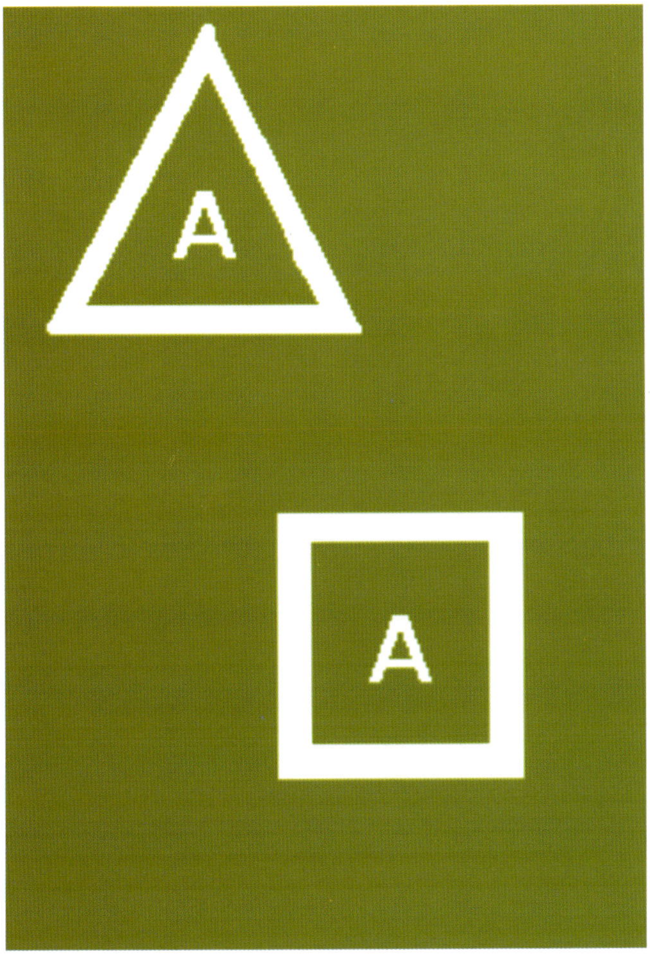

Example color turret markings for the 37th Armored Regiment, late 1941.

Example color turret markings for the 80th Armored Regiment, late 1941.

M2A4 Light Tank assigned to C Company Headquarters 37th Armored Regiment, during winter maneuvers in January 1942. The triangle and letter are in white.

LTC Robert Franklin, commander of the 80th Armored Regiment, in a headquarters tank of Company A of that regiment. Winter, 1941.

It should be noted here that the three regiments had been re-designated within a month of their creation, before unit tactical markings could even be assigned. Given that fact, the armored regiments were ultimately assigned the following colors. The 35th Armored Regiment was given red, the 37th Armored Regiment was designated with white, and the 80th was given blue. These markings first appeared in the winter of 1941-1942, but were soon replaced by the national emblem in April of 1942.

M3A1 Medium Tank assigned to Company C, 80th Armored Regiment. The square and letter are medium blue. Winter maneuvers, January 1942.

16

U.S. Marine Corps

The history of U.S. Marine Corps armored units during the 1920s and 1930s can be considered uneven at best. The successful use of armor in World War I had finally lead the Marine Corps to a decision to experiment with light tanks for amphibious operations. To this end, the Marine Corps organized the Marine Corps Light Tank Platoon, East Coast Expeditionary Force at Quantico, Virginia on the 5th of December 1923. Manned by two officers and twenty-four enlisted personnel, it was initially equipped with three M1917 Light Tanks, borrowed from the U.S. Army. Two mounted the Browning .30 cal. machine gun, while the third mounted the 37mm infantry gun.

On the 3rd of January 1924, after a month of training, the platoon was loaded onto the USS *Chamont* and transported to the island of Culebra, east of Puerto Rico, to participate in amphibious landing exercises. The exercise, which was designed to develop and perfect landing techniques, proved conclusively that the M1917 Light Tank was not suited for such operations. In spite of this, after its return from Culebra the Corps decided to borrow three additional M1917 Light Tanks – one machinegun tank, one 37mm gunned tank, and one signal tank – making the unit a true platoon.

Over the next three years the platoon grew in strength to two officers and thirty men, and also managed to borrow additional three vehicles – bringing the unit total up to eight – the same strength maintained by the average Army National Guard tank company.

In 1927, the platoon was detailed to overseas duty in China and on 6 April 1927, the platoon – with its five operational tanks – left Quantico, Virginia for the West Coast. Upon reaching San Diego on 12 April, the tanks were loaded aboard the USS *President Grant* and the ship departed for Olongapo, Philippine Islands, a few days later. In Olongapo, the tanks were transferred to another ship, the USS *Chaumont*, for the final run to Shanghai, China – arriving there on 21 May. The unit was sent up river by barge to Tientsin on the 6th of June, where was detailed to guard the Peking-Tientsin railway. There they performed this duty for the next fifteen months.

On September 15, 1928, the platoon was administratively detached and transferred to the Light Tank Platoon, Composite regiment, San Diego. The tanks were loaded onto barges for the trip down river to Shanghai, where they, once again, were placed aboard a ship, this time bound for San Diego. The ship left Shanghai on 18 September and arrived in San Diego on 1 November. On the 10th of November 1928 the platoon was disbanded and its men dispersed. The tanks themselves were shipped back to Quantico, Virginia, where they were finally declared excess and disposed of in 1935.

The Marine Corps remained interested in having their own tank units, and in 1934 a plan was proposed for two tank companies. The vehicle selected for these new units was the Marmon-Herrington CTL-3 Light Tank. On 1 March 1937, the 1st Tank Company, 1st Marine Brigade, was activated at Quantico. For much of its life, it remained a mere platoon, even though the Marine Corps eventually purchased a total of thirty-five Marmon-Herrington tanks before the outbreak of war in late 1941. In September of 1940, the Marines began to receive the new M2A4 Light Tank and later in 1941 – the even newer M3 Series Light Tanks.

Organization

Based on what information that is available, the Marines adopted the same unit organization as used by the U.S. Army. From 1923 to 1928, when the unit was deactivated, the single platoon contained five tanks, with a signal tank and an additional three light tanks as spares. When the 1st Tank Company was activated in 1937, it can be assumed that it also followed the Army model – three combat platoons of five tanks each, with two tanks in the headquarters. The Marines purchased enough tanks to outfit two light tank companies (the 1st and 2nd) prior to the outbreak of World War II.

In May of 1941, two additional tank companies were formed – the 3rd and 4th – that were assigned to the 3rd and 4th Fleet Marine Forces respectably. In November of 1941, the Marine Corps created the its first two tank battalions – the 1st and 2nd, assigned to the 1st and 2nd Marine Divisions. These two battalions originally contained only one tank company each and did not become fully formed until after the outbreak of World War II.

Markings

U.S. Marine Corps Light Tank Company

The tanks assigned to the USMC Light Tank Company were received from the United States Army in regulation olive drab and in whatever markings their previous unit had used. Photographs of one tank being loaded on board ship for China show the tank painted in olive drab with a full color Tank Corps emblem on the front armor, approximately twelve-inches tall. Painted on the road wheel suspension rail at either side of the hull is "U.S. MARINES" in red, six-inch tall lettering.

The single signal tank obtained from the army was painted with a large Marine Corps emblem (eagle, globe, and anchor) in white on the front armor plate – approximately twelve inches tall. Tanks in use in China exhibit a four-inch tall white lineal number centered on either side of the engine compartment near the top of the hull. The Marine Corps emblem, consisting of the eagle, globe and anchor was also painted in white on the nose of the hull sometime after their arrival in China.

On loan from the U.S. Army, an M1917 Light Tank is loaded aboard a vessel *enroute* to China for service with the U.S. Marine Corps. A full color Tank Corps emblem remains on the nose of the hull. 1927.

View of the other side of the same vehicle. A red stenciled "U.S. MARINES" is visible along the suspension on this side. The Tank Corps emblem is painted on the nose of the hull. 1927.

1st Tank Company, 1937-1941

When activated in 1937, the 1st Tank Company was initially equipped with at least a full platoon of brand new Marmon-Herrington CTL-3 Light Tanks – purchased specifically for the unit. The tanks were delivered in factory paint, but were soon repainted in the Marine Corps version of olive drab. A rectangular, stamped metal plate marked "U. S./MARINE CORPS" in two lines with the vehicle's registration number below was attached to the left rear of each tank. It too was painted in olive drab.

The Marines adopted a variation of the U.S. Army tactical marking system, using a square for the first platoon, a circle for the second platoon, and a diamond for the third platoon. With five tanks in a platoon, the vehicles were numbered from 1 to 5, with number one being the platoon leader. Since only one platoon was initially activated, the diamond was the most

An M1917 Light Tank awaiting off-loading from its transporter in China during 1929. The vehicle's lineal number is painted high on the side of the engine compartment in white. Notice the Marine Corps globe, eagle, and anchor painted on the side of the truck. This is repeated on the nose of the tank hull. 1928.

Column of USMC tank transporters with their cargo of M1917 Light Tanks in China in 1928.

common marking. With only one or two photographs available I can only conjecture the full marking scheme. The tactical markings were approximately ten-inches tall and centered on all four sides of the vehicle. The figures are hollow, the lines being about one to one and one-half inch thick. The background is a yellow, with the figure itself being a red color. The vehicle number was placed at the center in black. There were no other markings.

The history of this company becomes quite confusing at this point. Some sources state that it was re-designated as the 3rd Tank Company on 1 August 1940. At that point the unit began receiving new M2A4 Light Tanks, which were arriving from the American Car and Foundry Company in Army olive drab paint and marked with Army registration numbers. The markings applied to these vehicles were much less colorful than before. They consisted of the same geometric figures, but

U.S. Marine Corps M1917 Signal Tank in 1928.

Testing the new Marmon-Herrington Light Tanks for amphibious operations in 1938. The vehicle is, as yet, unpainted as it is loaded onto the small landing craft.

were applied only in white. The unit continued to use the Marmon-Herrington Light Tanks until nearly 1943, when they were finally abandoned. They were never used in combat, but rather in occupation duty in American Samoa.

On 1 May 1941 the company was again re-designated, this time as Company A, 1st Tank Battalion. The battalion itself was not stood up until November 1st of that year and consisted initially of only the HQ and HQ Company (known by the Marines as the H&S Company), Company A and Company B. The battalion would not become full operational until early 1942.

The same vehicle cruising along the beach during operational testing for the U.S. Marine Corps in 1938.

CTL-3 Marmon-Herrington Light Tank assigned to the 1st Platoon, 1st Tank Company, USMC in 1938. Note the diamond marking on the front and side of the hull in yellow and red.

2nd Tank Company
Little is known of this company, except that it was in existence by September of 1939 and was assigned to the 2nd Marine Brigade.

3rd Tank Company
This company was supposedly re-designated from the 1st Tank Company on the 1st of May 1941 and subsequently re-designated as Company A, 1st Tank Battalion, 1st Marine Division in November of 1941. It retained the equipment it had as the 1st Tank Company and also received a number of M2A4 Light Tanks prior to deployment to American Samoa in 1942. It retained the use of the white geometric figures and numbers.

4th Tank Company
Stood up on 1 May 1941, the company was sent to Iceland as part of a Marine Corps Provisional Task Force in July of 1941. In November, it was re-designated as Company A, 2nd Tank Battalion, 2nd Marine Division. As with most of the Marine tank companies, little or nothing is known of its equipment and markings.

Rear view of the same vehicle showing the markings on the side and read of the vehicle superstructure. The U.S. Marine Corps license plate, painted olive drab, is bolted to the rear of the engine compartment under the tools.

Marmon-Herrington Light Tanks assigned to 1st, 2nd, and 3rd Platoons of Company A, 1st Tank Battalion at Tutuila, American Samoa in early 1942. The white tactical markings are visible on sides of the hull or turret (depending on the model).

Appendix A: Tables of Organization 1936-1942

OET = Ordnance Equipment Table
P = Peace Time
Spec. = Special
Tent. = Tentative
T/O = Table of Organization
W = War Time

Tank Corps

OET 250	Army Tank Corps	16 October 1918
OET 251	General HQ, Tank Corps	16 October 1918
OET 252	Army Tank HQ, Tank Corps	17 October 1918
OET 253	HQ Brigade or Tank Center, Tank Corps	16 September 1918
OET 255	Light Tank Battalion, Tank Corps	16 September 1918
OET 256	Tank Brigade, Tank Corps	16 October 1918
OET 257	Heavy Tank Battalion, Tank Corps	16 September 1918

Infantry (Tanks)

T/O 10-W	Light Tank Company, Infantry Division	30 April 1921
T/O 509-W	Heavy Tank Group	6 Sept 1927
T/O 509-1/2 W	Light Tank Group	6 Sept 1927
T/O 510-P	HQ & HQ Company, Tank Group	6 June 1925
T/O 510-W	HQ & HQ Company, Tank Group (light or heavy)	6 Sept 1927
T/O 511-P	Heavy Tank Battalion	7 Dec 1925
T/O 511-W	Heavy Tank Battalion	6 Sept 1927
T/O 512-P	HQ & HQ Company, Heavy Tank Battalion	7 Dec 1925
T/O 512-W	HQ & HQ Company, Heavy Tank Battalion	6 Sept 1927
T/O 513-P	Heavy Tank Company	7 Dec 1925
T/O 513-W	Heavy Tank Company	6 Sept 1927
T/O 514-P	Light Tank Battalion	6 June 1925
T/O 514-W	Light Tank Battalion	6 Sept 1927
T/O 515-P	HQ & HQ Company, Light Tank Battalion	6 June 1925
T/O 515-W	HQ & HQ Company, Light Tank Battalion	6 Sept 1927
T/O 516-P	Light Tank Company, Light Tank Battalion	6 June 1925
T/O 516-W	Light Tank Company, Light Tank Battalion	6 Sept 1927
T/O 516-1/2 W	Heavy Tank Maintenance Company	6 Sept 1927
T/O 517-P	Tank Maintenance Company	6 June 1925
T/O 517-P	Light Tank Maintenance Company	6 Sept 1927
T/O 10 W	Light Tank Company, Infantry Division	1 July 1929
T/O 509-1/2 W	Light Tank Group	1 July 1929

T/O 510 W	HQ & HQ Company, Tank Group (Light or Heavy)	1 July 1929
T/O 511 W	Heavy Tank Battalion	1 July 1929
T/O 512 W	HQ & HQ Company, Heavy Tank Battalion	1 July 1929
T/O 513 W	Heavy Tank Company	1 July 1929
T/O 514 W	Light Tank Battalion	1 July 1929
T/O 515 W	HQ & HQ Company, Light Tank Battalion	1 July 1929
T/O 516 W	Light Tank Company, Light Tank Battalion	1 July 1929
T/O 516-1/2 W	Heavy Tank Maintenance Company	1 July 1929
T/O 7-8	Infantry Company, Light Tanks, Division	1938
T/O 7-8-3	Separate Light Tank Platoon, Infantry Company, Light Tanks, Division	1938
T/O 7-71	Infantry Regiment, Medium Tanks	1 October 1939
T/O 7-81	Infantry Regiment, Light Tanks	17 March 1938
T/O 7-82	HQ & HQ Company, Infantry Regiment, Light Tanks	17 March 1938
T/O 7-85	Infantry Battalion, Light Tanks	17 March 1938
T/O 7-87	Light Tank Company, Infantry Battalion	17 March 1938

Mechanized Cavalry

T/O 414-P	Armored Car Troop, Cavalry Division	1930
T/O 414 P (Spec.)	Armored Car Troop, Cavalry Regiment (Mechanized)	1933
T/O 415 P (Spec.)	Scout Troop, Cavalry Regiment (Mechanized)	1933
T/O 423 P (Spec.)	Cavalry Regiment (Mechanized)	1933
T/O 424 P (Spec.)	HQ & HQ Troop, Cavalry Regiment (Mechanized)	1933
T/O 426 P (Spec.)	Covering Squadron, Cavalry Regiment (Mechanized)	1933
T/O 427 P (Spec.)	Combat Car Squadron, Cavalry Regiment (Mechanized)	1933
T/O 428 P (Spec.)	Combat Car Troop, Cavalry Regiment (Mechanized)	1933
T/O 430 P (Spec.)	Machine Gun Troop, Cavalry Regiment (Mechanized)	1933

Armored Force 1940-1942

T/O 17	Armored Division	1 March 1942
T/O 17-1	Division HQ, Armored Division	15 Nov. 1940
T/O 17-1	Division HQ, Armored Division	1 March 1942
T/O 17-2	HQ Company, Armored Division	15 Nov. 1940
T/O 17-2	HQ Company, Armored Division	1 March 1942
T/O 17-3	Service Company, Armored Division	1 March 1942
T/O 17-10P	Armored Brigade	31 July 1940
T/O 17-10	Armored Brigade	15 Nov. 1940
T/O 17-11P (tent.)	Armored Regiment, Light	18 July 1940
T/O 17-11	Armored Regiment, Light	15 Nov. 1940
T/O 17-11	Armored Regiment	1 March 1942
T/O 17-12P (tent.)	Armored HQ & HQ Company, Regiment, Light	18 July 1940
T/O 17-12	Armored HQ & HQ Company, Regiment, Light	15 Nov. 1940
T/O 17-12	HQ & HQ Company, Armored Regiment	1 March 1942
T/O 17-13	Service Company, Armored Regiment, Light	15 Nov. 1940
T/O 17-13	Service Company, Armored Regiment	1 March 1942
T/O 17-14	Maintenance Company, Armored Regiment	1 March 1942
T/O 17-21P (tent.)	Armored Regiment, Medium	16 July 1940
T/O 17-21	Armored Regiment, Medium	15 Nov. 1940
T/O 17-32	Service Company, Armored Regiment, Medium	15 Nov. 1940
T/O 17-35	Armored Reconnaissance Battalion	15 Nov. 1940
T/O 17-35	Armored Reconnaissance Battalion	1 March 1942
T/O 17-36	HQ & HQ Company, Armored Reconnaissance Battalion	1 March 1942
T/O 17-37P (tent.)	Armored Company, Regiment, Light	18 July 1940
T/O 17-37	Armored Company, Reconnaissance Battalion OR Armored Company, Regiment, Light	15 Nov. 1940
T/O 17-37	Armored Company, Armored Regiment OR Armored Reconnaissance Battalion	1 March 1942
T/O 17-46	Armored HQ & HQ Company, Battalion, Tank, Medium, GHQ Reserve	15 Nov. 1940
T/O 17-60	Armored Division Trains	1 March 1940
T/O 170-1	HQ, Armored Corps	15 Nov. 1940
T/O 170-2	HQ Company, Armored Corps	15 Nov. 1940

Appendix B: Organizations (and their Lineage)

Tank Corps Battalions

1st Heavy Tank Battalion 3-18-18 to 4-9-18 (see 41st Heavy Battalion)
A Company – 16 Mar 1918
Re-designated A 41st Heavy Tank
Re-designated A Co., 301st Tank Battalion 25 Apr 1918
Reorganized and Re-designated Co B 15th Tank Battalion 22 June 1921
Re-designated Co E, 1st Tank Regiment 1 Sept 1929
Reorganized and re-designated Co. E, 66th Infantry (Tanks) 10/25/32
B Company – 16 Mar 1918
Re-designated B 41st Heavy Tank
Re-designated B Company, 301st Tank Battalion 25 Apr 1918
C Company – 16 Mar 1918
Re-designated C 41st Heavy Tank
Re-designated C Co., 301st Tank Battalion 25 Apr 1918
Reorganized and Re-designated Cos. A, B, & C, 16th Tank Bn. 22 June 1921

301st Heavy Tank Battalion, Tank Corps 6-11-18 to 6-22-21 (see 17th Tank Bn.)
Unit consolidated with 303rd Tank Battalion and re-designated
17th Tank Battalion (Heavy) 22 June 1921
A Company – 25 Apr 1918
Reorganized and re-designated Co B 15th Tank Bn. 22 June 21
B Company – 25 Apr 1918
C Company – 25 Apr 1918
Reorganized and Re-designated Cos. A, B, & C, 16th Tank Bn., 22 June 1921

302nd Provisional Bn, Tank Corps 9-1-18 to 10-24-18 (see 306th Tank Bn)

302nd Tank Battalion, Tank Corps 6-12-18 to 9-1-18 (see 302nd Provisional Bn)

303rd Heavy Tank Battalion, Tank Corps
Unit consolidated with 301st Heavy Tank Battalion and re-designated
17th Tank Battalion (Heavy) 22 June 1921

306th Tank Battalion, Tank Corps 10-24-18 to 10-14-19 (see 306th Heavy)

326th Tank Battalion, Tank Corps 6-6-18 to 9-12-18 (see 344th Tank Bn)
A Company – 6 June 1918
Reorganized and re-designated Co A 15th Tank Bn 22 June 1921
Re-designated D Co. 1st Tank Regiment 1 Sept 1929

Converted, Reorganized, re-designated D Co. 66th Infantry (Tanks) 10/25/32
Re-designated D Co. 66th Armor in 1940
B Company – 6 June 1918
Re-designated B Co. 344th Tank Bn 9/1/18
Re-designated 5th Tank Co. 8 Jan 1921 (RA)
Consolidated w/6th Tank Co. and re-designated C Co. 68th Infantry (Tanks) 1 Jan 1940
Re-designated C Co. 68th Armor 1940
Re-designated I Co. 67th Armor 1940
Re-designated C Co. 69th Armor 1941
C Company – 6 June 1918
Re-designated C Co. 344th Tank Bn 9/12/18)
Re-designated C Co. 15th Tank Bn. 28 Feb 1921
Reorganized and re-designated F Co. 1st Tank Regiment
Converted, reorganized and re-designated F Co. 66th Infantry (Tanks) 25 Oct 1932
Re-designated F Co. 66th Armor (1940)

327th Tank Battalion, Tank Corps 6-6-18 to 9-12-18 (see 345th Tank Bn)
A Company – 7 June 1918
Re-designated A Co. 345th Tank Bn 9/12/18
Re-designated 1st Tank Co. 8 Jan 1921 (RA)
Re-designated A Co. 68th Infantry (Tanks) 1 Jan 1940
Re-designated A Co. 68th Armor 1940
Re-designated G Co. 67th Armor 1940
Re-designated A Co. 69th Armor 1941
B Company – 6 June 1918
Re-designated B Co. 345th Tank Bn 9/1/18
Re-designated 7th Tank Co. 8 Jan 1921 (RA)
Re-designated F Co. 68th Infantry (Tanks) 1 Jan 1940
Re-designated F Co. 68th Armor 1940
C Company – 7 June 1918
Re-designated C Co. 345th Tank Bn 9/12/18
Re-designated 8 Jan 1921 as 2nd Tank Co. (RA)
Re-designated D Co. 68th Infantry (Tanks) 1 Jan 1940
Re-designated D Co. 68th Armor 1940

328th Tank Battalion, Tank Corps 4-18 to 1921
A Company – April 1918
Re-designated 3rd Tank Co. 8 Jan 1921 (RA) 3rd ID
Re-designated E Co. 68th Infantry (Tanks) 1 Jan 1940
Re-designated E Co. 68th Armor 1940
B Company – April 1918
Re-designated 6th Tank Co. 8 Jan 1921 (RA) 6th ID
C Company – April 1918
Re-designated 4th Tank Company 8 Jan 1921 (RA) 4th ID
Inactivated 27 Sept 1921
Reactivated 15 Sept 1931
Re-designated B Co. 68th Infantry (Tanks) 1 Jan 1940
Re-designated B Co. 68th Armor 1940
Re-designated H Co. 67th Armor 1940
Re-designated B Co. 69th Armor 1941

329th Tank Battalion, Tank Corps 5-18 to 7-1-21 (see 18th Tank Bn.)
A Company – May 1918
Re-designated Co. A 18th Tank Battalion 1 July 1921.
Inactivated 29 July 1922
Re-designated G Co. 1st Tank Regiment 1 Sept 1929

Reactivated as G Co. 1st Tank Regiment 16 Sept 1931
Converted, reorganized, re-designated as Co. G, 66th Inf. (Tanks) 25 Oct 1932
Re-designated Co. G. 66th Armor 1940

344th Tank Battalion, Tank Corps 9-12-18 to 6-22-21 (see 15th Tank Bn)

345th Tank Battalion, Tank Corps 9-12-18 to 6-22-21 (see 16th Tank Bn)

301st Tank Brigade (formed of 301st & 303rd Heavy Tank Bns) 1919-1920
(See 16th Light Tank Bn, 17th Heavy Tank Bn, and 15th Composite Tank Bn)

15th Tank Battalion, 1st Tank Group 6-22-21 to 9-1-29 (see 2/1 Tank Regiment)

15th Composite Tank Battalion 1920-1931 (see 2/1 Tank Regiment)

16th Tank Battalion, 1st Tank Group 6-22-21 to 9-1-29 (see 1/1 Tank Regiment)

16th Light Tank Battalion 1921-1929

17th Tank Battalion, 6-22-21 to 9-1-22 (see 2/2 Tank Regiment)
A Company – 22 June 1922: formed from A Company, 303rd Tank Bn
Re-designated E Company, 2nd Tank Regiment 1 Sept 1929
Inactivated 10-15-31
Re-designated E Company, 67th Infantry (Medium Tanks) 31 October 1932
B Company – 22 June 1922:

17th Heavy Tank Battalion (active) 1920-1931 (see 2/2 Tank Regiment & 3/1 Tank Regiment)

18th Tank Battalion, 7-1-21 to 9-1-29 (see 3/1 Tank Regiment)

19th Tank Battalion, Heavy (inactive) 3-24-23 to 9-1-29 (see 1/2 Tank Regiment)
A Company – 24 March 1923
Re-designated A Co. 2nd Tank Regiment 1 Sept 1929
Re-designated A Co., 67th Infantry (Tanks, Medium) 31 Oct 1932
B Company – 24 March 1923
Re-designated B Co. 2nd Tank Regiment 1 Sept 1929
Re-designated B Co., 67th Infantry (Tanks, Medium) 31 Oct 1932
C Company – 24 March 1923
Re-designated C Co. 2nd Tank Regiment 1 Sept 1923
Re-designated C Co., 67th Infantry (Tanks, Medium) 31 Oct 1932

Regular Army Tank Regiments

1st Tank Regiment
1 September 1929 to October 25 1932

Headquarters & HQ Company: Formed from HQ & HQ Company, 1st Tank Group
1st Battalion: Formed from 16th Tank Battalion 9-1-21 to 10-25-32 (see 1/66 Infantry)
2nd Battalion: Formed from 15th Tank Battalion 9-1-21 to 10-25-32 (see 2/66 Infantry)
3rd Battalion: Formed from 18th Tank Battalion (inactivate until 9-16-31) 9-1-29 to
Headquarters & Headquarters Company: Formed from HQ 17th Tank Battalion
G Company formed from A & C Companies 17th Tank
H Company formed from A & C Companies 17th Tank
I Company formed from A & C Companies 17th Tank
All re-designated as 66th Infantry Regiment (Light Tanks) October 25, 1932

2nd Tank Regiment
1 September 1929 – 31 September 1932

1st Battalion (Inactive): Formed from 19th Tank Battalion (Inactive) 9-1-29
2nd Battalion (Active): Formed from 17th Heavy Tank Battalion (active) 9-1-29
F Company formed from B Company 17th Tank Battalion
Re-designated F Company 67th Infantry Regiment (Medium Tanks) 1932
Inactivated 15 Sept 1931
3rd Battalion (Inactive): Newly constituted 9-1-29
All re-designated as 67th Infantry Regiment (Medium Tanks) October 25, 1932

Regular Army Tank Companies, 1921-1940

1st Tank Company, RA 1st Division – Activated February 1921
Assigned to Miller Field, NY – 2 September 1922
Ordered to concentrate at Fort Benning, GA 10 January 1940
Re-designated Company A, 68th Infantry (Light Tanks) 1 January 1940
Re-designated Company G, 67th Infantry (Medium Tanks) 5 June 1940
Re-designated Company G, 67th Armored Regiment (Medium) 15 July 1940
Re-designated Company A, 69th Armored Regiment (Medium) 31 July 1940
(company also twinned to start Company D, 69th Armored Regiment)

2nd Tank Company, RA 2nd Division
– 1921 to 1-1-40
Assigned to Fort Sam Houston, TX
Ordered to concentrate at Fort Benning, GA January 1940
Re-designated Company D, 68th Infantry (Light Tanks) 1 January 1940
Re-designated Company D, 68th Armored Regiment (Light) 15 July 1940

3rd Tank Company, RA 3rd Division – 1921 to 1-1-40
Assigned to Fort Lewis, WA
Ordered to concentrate at Fort Benning, GA January 1940 does not arrive until after April 1940
Re-designated Company E, 68th Infantry (Light Tanks)
Re-designated Company E, 68th Armored Regiment (Light)

4th Tank Company, RA 4th Division – Activated January 1921
Assigned to Fort Lewis, WA – January 1921
Inactivated 21 September 1921
Tank Platoon Number 4 activated at Camp Jackson, SC, late in 1921
Assigned to Fort Oglethorpe, GA late in 1921
Assigned to Camp McClellan, GA 27 March 1922
Reactivated as 4th Tank Company 15 September 1931
Ordered to concentrate at Fort Benning, GA 3 January 1940
Re-designated Company B, 68th Infantry (Light Tanks) 1 January 1940
Re-designated Company H, 67th Infantry (Medium Tanks) 5 June 1940
Re-designated Company H, 67th Armored Regiment (Medium) 15 July 1940
Re-designated Company A, 69th Armored Regiment (Medium) 31 July 1940
(Company also twinned to start Company E, 69th Armored Regiment)

5th Tank Company, RA 5th Division – Activated as 1st Platoon, 5th Tank Company – 1923
Assigned to Fort Benjamin Harrison, IN – 1923
Ordered to concentrate at Fort Benning, GA – January 1940
Combined with 2nd Platoon, 6th Tank Company and re-designated Company C, 68th Infantry (Light Tanks), 1 January 1940
Re-designated Company I, 67th Infantry (Medium Tanks) 5 June 1940
Re-designated Company I, 67th Armored Regiment (Medium) 15 July 1940
Re-designated Company C, 69th Armored Regiment (Medium) 31 July 1940
(Company also twinned to start Company F, 69th Armored Regiment)

6th Tank Company, RA 6th Division – Activated as 1st Tank Platoon at Camp Grant, IL
September 1921
2nd Platoon inactivated September 1927 and 1st Platoon, 7th Tank Company
re-designated at 2nd Platoon, 6th Tank Company at that same time and
assigned to Jefferson Barracks, MO
6th Tank Company – less 2nd Platoon – inactivated 1 October 1933
2nd Platoon ordered to concentrate at Fort Benning, GA, January 1940, arriving on 2 February 1940
Combined with 1st Platoon, 5th Tank Company and re-designated Company C,
68th Infantry (Light Tanks) 1 January 1940
Re-designated Company I, 67th Infantry (Medium Tanks) 5 June 1940
Re-designated Company I, 67th Armored Regiment (Medium) 15 July 1940
Re-designated Company C, 69th Armored Regiment (Medium) 31 July 1940
(Company also twinned to start Company F, 69th Armored Regiment)

7th Tank Company, RA 7th Division
– 1918 to 1-1-40 (see 1/68 Armor)
Ordered to concentrate at Fort Benning, January 1940
Re-designated Company F, 68th Infantry (Light Tanks) 1 January 10940
Re-designated Company F, 68th Armored Regiment 15 July 1940

10th Tank Company RA 1st Cavalry Division 1921-1928 and 1939-1940 Never equipped

11th Tank Company RA Hawaii 1921-1940

National Guard Infantry (Tank) Companies) 1921-1940

1st Army Area
26th Tank Company, MA NG 26th Division 3-11-24 to 9-1-40 (B/191st Tank Bn)
27th Tank Company, NY NG 27th Division 9-1-21 to 9-1-40 (A/191st Tank Bn)
28th Tank Company, PA NG 28th Division 1921 – 1940
29th Tank Company, VA NG 29th Division 10-17-21 to 9-1-40 (C/191st Tank Bn)
43rd Tank Company, CT NG 43rd Division 5-1-31 to 9-1-40 (D/191st Tank Bn)
44th Tank Company, NJ NG, 44th Division 1939-1940

2nd Army Area
32nd Tank Company, WI NG 32nd Division 11-30-21 to 9-1-40 (A/192nd Tank Bn)
33rd Tank Company, IL NG 33rd Division 12-13-21 to 9-1-40 (B/192nd Tank Bn)
37th Tank Company, OH NG 37th Division 7-1-21 to 9-1-40 (C/192nd Tank Bn)
38th Tank Company, KY NG 38th Division 3-29-21 to 9-1-40 (D/192nd Tank Bn)

3rd Army Area
30th Tank Company, GA NG 30th Division 8-15-24 to 9-1-40 (A/193rd Tank Bn)
31st Tank Company, AL NG 31st Division 7-1-23 to 9-1-1940 (B/193rd Tank Bn)
36th Tank Company, TX NG 36th Division 4-19-37 to 9-1-40 (C/193rd Tank Bn.)
39th Tank Company, AL NG 39th Division 12-20-20 to 7-1-23 (see 31st Tank Co.)
45th Tank Company, CO NG 45th Division 11-1-21 to 9-1-40 (D/193rd Tank Bn)

4th Army Area
34th Tank Company, MN NG 34th Division 6-10-36 to 9-1-40 (A/194th Tank Bn)
35th Tank Company, MO NG 35th Division 3-5-23 to 9-1-40 (B/194th Tank Bn)
602nd Tank
40th Tank Company, CA NG 40th Division 6-18-24 to 9-1-40 (C/194th Tank Bn)
41st Tank Company, WA NG 41st Division 1921-1940 (Disposition Unknown)

Regular Army Infantry (Tank) Regiments 1932-1940

66th Infantry Regiment
(Light Tanks) – formed from the 1st Tank Regiment

Headquarters & HQ Company
1st Battalion 10-25-32 to 7-15-40
2nd Battalion 10-25-32 to 7-15-40
3rd Battalion 10-25-32 to 7-15-40 (HQ & HQ Company not activated 1940)

67th Infantry Regiment (Heavy Tanks – later Medium Tanks) formed from the 2nd Tank Regiment

Headquarters and HQ Company
1st Battalion,10-31-32 (Not activated until 1940)
 Headquarters & HQ Company activated 1 Oct 1939
 A Company
 B Company
 C Company
2nd Battalion 10-31-32 (Not activated until 1940)
 D Company activated 1 Oct 1939
 E Company
 F Company – activated 10-31-32
3rd Battalion 1940
 G Company – Company A, 68th Infantry Regiment (Light) 6-5-40
 H Company – Company B, 68th Infantry Regiment (Light) 6-5-40
 I Company – Company C, 68th Infantry Regiment (Light) 6-5-40

68th Infantry Regiment (Light Tanks)
Headquarters & HQ Company Constituted 10-1-33 (not activated until 1940)
1st Battalion Constituted 10-1-33 (Not activated until 1940)
 A Company – 1st Tank Company
 B Company – 4th Tank Company
 C Company – 5th and 6th Tank Companies
2nd Battalion Constituted 10-1-33 (Not activated until 1940)
 D Company – 2nd Tank Company
 E Company – 3rd Tank Company
 F Company – 7th Tank Company
3rd Battalion Constituted 10-1-33 (Not activated until 1940)

Armored Regiments

1st Armored Regiment (Light) 10 July 1940 (1st AD)
2nd Armored Regiment (Light) 15 April 1941(3rd AD)
3rd Armored Regiment (Light) 15 April 1941 (3rd AD)
4th Armored Regiment (Medium) 15 April 1941 (3rd AD)
5th Armored Regiment (Light) 15 April 1941 (4th AD)
7th Armored Regiment (Light) 15 April 1941 (4th AD)
8th Armored Regiment (Medium) 15 April 1941 (4th AD)
13th Armored Regiment (Light) 10 July 1940 (1st AD)
31st Armored Regiment (Light) 1 October 1941 (5th AD)
32nd Armored Regiment (Light) 12 May 1941 (from 2nd Armored Regiment 3rd AD)
33rd Armored Regiment (Light) 12 May 1941 (from 3rd Armored Regiment 3rd AD)
34th Armored Regiment (Light) 1 October 1941 (5th AD)
35th Armored Regiment (Light) 8 May 1941 (from 5th Armored Regiment 4th AD)
37th Armored Regiment (Light) 8 May 1941 (from 7th Armored Regiment 4th AD)
40th Armored Regiment (Medium) 12 May 1941 (From 4th Armored Regiment 3rd AD)
66th Armored Regiment (Light) 10 July 1940 (2nd AD
67th Armored Regiment (Medium) 10 July 1940 (2nd AD)
68th Armored Regiment (Light) 10 July 1940 (2nd AD)
69th Armored Regiment (Medium) (1st AD)
80th Armored Regiment (Medium) 8 May 1941 (from 8th Armored Regiment 4th AD)
81st Armored Regiment (Medium) 1 October 1941 (5th AD)

Organized Reserve Corps

Tank Battalions 1921-1928

301st Tank Battalion (Heavy)	7-29-21 to 10-6-28 I and V Corps
302nd Tank Battalion (Heavy)	7-29-21 to 5-20-30 (1/311 Tank) IV Corps
303rd Tank Battalion (Light)	7-29-21 to 5-20-30 (1/306 Tank) II Corps
304th Tank Battalion (Light)	7-29-21 to 5-20-30 (2/306 Tank) II Corps
305th Tank Battalion (Light)	7-29-21 to 5-20-30 (3/306 Tank) II Corps
306th Tank Battalion (Heavy)	7-29-21 to 10-6-28 II Corps
307th Tank Battalion (Light)	7-29-21 to 5-20-30 (1/307th Tank) III Corps
308th Tank Battalion (Light)	7-29-21 to 5-20-30 (2/307th Tank) III Corps
309th Tank Battalion (Heavy)	7-29-21 to 5-20-30 (1/310th Tank) III Corps
310th Tank Battalion (Heavy)	7-29-21 to 5-20-30 (2/310th Tank) III Corps
311th Tank Battalion (Light)	7-29-21 to 5-20-30 (3/307th Tank) III Corps
312th Tank Battalion (Heavy)	7-29-21 to 5-20-30 (3/310th Tank) III Corps
313th Tank Battalion (Light)	7-29-21 to 5-20-30 (2/311th Tank) IV Corps
314th Tank Battalion (Light)	7-29-21 to 10-6-28 IV Corps
315th Tank Battalion (Light)	7-29-21 to 5-20-30 (1/308th Tank) V Corps
316th Tank Battalion (Light)	7-29-21 to 5-20-30 (2/308th Tank) V Corps
317th Tank Battalion (Light)	7-29-21 to 5-20-30 (3/308th Tank) V Corps
318th Tank Battalion (Light)	7-29-21 to 5-20-30 (3/311th Tank) V Corps
319th Tank Battalion (Heavy)	7-29-21 to 5-20-30 (1/312th Tank) VI Corps
320th Tank Battalion (Light)	7-29-21 to 5-20-30 (1/309th Tank) V Corps
321st Tank Battalion (Light)	7-29-21 to 5-20-30 (2/309th Tank) V Corps
322nd Tank Battalion (Light)	3-31-24 to 5-20-30 (3/309th Tank) V Corps
323rd Tank Battalion (Heavy)	3-31-24 to 5-20-30 (2/312th Tank) VI Corps
324th Tank Battalion (Heavy)	3-31-24 to 4-20-30 (3/312th Tank) VI Corps

Tank Regiments 1930-1932

306th Tank Regiment (Light) New York
Headquarters & HQ Company (6th Tank Group) New York, New Jersey

1st Battalion (303rd Tank Battalion – Light)	5-20-30 to 10-25-32 (424th INF)
2nd Battalion (304th Tank Battalion- Light)	5-20-30 to 10-25-32 (424th INF)
3rd Battalion (305th Tank Battalion -Light)	5-20-30 to 10-25-32 (424th INF)

307th Tank Regiment (Light)

Headquarters & HQ Company (7th Tank Group)	5-20-30 to 10-25-32
1st Battalion (307th Tank Battalion – Light)	5-20-30 to 10-25-32 (425th INF)
2nd Battalion (308th Tank Battalion – Light)	5-20-30 to 10-25-32 (425th INF)
3rd Battalion	5-20-30 to 10-25-32 (425th INF)

308th Tank Regiment (Light) West Virginia

Headquarters & HQ Company (8th Tank Group) WV	5-20-30 to 10-25-32
1st Battalion (315th Tank Battalion – Light)	5-20-30 to 10-25-32 (426th INF)
2nd Battalion (316th Tank Battalion – Light)	5-20-30 to 10-25-32 (426th INF)
3rd Battalion (317th Tank Battalion – Light)	5-20-30 to 10-25-32 (426th INF)

309th Tank Regiment (Light) Illinois

Headquarters & HQ Company (9th Tank Group)	5-20-30 to 10-25-32
1st Battalion (320th Tank Battalion – Light)	5-20-30 to 10-25-32 (420th INF)
2nd Battalion (321st Tank Battalion – Light)	5-20-30 to 10-25-32 (420th INF)
3rd Battalion (322nd Tank Battalion – Light)	5-20-30 to 10-25-32 (420th INF)

310th Tank Regiment (Heavy) Pennsylvania

Headquarters & HQ Company (10th Tank Group)	5-20-30 to 10-25-32
1st Battalion (309th Tank Battalion – Heavy)	5-20-30 to 10-25-32 (421st INF)
2nd Battalion (310th Tank Battalion – Heavy)	5-20-30 to 10-25-32 (421st INF)
3rd Battalion (312th Tank Battalion – Heavy)	5-20-30 to 10-25-32 (421st INF)

311th Tank Regiment (Heavy) Georgia, Alabama, Kansas, Indiana	
Headquarters & HQ Company (11th Tank Group – GA)	5-20-30 to 10-25-32
1st Battalion 311th Tank Regiment (Heavy) KS	5-20-30 to 10-25-32 OR (422nd INF)
2nd Battalion (313th Tank Battalion – Light) AL	5-20-32 to 10-25-32 OR (422nd INF)
3rd Battalion (318th Tank Battalion – Light) IN	5-20-30 to 10-25-32 OR (422nd INF)

312th Tank Regiment (Heavy) Wisconsin	
Headquarters & HQ Company (12th Tank Group – WI)	5-20-30 to 10-25-32
1st Battalion (319th Tank Battalion – Heavy)	5-20-30 to 10-25-32 (423rd INF)
2nd Battalion (323rd Tank Battalion – Heavy)	5-20-30 to 10-25-32 (423rd INF)
3rd Battalion (324th Tank Battalion – Heavy)	5-20-30 to 10-25-32 (423rd INF)

Infantry (Tanks) Regiments 1932-1942

420th Infantry (Light Tanks)	10-25-32 to 1-30-42 (792nd Tank) V Corps
421st Infantry (Light Tanks)	10-25-32 to 1-30-42 (782nd Tank) III Corps
422nd Infantry (Heavy Tanks)	10-25-32 to 1-30-42 (790th Tank) IV Corps
423rd Infantry (Heavy Tanks)	10-25-32 to 1-30-42 (793rd Tank) VI Corps
424th Infantry (Light Tanks)	10-25-32 to 1-30-42 (781st Tank) II Corps
425th Infantry (Light Tanks)	10-25-32 to 1-30-42 (783rd Tank) III Corps
426th Infantry (Light Tanks)	10-25-32 to 1-30-42 (791st Tank) V Corps
427th Infantry (Light Tanks)	10-1-33 to 1-30-42 (794th Tank) VII Corps

Tank Corps

6th Tank Group II Corps Area (NY, NJ)	10-15-1921 to 5-20-1930 (306th Tank Regt.)
7th Tank Group III Corps Area (PA)	10-15-1921 to 5-20-1930
8th Tank Group V Corps Area (WV)	10-15-1921 to 5-20-1930 (308th Tank Regt.)
9th Tank Group V Corps Area (IL)	10-15-1921 to 5-20-1930 (309h Tank Regt.)
10th Tank Group III Corps Area (PA)	10-15-1921 to 5-20-1930 (310th Tank Regt.)
11th Tank Group IV Corps Area (AL, GA, IN, KS)	9-5-1928 to 5-20-1930 (311th Tank Regt)
12th Tank Group VI Corps Area (IL, WI)	9-5-1928 to 5-20-1930 (312th Tank Regt.)

GHQ Reserve Tank Battaltions

191st Tank Battalion (Light) – First Army

A Company: 27th Tank Company, NY NG 27th ID
B Company: 26th Tank Company, MA NG 26th ID
C Company: 29th Tank Company, VA NG 29th ID
D Company: 43rd Tank Company, CN NG 43rd ID

192nd Tank Battalion (Light) – Second Army

A Company: 32nd Tank Company, WI NG 32nd ID
B Company: 33rd Tank Company, IL NG 33rd ID
C Company: 37th Tank Company, OH NG 37th ID
D Company: 38th Tank Company, KY NG 38th ID

193rd Tank Battalion (Light) – Third Army

A Company: 30th Tank Company, GA NG 30th ID
B Company: 31st Tank Company, AL NG 31st ID
C Company: 36th Tank Company, TX NG 36th ID
D Company: 45th Tank Company, CO NG 45th ID

194th Tank Battalion (Light) – Fourth Army

A Company: 34th Tank Company, MN NG 34th ID
B Company: 35th Tank Company, MO NG 35th ID
602nd Separate Tank Company, April 1942
C Company: 40th Tank Company, CA NG 40th ID

70th Tank Battalion (Medium)
HQ Company: HQ & HQ Company, 1st Battalion, 66th Infantry (Light Tanks)
A Company: A Company, 66th Infantry (Light Tanks)
B Company: B Company, 66th Infantry (Light Tanks)
C Company: C Company, 66th Infantry (Light Tanks)
D Company: New activation

Separate Tank Battalions

71st Tank Battalion (Medium)
Created 1 January 1941
Re-designated 751st Tank Battalion (Medium) 8 May 1941
Activated 1 June 1941 – Fort Benning, GA

72nd Tank Battalion (Medium)
Created 1 January 1941
Re-designated 752nd Tank Battalion (Medium) 8 May 1941
Activated 1 June 1941 – Fort Lewis, WA

73rd Tank Battalion (Medium)
Created 1 January 1941
Re-designated 753rd Tank Battalion (Medium) 8 May 1941
Activated 1 June 1941 – Fort Benning, GA

74th Tank Battalion (Medium)
Created 1 January 1941
Re-designated 754th Tank Battalion (Medium) 8 May 1941
Activated 1 June 1941 – Fort Knox, KY

75th Tank Battalion (Medium)
Created 1 January 1941
Re-designated 755th Tank Battalion (Medium) 8 May 1941
Activated 1 June 1941 – Camp Bowie, TX

76th Tank Battalion (Light)
Created 1 January 1941
Re-designated 756th Tank Battalion (Light) 8 May 1941
Activated 1 June 1941 – Fort Lewis, WA

77th Tank Battalion (Light)
Created 1 January 1941
Re-designated 757th Tank Battalion (Light) 8 May 1941
Activated 1 June 1941 – Fort Ord, CA

78th Tank Battalion (Light) (Colored)
Created 1 January 1941
Re-designated 758th Tank Battalion (Light) (Colored) 8 May 1941
Activated 1 June 1941 – Fort Knox, KY

79th Tank Battalion (Light)
Created 1 January 1941
Re-designated 759th Tank Battalion (Light) 12 May 1941
Activated 1 June 1941 – Fort Knox, KY

80th Tank Battalion (Light)
Created 1 January 1941
Re-designated 760th Tank Battalion (Light) 8 May 1941
Activated 1 June 1941 – Camp Bowie, TX

Appendix C: Federal Standard Color Equivalents

American Vehicle Paints

Color	Used for	Closest FSC Match
Medium Blue (flat)	Registration Numbers	35231
Yellow (flat)	Tactical Markings	33655
Yellow Striping (gloss)	Tactical Markings	13538
Red Striping (semi-gloss)	Tactical Markings	21400
Red Striping (gloss)	Tactical Markings	11400
Blue Striping (semi-gloss)	Tactical Markings	25102
Blue Striping (gloss)	Tactical Markings	15102
Olive-drab (gloss)	Base Coat	14079
Olive-drab (flat)	Base Coat	34079
White (flat)	Tactical/Registration Markings	
White (gloss)	Interior	
French World War I Colors (Closest Matches – all drab unless noted)		
Orange-red Lead Primer	Primer/Camouflage	32473
Armee vert (olive-drab)	Base coat	34088
Ochre	Camouflage	20260
Dark Yellow	Camouflage	37855
Blue-green (light)	Camouflage	34325
Blue-green (faded)	Camouflage	34491
Interior Gray	Lower Interior	36307
Interior Gray	Lower Interior	36320
Blue-gray	Camouflage	24233
Black	Engine compartment/Engine	26188

Endnotes

Chapter 1 Endnotes

1. *Order of Battle of the United States Land Forces in the World War*, Zone of the Interior, Vol. 3, Part 1, U.S. GPO, CMH Pub 23-3, 1949, Pg. 492.
2. Dale E. Wilson, *Treat 'Em Rough*, Presidio Press, 1989, pg. 23.
3. *Order of Battle of the United States Land Forces in the World War*, Zone of the Interior, Vol. 3, Part 1, U.S. GPO, CMH Pub 23-3, 1949, Pg. 492.
4. Ibid.
5. Ibid, pg. 494-495.
6. Dale E. Wilson, *Treat 'Em Rough*, Presidio Press, 1989, pg. 27 and 51-52.
7. *Order of Battle of the United States Land Forces in the World War*, Zone of the Interior, Vol. 3, Part 1, U.S. GPO, CMH Pub 23-3, 1949, Pg. 494.
8. Ibid, Volume 3 part 3, pgs.1541-1542.
9. Dale E. Wilson, *Treat 'Em Rough*, Presidio Press, 1989, pg. 29-34.
10. A total of 225 FT17 and 57 heavy tanks (mixed types) Untitled Pamphlet, *General History, Production, and Weapons System Data and Tank Corps Training* c1920, Author Unknown, COL. Viner Collection, Patton Museum, pages 12-13
11. Dale E. Wilson, *Treat 'Em Rough* Presidio Press, pg. 86
12. Ibid, pages 221-222 (other sources say 214 Light Tanks and 33 Heavy Tanks).
13. Based on photographs supplied by Mr. Mark Beveridge, Dwight D. Eisenhower Library. A series of shots also exists of a single tank that climbed Pike's Peak in Colorado in 1920.
14. Untitled Pamphlet, *General History, Production, and Weapons System Data and Tank Corps Training* c1920, Author Unknown, COL. Viner Collection, Patton Museum, pages 24-25.
15. *National Defense Act Approved 3 June 1916 as Amended by Act Approved 4 June 1920*, Washington DC, GPO, 1920, pg. 15.
16. *Extracts from General Orders and Bulletins, January 1 to August 31, 1917, Relating to Regimental and Company Administration*, GPO, 1917, Pg. 55-58.
17. For example, the 1st Tank Brigade AEF was re-designated the 301st Tank Brigade.
18. Ordnance Equipment Table 257 *Heavy Tank Battalion, Tanks Corps*, dated 16 SEP 1918. This authorizes 23 heavy tanks and 1 signals tank per company, as well as a signals tank for the BN HQ.
19. This is based on existing photographic evidence.
20. U.S. Army Signal Corps Photographs, WWI, Patton Museum Archives Collection, Numbers 20951, 22493, 23893, 23952, 24439, 24724, 27159, 27424, 28385, 29504, 29506, 31858, 32330, 50125.
21. U.S. Army Signal Corps Photographs, WWI, Patton Museum Archives Collection, Numbers: 20951, 23952, 24439, 27159, 27424,28385, 29504, 29506.
22. Dale E. Wilson, *Treat Em' Rough*, Presidio Press, 1989, pg. 133.
23. Ibid, pg. 103.
24. *Histoire De L'Armee Motorisee*, Andre' Duvignac, Imprimrie Nationale, Paris, 1947, pg. 305-306, Icks Collection, Patton Museum; Untitled Pamphlet, *General History, Production Weapons Systems Data, and Tank Corps Training, Post WWI*, Author Unknown, c1920, Item #1, COL Viner Collection, Patton Museum of Cavalry Armor, Ft Knox, KY.
25. Ordnance Equipment Table 255 *Light Tank Battalion, Tank Corps*, dated 16 SEP 1918. This document authorizes 24 combat tanks and one signals tank per company with no tanks authorized for the battalion headquarters. Technically, this should give each battalion a total of 75 tanks, not 72.
26. *Historie De L'Armee Motorisee*, Andre' Duvignac, Imprimrie Nationale, Paris, 1947, pg. 305-306, Icks Collection, Patton Museum.
27. Also known as the 41st Heavy Tank Company, as well as the 1st Separate Tank Battalion, 65th Engineers.
28. Ordnance Equipment Table 257 *Heavy Tank Battalion, Tanks Corps*, dated 16 SEP 1918. This authorizes 23 heavy tanks and 1 signals tank per company, as well as a signals tank for the BN HQ.
29. *Treat 'Em Rough*, Dale E. Wilson, Presidio Press, 1989, pg. 187-211.
30. *301st Tank Battalion After Action Report*, MAJ Sasse, 1918, Icks Collection, Patton Museum Archives.
31. Male tanks are armed with a single 6 lbr (57mm) gun in the each side sponson in combination with light machineguns overall.

Female tanks are armed entirely with light machineguns. Composite tanks (also called hermorphidites) have one sponson armed with a 57mm gun and the other with a machinegun.

32. Photographs of 301st Heavy Tank Battalion Tank Park, taken circa 1919.

Endnotes for Introduction to Chapters 2-5

1. National Defense Act Approved 3 June 1916 as Amended by Act Approved 4 June 1920, Washington DC, GPO, 1920, pg. 15.
2. 1st-4th, 6th, and 7th Tank Companies.
3. *Fort Geo. G. Meade, Tank School, 1930*, booklet published by the Tank School, pg. 25-29.
4. Camp Meade, MD became Fort George G. Meade in 1928.
5. 1st through 7th Tank Companies and two new companies – the 10th assigned to the 1st Cavalry Division and the 11th assigned to the Hawaiian Department.
6. A light tank company was normally assigned to an Infantry Division and according to T/O 10 W dated 1 JUL 1929, contained a total of 24 tanks 5 in each platoon, and 9 in the HQ platoon. These companies were all re-designated on 8 January 1921.
7. 1st Tank Regiment was formed in 1929 from the 15th, 16th and 18th Tank Battalions while the 2nd Tank Regiment was formed from the 17th and 19th Tank Battalions, *Tank Battalions of the U.S. Army*, James A. Sawicki, 1983.

Chapter 2 Endnotes

1. Untitled Pamphlet, *General History, Production, and Weapons System Data and Tank Corps Training* circa 1920, Author Unknown, COL. Viner Collection, Patton Museum; M1917 Light Tank was also known as the Six-ton Special Tractor, Model 1917.
2. On June 6, 1925 Table 514-P *Light Tank Battalion*, was adopted, which gave the authorized strength of a light tank battalion as 72 tanks in 3 companies of 24 tanks. (3 platoons of 5 with 9 spares in Co. HQ. This is modified on 6 SEPT 1927 to add 1 signals tank to BN HQ. (Table 514-W).
3. Table 511-P *Heavy Tank Battalion*, dated 7 DEC 1926, gives battalion tank strength as 45 combat tanks; 15 combat tanks per company, 3 per platoon with 6 spares in the each company HQ platoon.
4. *Manual for the Quartermaster Corps*, 1916 with changes to 1917, Vol. I, GPO, 1917, pg. 485.
5. *Military Modeling Magazine* "Olive Drab for Modelers" Steve Zaloga, 2001.
6. *Specifications for Interior Painting of Tanks*, OMT 470.8/1330 dated Jan 20, 1920. This memo mentions several options in the painting of interiors, but specifically mentions that normal practice was to paint the interior white with the doors painted OD. Other options included painting it all OD, or all but the turrets OD.
7. *Proposed Authorization to Use Varnish on Surfaces Normally Painted Olive Drab*, Item 7173, Sub-Committee on Mobile Artillery, Aug. 17, 1928. Approved Aug. 23, 1928. This memo covered ALL types of Ordnance equipment, including tanks specifically.
8. OCM 14022, November 1937 recommended that long oil enamel be adopted as a substitute standard for peacetime use only.
9. AR 850-5 *Marking of Equipment, Vehicles, and Property*, War Department, 15 May 1926 "8. Tractors and Tanks. a) These vehicles may be marked as prescribed in paragraph 6.... b) Such markings are not required but, if used, must be uniform throughout the unit."
10. Photographs taken ca1929, Fort George Meade MD, 17th Tank Battalion Folder, Patton Museum Archives
11. Ibid. It is probable that this number was painted in the color assigned to the company or battalion to which the tank was attached.
12. *Tank Notes*, Volume IV, Number 1, July 1927, Tank School Library Camp Meade, MD, pg. 44. This system was based on one in use at Fort Benning, but Benning's system was not specifically described in the article.
13. Location nomenclature for the M1917 Light Tank is taken from *Handbook of the Six-Ton Special Tractor Model 1917*, War Department Book No. 1995, circa 1919. In this case, the tower is the turret cupola.
14. *Tank Notes*, Volume IV, Number 1, July 1927, Tank School Library, Camp Meade, MD, pg. 44. The front of the tank was marked on the plate above the driver's feet; the rear number was painted on the either side of the rear of the engine compartment.
15. Photographs of the 66th Infantry (Light Tanks) clearly show that the stripe markings were still being used by the 1st Battalion. The vehicle numbers also continued to be painted in the company colors, the dark colors being shaded in white.

Endnotes for Chapter 3

1. *Order of Battle of the United States Land Forces in the World War*, Zone of the Interior, Vol. 3, Part 1, U.S. GPO, CMH Pub 23-3, 1949, pg. 492.
2. Dale E. Wilson, *Treat 'Em Rough*, Presidio Press, 1989, pg. 23.
3. *Order of Battle of the United States Land Forces in the World War*, Zone of the Interior, Vol. 3, Part 1, U.S. GPO, CMH Pub 23-3, 1949, Pg. 492.
4. Ibid.
5. Ibid, pg. 494-495.
6. Wilson, Dale E. *Treat 'Em Rough*, Presidio Press, 1989, pg. 27 and 51-52.
7. Order of Battle of the United States Land Forces in the World War, Zone of the Interior, Vol. 3, Part 1, U.S. Government Printing Office, U.S. Army Center of Military History Publication 23-3, 1949, pg. 494
8. Ibid, Volume 3 part 3, pgs.1541-1542.
9. Wilson, Dale E. *Treat 'Em Rough*, Presidio Press, 1989, pg. 29-34.
10. A total of 225 FT17 and 57 heavy tanks (mixed types) Untitled Pamphlet, *General History, Production, and Weapons System Data and Tank Corps Training* circa 1920, Author. Unknown, COL. Viner Collection, Patton Museum, pages 12-13.
11. Wilson, Dale E., *Treat 'Em Rough*, pg. 86.
12. Ibid, pages 221-222 (other sources say 214 Light Tanks and 33 Heavy Tanks).
13. Based on photographs supplied by Mr. Mark Beveridge, Dwight D. Eisenhower Library. A series of shots also exists of a single tank that climbed Pike's Peak in Colorado in 1920.
14. Untitled Pamphlet, *General History, Production, and Weapons System Data and Tank Corps Training* c1920, Author Unknown, COL. Viner Collection, Patton Museum, pages 24-25.
15. National Defense Act Approved 3 June 1916 as Amended by Act Approved 4 June 1920, Washington DC, GPO, 1920, pg. 15.
16. War Department, *Extracts from General Orders and Bulletins, January 1 to August 31, 1917, Relating to Regimental and Company Administration*, GPO, 1917, Pg. 55-58. For example,

the 1st Tank Brigade AEF was re-designated the 301st Tank Brigade Ordnance Equipment Table 257 *Heavy Tank Battalion, Tanks Corps*, dated 16 SEP 1918. This authorizes 23 heavy tanks and 1 signals tank per company, as well as a signals tank for the BN HQ.

17. This is based on existing photographic evidence.
18. U.S. Army Signal Corps Photographs, WWI, Patton Museum Archives Collection, Numbers 20951, 22493, 23893, 23952, 24439, 24724, 27159, 27424, 28385, 29504, 29506, 31858, 32330, 50125.
19. U.S. Army Signal Corps Photographs, WWI, Patton Museum Archives Collection, Numbers: 20951, 23952, 24439, 27159, 27424,28385, 29504, 29506.
20. *Treat 'Em Rough*, Dale E. Wilson, Presidio Press, 1989, pg. 133.
21. Ibid, pg. 103.
22. *Histoire De L'Armee Motorisee*, Andre' Duvignac, Imprimrie Nationale, Paris, 1947, pg. 305-306, Icks Collection, Patton Museum; Untitled Pamphlet, *General History, Production Weapons Systems Data, and Tank Corps Training, Post WWI*, Author Unknown, c1920, Item #1, COL Viner Collection, Patton Museum of Cavalry Armor, Ft. Knox, KY.
23. Ordnance Equipment Table 255 *Light Tank Battalion, Tank Corps*, dated 16 SEP 1918. This document authorizes 24 combat tanks and one signals tank per company with no tanks authorized for the battalion headquarters. Technically, this should give each battalion a total of 75 tanks, not 72.
24. *Historie De L'Armee Motorisee*, Andre' Duvignac, Imprimrie Nationale, Paris, 1947, pg. 305-306, Icks Collection, Patton Museum.
25. Also known as the 41st Heavy Tank Company, as well as the 1st Separate Tank Battalion, 65th Engineers.
26. Ordnance Equipment Table 257 *Heavy Tank Battalion, Tanks Corps*, dated 16 SEP 1918. This authorizes 23 heavy tanks and 1 signals tank per company, as well as a signals tank for the BN HQ.
27. *Treat 'Em Rough*, Dale E. Wilson, Presidio Press, 1989, pg. 187-211.
28. *301st Tank Battalion After Action Report*, MAJ Sasse, 1918, Icks Collection, Patton Museum Archives.
29. Male tanks are armed with a single 6 lbr (57mm) gun in the each side sponson in combination with light machineguns overall. Female tanks are armed entirely with light machineguns. Composite tanks (also called hermorphidites) have one sponson armed with a 57mm gun and the other with a machinegun.
30. Photographs of 301st Heavy Tank Battalion Tank Park, taken circa 1919.

Endnotes for Chapter 4

1. This description is based on photographs taken in 1929-1931.
2. Photographs of tanks assigned to the 40th Tank Company (Cal NG) and the 3rd Tank Company RA, both taken in the late 1920s and early 1930s show this variation.
3. *Wisconsin Magazine of History*, Vol. 75, No. 4, summer, 1992, Wisconsin State Historical Society, pg. 249.

Endnotes for Chapter 5

1. The 1st Tank Regiment was re-designated at the 66th Infantry Regiment (Light Tanks) while the 2nd Tank Regiment was re-designated at the 67th Infantry Regiment (Heavy Tanks).

Endnotes for Chapter 6

1. War Department Letter, May 1 1931, SUBJ: *General Principles to Govern Mechanization and Motorization Throughout the Army*, AG 537.3 AG Central Files, NA, RG 94.
2. Ibid, pg. 32.
3. The units added to the Brigade included the 68th Field Artillery Battalion and 19th Ordnance Company.

Endnotes for Chapter 7

1. In April 1936, the Ordnance Committee recommended canceling the requirement for the Heavy Tank. This was approved on 7 May 1936.
2. The 67th Inf. (Medium Tanks) consisted on a single company of M2 series medium tanks. The 68th Inf. (Light Tanks) was made up of the 1st, 2nd, 3rd, 4th, 5th, 6th, and 7th Tank Companies, consolidated especially for these maneuvers. The 66th Inf. (Light Tanks) was full strength and consisted of three battalions.
3. COL Alvan C. Gillem Jr., *Conference of 2nd Armored Division* October 7, 1940, G-3 Conference file, War Dept. General Staff Records, NA RF 165.
4. *Military Modeling Magazine*, *Olive Drab for Modelers*, Steve Zaloga, 2002.
5. Ibid.

6 Company F, 67th Infantry Regiment (Medium Tanks).

7. AR 850-5 *Marking of Equipment, Vehicles, and Property*, dated 25 September 1936. It specifically prescribes the placing of registration numbers on all Army owned vehicles.
8. Letter from the Office of the Chief of Infantry, 10 March 1936, SUBJ: *Assignment and Preservation of Tanks.*
9. Black and white films transferred to VHS format. *66th Light Tanks in Louisiana Maneuvers, 1940*, and training film, T55-145, dated 1940, *Armored Combat Vehicles*, Patton Museum Library Collection.

Endnotes for Chapter 8

1. *Table of Organization and Reference Data 1939*, Command and General Staff School, Fort Leavenworth KS, 1939. This is one more tank than was allowed the Regimental tank company.
2. In AR 850-5, all markings were applied in either white or black paint. It would seem that most units continued this practice with their tactical markings.
3. AR 850-5 *Marking of Equipment, Vehicles, and Property*, dated 25 September 1936. It specifies makeup and placement of unit markings.
4. *Provisional Tank Brigade in the Louisiana Maneuvers, 1940*, 8mm black and white transferred to VHS, Patton Museum Library Collection.

Endnotes for Chapter 9

1. Phone interview with COL James Leach (USA Ret). COL Leach was a SGT with the 36th Tank Company in 1939 and was with the unit when it was converted to C Company, 193rd Tank Battalion in 1940.

Endnotes for Chapter 10

1. M1 Combat Cars were actually light tanks. The regulations did not allow the Cavalry branch to have tanks, so this subterfuge of calling tanks combat cars got around the restriction.

Endnotes for Chapter 11

1. Transcribed notes. Fort Knox History Collection, Patton Museum Library.
2. Ibid.
3. AR 850-5 side note in change dated 1942 referring to AG.400.161 (7-18-41) which authorizes the use of the blue paint.
4. Each of the tank companies was instructed to bring two of their own tanks with them from their home stations. The 70th, on the other hand, was issued with brand new M2A4 Light Tanks.
5. 192nd and 193rd GHQ Reserve Tank Battalions.
6. Interview with COL. James Leach in May of 1996. COL Leach began his career as a Sargeant with the 193rd Tank Battalion, before being transferred to the 3rd Armored Division and later the 4th Armored Division, where he ended the war as a Company Commander.
7. C for Commander, S for Staff.
8. The company system used only the numbers 1-5.
9. *Janesville Tankers.*

Endnotes for Chapter 12

1. The 3rd and 4th Armored Divisions were activated on 15 April 1941. The 5th AD was activated on 1 October 1941.
2. A.G. Memo 400.161 dated July 18, 1941 authorized the change in AR 850-5 to change from white to lusterless blue paint for registration markings.
3. *The Reconnaissance Battalion*, MAJ H.H.D. Heiberg, Officer's School, 1st Armored Division, Conference #7, 1 April 1941 Heiberg Collection, Box 1 Folder 9.
4. *Historical and Pictorial Review, First Armored Division*, The Army and Navy Publishing Co., 1941.
5. The lack of medium tanks forced the unit to be filled out with M2A1, M2A2 and M2A3 Light Tanks until enough M2/M3 Mediums were available.
6. In 1941, the M1, M1A1, and M2 Combat Cars were reclassified as M1 and M1A1 Light Tanks.
7. M3 Light Tank in the collection of the Patton Museum; 1st Armored Division Photographs SEP 1941, Patton Museum Collection.
8. *Historic Fort Knox, The Thornsbury Film*, 8mm Color Film, Home movie shot by MAJ. S. Thornsbury at Fort Knox, 1940-1941.
9. HQ, 2nd Armored Division, Division Officer's School, *G3 Conference on Organization*, 26 August 1940, Fort Benning, GA, Patton Museum Archives, Fort Knox, KY. Located in Bin 49-6. The two armored divisions used the same organization charts.
10. *AR 850-5, Marking of Equipment, Vehicles, and Property*, This regulation mandated the use of white markings. In practice, the size of these markings ranged from 3" tall to upwards of 6" tall, dependent on the battalion.
11. *Historic Fort Knox, The Thornsbury Film*, 8mm color footage taken at Fort Knox in late 1940 - mid 1941. MAJ Thornsbury, 1st Armored Division, Patton Museum Collection.
12. *The Tanks are Coming*, 16mm Color Film, A recruiting film shot for the War Department by Warner Brothers, circa April 1941.
13. *192nd Tank Battalion, 1940-1941*, 8mm B/W & Color Film, Home movie footage taken at Fort Knox by members of the 192nd Tank Bn. The white stripes designating them as medium tanks were retained.
14. Ibid.
15. *Historic Fort Knox, The Thornbury Film*, 8mm Color Film, Home movie taken at Fort Knox by MAJ. S. Thornsbury 1940-1941.
16. Organization as of 1941: *The Reconnaissance Battalion*, MAJ H.H.D. Heiberg, Officer's School, 1st Armored Division, Conference #7, 1 April 1941 Heiberg Collection, Box 1 Folder 9
17. M2A1, M2A2, M2A3, M2A4 Light Tanks, M1, M1A1 & M2 Combat Cars (later re-designated M1A1 & M1A2 Light.

Endnotes for Chapter 13

1. *Table of Organization and Reference*, Command and Staff School, Fort Leavenworth, KS 1939.
2. HQ 2nd Armored Division, Division Officer's School, *G3 Conference on Organization*, 26 AUG 1940, Fort Benning, GA. Patton Museum Archives, Fort Knox, KY, Bin 49 Folder 6.
3. Ibid.
4. *Table of Organization and Equipment "A"*, dated 22 December 1941 to take affect on 1 January 1942, Armored Force Headquarters, Fort Knox, KY.
5. Ibid, Pg. 12-13.
6. Based on the examination of an M3 Light Tank, Serial Number 158 in the collection of the Patton Museum. It retains its original coat of paint, as well as the paint scheme applied to it for the maneuvers of 1941.
7. Until June of 1941, when it was directed that registration numbers would be stenciled in lusterless blue paint.
8. *Home Movie, BG Patton, 2nd AD*, 8mm B&W Film taken at Fort Benning, GA of the 2nd Armored Division circa September 1940 - early 1941.
9. *Life Magazine*, April 1941 showing MG George S. Patton JR's M1 Light Tank in the divisional HQ colors.
10. Black and white film transferred to VHS -*66th Infantry Regiment (Light Tanks), 1940.*
11. Roll Again Second Armored, MAJ Norris Perkins and Michael Rogers Pg. 59 & 67.
12. C Troop was the Light Tank troop within the Reconnaissance Battalion.

Bibliography

United States War Department, *Order of Battle of the United States Land Forces in the World War, Zone of the Interior*, Volume 3, Part 1, Washington DC: Government Printing Office, Center of Military History Publication 23-3, 1949

Duvignac, Andre', *Historie De L'Armee Motorisee*, Paris France; Imprimrie Nationale, 1947

United States Congress, *National Defense Act Approved 3 June 1916 as Amended by Act Approved 4 June 1920*, Washington DC: Government Printing Office, 1920

United States War Department, *Extracts from General Orders and Bulletins, January 1 to August 31, 1917, Relating to Regimental and Company Administration*, Washington DC: Government Printing Office, 1917

Sasse, Major, *301st Tank Battalion After Action Report,* France, 1918

Wilson, Dale E., *Treat 'Em Rough*, Presidio Press, 1989

United States War Department, *Ordnance Equipment Table 255, Light Tank Battalion, Tank Corps*, Washington DC: Government Printing Office, 16 September 1918

United States War Department, *Ordnance Equipment Table 257, Heavy Tank Battalion, Tank Corps*, Washington DC: Government Printing Office 16 September 1918

Unknown, *Fort Geo. G. Meade, Tank School, 1930,* Fort George G. Meade Maryland: The Tank School, 1930

Sawicki, James A, *Tank Battalions of the U.S. Army*, 1983

United States War Department, *Table 514-P Light Tank Battalion*, Washington DC: Government Printing Office, 6 June 1925

United States War Department, *Table of Organization T/O 10 W Light Tank Company*, Washington DC: Government Printing Office, 1 JUL 1929

United States War Department, *Table 514-W Light Tank Battalion*, Washington DC: Government Printing Office, 6 September 1927

United States War Department, *Table 511-P Heavy Tank Battalion*, Washington DC: Government Printing Office, 7 December 1926

United States War Department, *Manual for the Quartermaster Corps*, 1916 with changes to 1917, Volume I, Washington DC: Government Printing Office, 1917.

United States War Department, *Army Regulation 850-5 Marking of Equipment, Vehicles, and Property*, Washington DC: Government Printing Office, 15 May 1926

United States War Department, *Army Regulation 850-5 Marking of Equipment, Vehicles, and Property*, Washington DC: Government Printing Office, 25 September 1936

Zaloga, Steve *Military Modeling Magazine* "Olive Drab for Modelers", 2001

Unknown, *Tank Notes*, Volume IV, Number 1, July 1927, Camp Meade, Maryland: Tank School Library, 1927

United States War Department, *Handbook of the Six-Ton Special Tractor Model 1917*, War Department Book No. 1995, Washington DC: Government Printing Office, circa 1919

Command and General Staff School, *Table of Organization and Reference Data 1939,* Fort Leavenworth Kansas: C and GS School, 1939.

Schutt, Donald A., *Janesville Tankers on Bataan*, Master of Science Thesis, University of Wisconsin – Madison, 1967

Powlett, Dr. Alvin C., MD, *Kentucky's Fighting 192nd Light GHQ Tank Battalion*, Quality Lithographing Company, Newport KY, 1981

Blaker, Gordon, *Iron Knights*, Burd Street Press, 1999

67th Armored Regiment, *History of the 67th Armored Regiment*, Georg Westermann Publisher, Brunswick GE, 1945

33rd Armored Regiment, 33rd Armored Regiment Yearbook for 1942

Perkins, Norris and Rogers, Michael, *Roll Again Second Armored*

Historical and Pictorial Review, First Armored Division, The Army and Navy Publishing Co., 1941

Gillem, Colonel Alvan C. Jr., *Conference of 2nd Armored Division*, October 7, 1940, G-3 Conference file, War Dept. General Staff Records, NA RF 165

Heiberg, Major H.H.D., *The Reconnaissance Battalion*, Officer's School, 1st Armored Division, Conference #7, 1 April 1941 Heiberg Collection, Box 1 Folder 9

Office of Motor Transport, Specifications for Interior Painting of Tanks, OMT 470.8/1330 dated Jan 20, 1920.

Sub-Committee on Mobile Artillery, Proposed Authorization to Use Varnish on Surfaces Normally Painted Olive Drab, Item 7173, Aug. 17, 1928. Approved Aug. 23, 1928.

United States War Department, *Tanks*, Government Printing Office, 1920

War Department Letter, May 1 1931, SUBJ: General Principles to Govern Mechanization and Motorization Throughout the Army, AG 537.3 AG Central Files, NA, RG 94

Letter from the Office of the Chief of Infantry, 10 March 1936, SUBJ: Assignment and Preservation of Tanks

HQ, 2nd Armored Division, Division Officer's School, Handout - G3 Conference on Organization, 26 August 1940, Fort Benning GA, A.G. Memo 400.161 dated July 18, 1941

Armored Force Headquarters, Fort Knox KY, *Table of Organization and Equipment "A"*, 22 December 1941.

LIFE Magazine, April 1941

Wilfong, William T., *Military Collector and Historian*, VOL xxxviii no. 3, Fall 1986, "Armor Comes to Pennsylvania"

Hall, Rolo, *Marine Corps Tanker's Association Newsletter,* April 1999, Article – "March Newsletter Surprise"

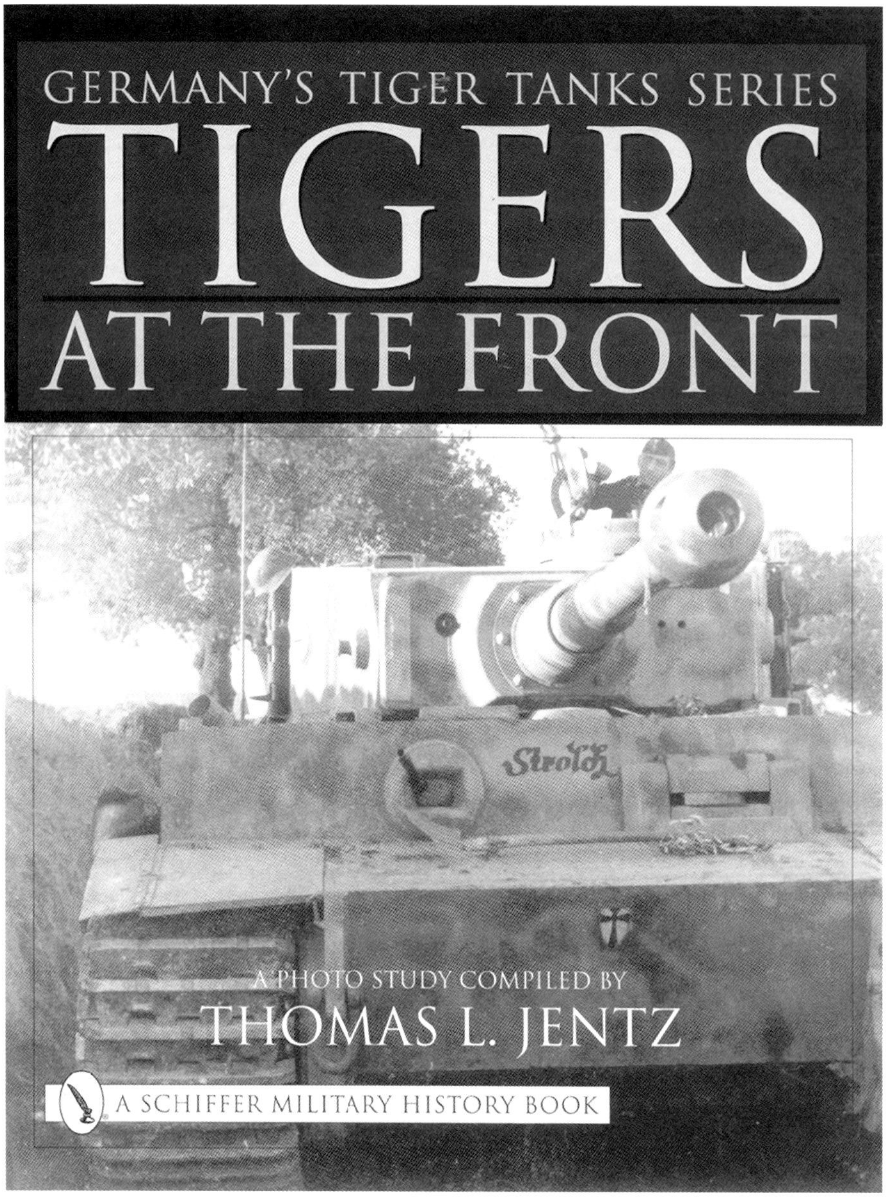

Germany's Tiger Tank Series
Tigers at the Front
A Photo Study Compiled by Thomas L. Jentz

Tiger! The very name that Allied troops feared. It came to symbolize the superiority of German tank design. This book has been created as a photo essay showing the best available and rare photographs of Tigers with units at the front. No tank that the Allies fielded in World War II was comparable to this combination of the 88mm gun with massive armor protection. Allied tankers didnÕt think that they stood a chance of defeating these formidable Tigers. They only hoped that these heavy tanks would breakdown, become immobilized in soft ground, or be damaged by lucky hits on vulnerable points.

Size: 8 1/2" x 11"
Illustrations: over 270 b/w photographs
Pages: 208 pages
ISBN: 0764313398 hard cover $29.95